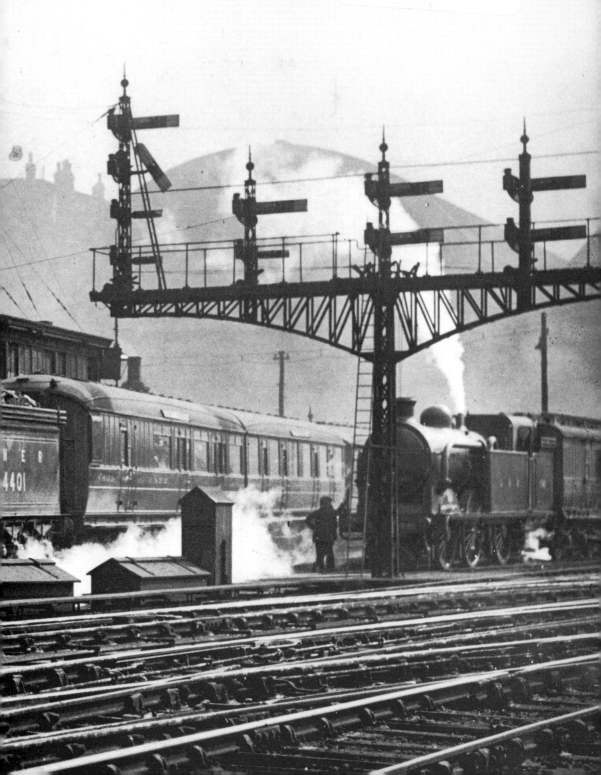

*Shortly a............................ngs
Cross wi........................hat
the 0-6-2.................................VR'
(Rail Ar.....

CLASSIC LOCOMOTIVES
GREAT NORTHERN 4-4-2 'ATLANTICS'

O.S.Nock

*A celebrated Kings Cross 'Pullman' engine, No 4444,
here seen on the 5:35 pm Hull express near Potters Bar
(Rail Archive Stephenson).*

CLASSIC LOCOMOTIVES

GREAT NORTHERN
4-4-2 'ATLANTICS'

O.S. Nock

Patrick Stephens, Wellingborough

First published in 1984

British Library Cataloguing in Publication Data

Nock, O.S.
    The Great Northern 'Atlantics'.—(Classic
    locomotives; 2)
    1. Great Northern Railway
    2. Locomotives—England
    I. Title   II. Series
    385'.361'09426   TJ603.4.G72G72

    ISBN 0-85059-683-1

*Patrick Stephens Limited is part of the
Thorsons Publishing Group.*

Photoset in 10pt Plantin by MJL Typesetting,
Hitchin, Herts. Printed in Great Britain on 115 gsm
Fineblade, and bound, by William Clowes Limited,
Beccles, Suffolk, for the publishers, Patrick Stephens
Limited, Denington Estate, Wellingborough,
Northants, NN8 2QD, England.

Contents

Preface

In choosing the Great Northern 'Atlantics' for the second volume in this series of 'Classic Locomotives', I do not think there will be many who would, in general terms, dispute the place that these engines occupy in the history of British Locomotive development. The small-boilered engine No 990 was the first tender locomotive of the 'Atlantic' type in Great Britain and a remarkably good engine design in itself, followed, in 1902, by the massive-looking 251, which was developed through several stages into one of the most remarkable engine classes that have ever run the rails in this country. I must join issue, however, with those, including so usually erudite an author as Cuthbert Hamilton Ellis, who persist in referring to the smaller-boilered variety as the 'Klondykes' (sic). Most of us will know of the Gold Rush of 1898 and how the first British 'Atlantic' built in that same year came to be associated with it; but I have been to the Canadian North-West, have read much about it and studied many maps, and without exception the spelling of that famous territory is Klondike, with an 'i' and not a 'y'.

In writing this book I have to thank very many friends both inside and outside the rail-

way service, who have given me unstinted help, with data, photographs and personal reminiscences. Many of them are mentioned at intervals in the text, but I remember particularly the late Edward G. Marsden, who for some years held the office we should now call Public Relations Officer of the LNER at Kings Cross, but who was then known as Information Agent. He was a great locomotive enthusiast himself, who not only arranged many privileges for me, but always delighted in having a personal report of the journeys I made and the things I saw, some of which had to be hushed up at the time! Through his good offices I met many of the senior officers of the LNER, and thereby gained a clearer insight into the design and operating features of the locomotives concerned. I never had occasion to ride on one of the 'Klondikes', but I count myself fortunate in having ridden on engines of the '251' class, in such exciting and demanding circumstances as the 'Queen of Scots' Pullman trains.

O.S. Nock
Batheaston, Bath
December 1983

Opposite *Front-end view of No 251, with stove-pipe chimney and no fewer than seven lamp irons, for the head-codes in use on GNR prior to adoption of Railway Clearing House standards* (British Railways).

Below *The pioneer 'Atlantic', No 990, after being named* Henry Oakley (British Railways).

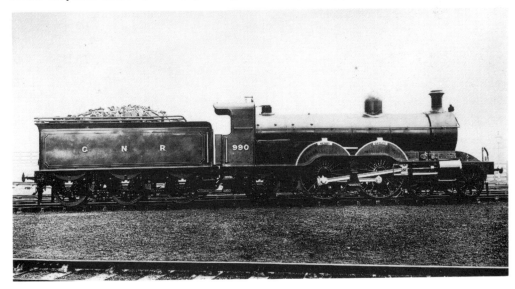

Above *Motive power when Ivatt arrived; an up East Coast express south of Hitchin, hauled by Stirling 8 ft 4-2-2 No 663* (Loco Publishing Co Ltd).

Below *The changing scene on the GNR. A Stirling 7 ft 7 in 2-2-2, rebuilt with domed boiler, on up stopping train near Hadley Wood* (C. Laundy).

Chapter 1
'990' — Start of a new era

On November 11 1895, Patrick Stirling died, still in office as Locomotive Superintendent of the Great Northern Railway, although in his 76th year. His death marked the end of an era and, at the same time, the beginning of a legend. Stirling's days at Doncaster and the locomotives introduced during them were to become venerated by a band of enthusiasts as keen, if not more so, than those who worshipped at the shrine of William Stroudley and his yellow Brighton engines. In the later 1930s, when the cult received a tremendous fillip from the restoration of the famous bogie 8-ft single No 1 to working order and her running on many excursion trains, I can remember an elderly enthusiast referring to Stirling with positively awed reverence as 'an artist in metal'. Stirling lived to see the second great 'Race to the North' and to urge his enginemen to ever faster running, and there is no doubt that the sympathies of the leading railway enthusiasts were on the side of the East Coast companies. The triumph of their rivals on the ever memorable night of August 22–23 was regarded as something of a Pyrrhic victory in that, by so drastically lightening the load, most of the passengers were left behind!

Stirling's death, at the relatively advanced age of nearly 76, had not taken the Great Northern's management entirely by surprise, though it would seem that little had been done within the company to provide for his succession. Stirling seems to have been in his usual vigorous frame of mind during the exciting period of the 'Race to the North' in the summer of 1895, but in the autumn of that year Sir Henry Oakley, General Manager of the GNR, took the unusual step of writing privately to J.A.F. Aspinall, then Chief Mechanical Engineer of the Lancashire and Yorkshire Railway, and asking if he thought H.A. Ivatt would be a suitable successor to Stirling. On the Great Southern and Western Railway in Ireland, Ivatt had been assistant to Aspinall, and had succeeded him as Locomotive Superintendent, when the latter went to the LYR in 1886. His answer to Sir Henry Oakley was contained in the one word, 'indubitably'! As the directors of the Great Northern Railway knew, however, there was more to it than just that.

The legend of Stirling on the Great North-
ern Railway went a good deal further than the ranks of the amateur enthusiasts. He was a father figure to the men of the Locomotive Department and any successor would have to tread warily. The railway's great partner, the North Eastern, had been through a tempestuous epoch when the immediate successor of Edward Fletcher, another father figure in the locomotive world, was unduly hurried in instituting some (admittedly needed) reforms. Yet in February 1896, at the half-yearly meeting of the Company, in explaining the Board's choice of a successor to Stirling, the Chairman, the Hon F.L. Jackson, afterwards Lord Allerton, said, 'We hold, as directors, that it is our duty, in the event of a vacancy arising, not necessarily to limit our selection to servants or officers of the Company, but it is our bounden duty to try and make the best appointment we can'. And they went to the very same Irish railway from which the would-be iconoclast of Gateshead had come; not only that, but to a man who had been appointed by and served under the ill-fated McDonnell (Fletcher's successor), and who was already steeped in the precepts that had been so successfully established on the Great Southern and Western Railway at Inchicore. But Henry A. Ivatt, as ardent and forward-looking a locomotive engineer as ever was McDonnell, had come to the top in Ireland after a spell as assistant to J.A.F. Aspinall, and the two close friends must have been saddened to see what happened when their former, greatly appreciated chief took up the reins at Gateshead. When the Great Northern Board put Ivatt in to succeed so legendary a figure as Patrick Stirling, in less discerning hands the situation at Doncaster could have been a repetition of what had happened at Gateshead, 12 years earlier.

Ivatt, however, was a diplomat as well as being a very able engineer and he enlisted the sympathy of the entire staff of his department with a message, early in 1896, in which he said that he was following in the footsteps of a very great engineer and, while there would eventually be changes, he assured the footplate men particularly that they would have plenty of steam. The locomotive stock, as Stirling left it, was really something of an anachronism in 1895. The express passenger service was worked entirely by single-wheelers. From the viewpoint of nominal tractive effort these — and particularly the final batch of outside-cylindered bogie 4-2-2s — were considerably more powerful than any of the 2-4-0s, having 19½ in by 28 in cylinders, against 17½ in by 26 in in the latest of the coupled engines. But *force majeure*, in the form of heavier train loads, was tending to break down Stirling's rigid anti-piloting rule; and although the '1003' class of bogie 8-ft singles, built in 1894-5 were originally built without vacuum-brake connections on the front buffer beam, thus making it impossible to double-head them, it was not long before this equipment had to be added.

Ivatt was no stranger to bad track; but while it did not hamper locomotive design for the GS & WR in Ireland, with relatively small locomotives and light loads, it was another matter on the Great Northern, where the final batch of Stirling bogie 8-footers originally had no less than 19.2 tons on their driving axles. Not only were there no rails heavier than 85 lb per yard on the main line, but the track maintenance was none too good. There were two bad accidents with the '1003' class of 4-2-2s, both due to faulty permanent way, and one of Ivatt's first tasks on arrival at Doncaster was to arrange a redistribution of the weight of the bogie 8-footers, so as to reduce the loading on the driving axle. In the meantime, to meet the increased loading of many express passenger trains, recourse was had to double heading, frequently with a 4-2-2 and a 2-2-2. Contemporary photographs do not seem to have captured any instances in which the 6 ft 7 in 2-4-0s

were used to assist the single-wheelers. Nevertheless, Ivatt seems to have found a need for many more four-coupled engines, for in the first two years of his superintendence he built 41 further examples, all with 17½ in by 26 in cylinders, 10 of them of the 2-4-0 type. None of them however replaced the Stirling 'singles' on the principal express trains. Ivatt was planning something much bigger for his future development and it is interesting that in so doing he was in frequent touch with his former chief at Inchicore, his close personal friend, John A.F. Aspinall, who was also preparing for much larger passenger engines on the Lancashire and Yorkshire Railway.

Like Churchward on the Great Western, Ivatt attached great importance to the boiler, particularly as the Stirling engines had been so limited in that respect. It was not that they would not steam; in fact they steamed very freely, but they did not produce enough for the increasingly heavy demands of the traffic. But there was also the question of the 'engine', and this was a subject that Ivatt and Aspinall discussed together at some length. At Horwich they had standardised the Joy valve gear, and Ivatt borrowed one of the very speedy Aspinall 7 ft 3 in 4-4-0s for trials, it being fitted temporarily with a Great Northern tender. But both engineers felt that the ordinary valve motions, whether Stephenson's or Joy's, did not give as free an exhaust as desirable when running fast with the gear fully linked up; and, as a result of their discussions, Aspinall took out a patent for a supplementary exhaust valve, which was fitted experimentally to one of the standard 4-4-0s of

GNR Express Passenger Engines 1884–1900

Date:	1884	1892	1894	1898	1900
Type:	4-2-2	2-2-2	4-2-2	4-4-2	4-2-2
First of class:	771	871	1003	990	267
Cylinders					
diameter, ins	18	18½	19½	18¾	19*
stroke, ins	28	26	28	24	26
Driving wheel diameter, ft-in	8-1	7-7	8-1	6-7	7-8
Total heating surface, sq ft					
Tubes	936	936	910	1,302	1,143.8
Firebox	109	109	121.7	140	125.8
Grate area, sq ft	17.75	18.4	20	26.75	23.2
Boiler pressure psi	160	160	170	175	175
Total engine weight, tons	45.15	40.65	49.55	58	48.55
Adhesion weight, tons	17	17.4	19.2	31	17.75
Nominal tractive effort, lb	12,900	13,130	16,100	15,650	15,200

* The pioneer engine, built in 1898, had 18 in diameter cylinders.

the L & YR. But he, and Ivatt too, felt that the complications involved were not worth the candle; neither did his trials of the L & YR 4-4-0 convince Ivatt that there would be any advantage in changing to the Joy valve gear. In the meantime both engineers were busy designing large new express passenger engines of the 'Atlantic' type, though while Aspinall's was promised to be a development on a big scale of the standard 4-4-0, Ivatt's proved to be something entirely new. Furthermore, while Aspinall obtained authority to build a first batch of twenty, Ivatt's was to be a single prototype.

The extent to which Ivatt was breaking away from traditional Doncaster design in the pioneer 'Atlantic' engine can be appreciated from nothing more than a tabulated statement of its basic dimensions alongside those of the final batches of Stirling single-wheeler express engines and those of the 4-2-2 that Ivatt himself introduced later in 1898 and multiplied in 1900. Seeing that, ostensibly, provision was

being made for the haulage of considerably heavier trains one can indeed wonder why, in relation to the greatly enlarged boiler on No 990, the cylinders were made so small. Not only this, but this pioneer 'Atlantic' did not prove merely an experimental prototype. Ivatt was evidently satisfied with the performance of the engine to the extent that a production batch of ten, differing from the prototype in no more than minor constructional details, was built at Doncaster in 1900. Comparison of the tractive effort of No 990 with that of the Stirling '1003' class is not really a case of like for like. The 'Atlantic' with the greater adhesion weight would, theoretically, be more surefooted in getting away with a load, while the far greater boiler capacity would permit of a higher sustained effort at speed, provided the cylinders could use the steam effectively. This, of course, is the question both Aspinall and Ivatt had in mind when considering supplementary exhaust valves.

At this stage it is convenient to consider the

Grantham, South End, about 1902: a Stirling 8-footer, No 771, leaves for Kings Cross, while an Ivatt 4-2-2, No 264, and a Stirling 7 ft 7 in 2-2-2, No 876 (rebuilt with domed boiler), wait for succeeding trains (Rev R.A. Parley).

Above *The first Great Northern 'Atlantic', No 990, as first turned out from Doncaster Plant, in 1898, painted in 'shop grey'* (British Railways).

Below *Engine No 990 in standard GNR livery, but before naming, at York* (W.J. Reynolds).

Bottom *4-4-0s on Great Northern expresses: an Ivatt, No 1339, on a down train near Potters Bar* (O.S. Nock Collection).

design of engine No 990 in detail. As the first 10-wheeled locomotive to be built in Great Britain for express passenger work it created a great amount of interest, particularly as it was extensively featured in the two popular illustrated monthly magazines not long previously introduced. *The Locomotive Magazine* had an illustrated account of the engine in its issue of July 1898, while *The Railway Magazine*, anticipating the working appearance of the engine, had a magnificent colour plate, in the lithographed style, in its December 1898 issue. Not all the early colour plates in that journal were renowned for the accuracy of the colour rendering, but that of No 990 was superb. It was however noted that at the time of publication the engine was still running in its 'shop grey', albeit fully lined out in black and white. *The Locomotive Magazine* invited its readers to note 'a good many points in common with the latest American practice'; but what they were I have no idea, save that of the wheel arrangement. Although very large at the time, No 990 looked nothing but purely English. The journal ended its short article thus, 'No 990 looks like pulling and the driver who is fortunate to run her ought not to fear keeping time with a more than usually heavy load'. Actually she was at first allocated to Grantham shed, for working on the Anglo-Scottish expresses southwards to Kings Cross and northwards to York.

The commentary in *The Railway Magazine*, accompanying that superb colour plate, explained, in rather naive language, how the new locomotive, 'may be regarded as an advance in the direction of dealing with the problem of how to pull heavy trains at high speed. That the problem is not an easy one is admitted by those who know most about it. Bigger trains require larger engines, but the height and width to which the engine may extend is limited by bridges, platforms etc, so that increased length is the only direction in which there is room for expansion. Here, again, increased size is limited by the provision necessary for getting round curves, and also by the average strength of the fireman's arms. A firebox so long that it cannot be properly fired is manifestly out of the question.'

Then, in the succeeding issue of *The Railway Magazine*, Charles Rous-Marten in his characteristically breezy style also wrote of Mr Ivatt's problems. 'Coming from a quiet, easy-going railway like the Great Southern and Western of Ireland to an impetuous, high

pressure, energetic, go-ahead line such as the Great Northern of England, many men would have been almost dazed and bewildered by the perpetual rush and dash of a railway whose standard speed for expresses is not the dignified old forty miles an hour, but anything you like so long as it is over fifty. But Mr Ivatt quietly fitted himself at once to his surroundings, and promptly recognised that a new and difficult problem that had been steadily building itself up for some years met him with an imperative demand for its immediate solution.'

The problems on the Great Northern were not by any means his sole responsibility. Bustling and energetic though the operation might have been, he was appalled at the condition of the track. O.V.S. Bulleid, his son-in-law, recalling that he was always interested as much in locomotive running as in design, had told how, after taking over at Doncaster, Ivatt walked over the entire 156 miles between there and Kings Cross and having done so wished he was back in Ireland! It was not only the light section of the rails that alarmed him, but the way in which odd lengths were relaid with old and worn pieces. The rail that broke at St Neots on the day before Stirling died and derailed one of the '1003' class bogie 8-footers weighed no more than 70 lb per yard.

The 'Atlantic' engine No 990 was designed very much with poor track in mind. Although the boiler was considered huge the weight was very carefully distributed, with 15 tons on the bogie, 15 tons on the first pair of coupled wheels, 16 on the second and 12 tons on the trailing truck. It was not until Ivatt built his very first Great Northern design, the 4-4-0 engine No 400, in December 1896, that Doncaster had ever built a bogie engine; this was of the swing-link type, with the bogie pin 1½ in to the rear of the central position. This type of bogie had been used by Aspinall on the GS & WR in Ireland, and he took it to the Lancashire and Yorkshire. While it was satisfactory on the 4-4-0s it permitted too much rolling on the 'Atlantics' and was replaced by the Adams type. But the swing-link type proved satisfactory on the GNR and was used on the twenty 4-4-0s of the '1301' class built in 1897-8. as well as being incorporated on the 'Atlantic' No 990. Because of what was then considered the great length of the new engine, allowance was made for some lateral play in the trailing wheel axle-boxes so that the rigid wheelbase was no more than 6 ft 10 in, the distance apart of the coupled axles. Outwardly it might appear that the rigid wheelbase extended a further 8 ft back to the trailing axle which had outside bearings in a supplementary outside frame-plate.

The design of the trailing-wheel mountings which remained standard throughout the entire range of Great Northern 'Atlantics' and which were, I believe, also used on the Marsh 'Atlantics' of the London Brighton and South Coast, was not a trailing 'truck' in the usually understood form. The spring, mounted externally on the supplementary frame-plate, rested on a plate that was free to slide over the top of the axle-box. There was no side control by springs or other means to keep the trailing wheels central when the locomotive was running on a straight road. As vehicles these 'Atlantics' rode well and were easy on the track, but as will be told later in this book they could give their privileged guests some palpitating moments when speed ruled high. When No 990 first took the road, however, Ivatt did everything he could to restrain drivers from attaining high maximum speeds. It was not until radical improvements had been made to the track that there was any official relaxation in this respect.

While Ivatt himself paid the most careful attention to everything that concerned the behaviour of his large new engine as a vehicle, it was, somewhat naturally, the boiler that caused most comment from others. It looked longer than it really was, because the leading end of the barrel was recessed by 1 ft 11 in, to provide an extension of the smokebox capacity and, although the overall length externally was 14 ft 8½ in, the distance between the tube plates was no more than 13 ft 0 in. Aspinall did exactly the same on his L & YR 'High-flyers', with the same distance between the tubeplates; but although both friends used tubes of 2 in outside diameter, the Horwich boiler of larger diameter had 233 of them, against 191 on No 990. It was considered that the free gas area through the tubes, related to the grate area, was a measure — other things being equal — of the freedom with which an engine would steam. The Aspinall engine, with 26 sq ft of grate area, was the better of the two, with a ratio of 16:1, against the 13:1 of No 990; but the latter, fired on best quality, hard, Yorkshire coal steamed well enough for all current requirements on the GNR. The corresponding gas-area ratio on the '1003' class of Stirling bogie 8-footers was 12:1 and, as Sir Nigel Gresley once remarked in retrospect, 'Those engines had no boiler to speak of

and yet they steamed well enough!'

Both Ivatt and Aspinall were very conscious of the need to have a free exhaust and while the L & YR experiments with a supplementary exhaust valve came to nothing it is interesting to see how the cylinders and valves of No 990 were designed. In view of the state of the track it was essential to keep the weight of this large engine as low as possible, and something was saved by keeping the piston stroke down to 24 in and the cylinder diameter to 18¾ in. But with such small cylinders and a nominal tractive effort less than that of the largest Stirling 8-footers, if the potentialities of the much larger boiler were to be realised then those small cylinders had to use considerably more steam and use it effectively. The answer to that particular problem lay in having a free exhaust and Ivatt's design of balanced slide valves merits special attention. This was a straight adaptation of the Richardson type (also used by Aspinall) and was the only feature of engine No 990 that could be described as derived from American practice. In this design, four strips were let into four planed grooves on the back of the valve; these strips, projecting upwards, bore upon a plate held so as to be parallel to the valve face. The strips making contact with this plate were pressed up by springs. The area enclosed was under exhaust pressure only, because the back of the valve was kept in free communication with the blast pipe through a hole in the crown of the valve. The steam ports in the slide valve itself were 1½ in wide by 16 in long and the exhaust ports 3½ in by 16 in.

The Stephenson's link motion, inside the frames, provided a setting that was conventional at that period, with a positive lead of $\frac{3}{32}$ in in full gear and a maximum travel of 4⅜ in. An unusual feature was the design of the catch-block on the reversing lever. The usual form was to have a drop catch of substantial proportions, the adjustment of which made a change of 'one notch' represent an increase or decrease of about 10 per cent in the point of cut-off of steam in the cylinders. The Ivatt 'Atlantics' had instead a toothed catch block which made possible a much finer adjustment of the reversing lever position. Actually, however, no use was made of this feature in driving the locomotive — at any rate on the occasions when I was privileged to ride on the footplate. This, however, is anticipating experience that lay many years ahead of the time of which I am now writing. In the first production batch of these engines, built at

Doncaster in 1900, an arrangement for locking the reversing gear in any desired position was fitted. To my mind the advisability of having such a device is questionable and, in my own footplate experience on Great Northern 'Atlantics', I cannot recall its being used. It may have been introduced in the first place to eliminate the 'judder' that sometimes occurred with reversing gears of the notched lever type, caused by vibration off the motion.

The locking device designed for his 'Atlantic' engines by Mr Ivatt consisted of a small vacuum cylinder 6 in in diameter, of a similar type to that used for the vacuum brake, which was secured to the front of the cross-stay between the frames of the locomotive. On the back of the stay was fastened a cast-iron strap which embraced half the circumference of a cast-iron drum 8 in in diameter by 3 in wide. This drum was in halves bolted together and keyed into the reversing shaft. The movable part of the strap embracing the other half-circumference of the drum was of wrought iron. It was connected at the bottom, by a coupling link to a bell-crank lever, the latter being in its turn connected to the eye-bolt of the actuating vacuum cylinder. The driver's control device, nothing more than a simple turncock, enabled the clutch to be locked or released, by tightening the wrought iron strap on the locking drum. As details of my footplate journeys related in subsequent chapters of this book will show, very little adjustment of the reversing lever was made in fast and heavy express duty.

At this stage it is of interest to recall how No 990 and the subsequent 20 engines of her class got their celebrated nickname. Excitement from the great 'Race to the North' of 1895 had not entirely died down by 1898. The North Eastern had built two special 'racing' locomotives with 7 ft 7 in coupled wheels, similar otherwise to Class 'Q', and the London and North Western had demonstrated that, if necessary, they could run non-stop from Euston to Carlisle with one of the 7 ft Webb 3-cylinder compound engines. But the derailment of the West Coast 'Tourist' express at Preston in the late summer of 1896 had put a damper on speeding. Nevertheless, the enthusiasts were always looking for signs of renewed activity and, coincidentally, No 990 was 'out-shopped' from Doncaster just at the time when the attention of the world's press was rivetted on the breathless news from the far north-west of the North American continent. The 'Gold Rush' was on and it seemed that all

ordinary ideas of business development and wealth creation were collapsing overnight. On the British railways it seemed there was a parallel, in that No 990 of the Great Northern seemed to have far outstripped all existing standards of size and potential tractive ability.

Today, in Canada, the 'Trail of '98' is revered and pinpointed as an historic national site, and at a place with the eerie name of Dead Horse Gulch there is a memorial plaque erected by the government. It reads:

DISCOVERY CLAIM

Tipped off by veteran prospector Bob Henderson, George Carmack and his fishing partners, Snookum Jim and Tagish Charlie searched the creek gravels of this area. On August 17, 1896, they found gold and staked the first four claims. A few days later at Fortymile, Carmack, in his own name, registered the Discovery Claim where this monument stands. Within days Bonanza and Eldorado Creeks had been staked from end to end and when the news reached the outside the KLONDIKE GOLD RUSH was on.

And so, appropriately, the new epoch-marking British locomotives that were to lead the 'gold rush' on the Great Northern became known as the 'Klondikes'. Strangely enough, the nickname did not appear in any of the popular railway literature of the day. Rous-Marten, when he did mention nicknames, was always apt to scoff at them, as he did once, quite *in extenso*, over the happy little name of 'Jumbo', for the family of LNWR 2-4-0 express locomotives. In his opinion it detracted from their dignity. The Rev W.J. Scott, who frequently wrote in a light vein, once, to distinguish the 'Klondikes' from the larger boilered '251' class that followed, referred to them as 'the long-necked variety' of GN 'Atlantics'. Nicknames or not, through the columns of *The Railway Magazine* and that magnificent colour plate, the enthusiasts of the day could appreciate something of the profound impression that No 990 created. It was not until some time later that the engine was named *Henry Oakley*, after the General Manager of the GNR, and became the first ever Great Northern engine to be named. It is indeed fortunate that timely steps were taken to preserve this historic engine and to restore it, not only to its original livery but to full working order. There is much to be told of the engine's activities, since 1953, in later chapters of this book.

Chapter 2

The 'Klondikes' in service

The building of a production batch of the new 'Atlantics' in 1900, differing in no more than incidental details from the prototype No 990, seemed a sure sign that the first had been successful. The changes included a modification to the shape of the main framing at the front end and an alteration to the layout of the sanding gear. In No 990 sanding for forward running was applied only under the leading pair of coupled wheels, whereas in the production batch it was transferred to the rearward pair. Engine No 990 was at first stationed at Grantham, which was then generally considered the premier Great Northern shed for the East Coast traffic. It was not until a second production batch of these engines was built in 1902–03 that any of them were stationed at Kings Cross. Ivatt himself took great interest in running generally; from the earliest recorded examples of 'Atlantic' performance it is evident that he gave no encouragement to the attaining of high maximum speeds. There can be no doubt that he was apprehensive of the state of the track. Although photographs show the ballast piled

on top of the sleepers the way in which it was packed left much to be desired.

Not long after No 990 has been put into service, something of a 'show' run was made from Kings Cross to Grantham to which Charles Rous-Marten was invited. The load, quoted as 214 tons, was little more than those that the Stirling bogie 8-footers tackled regularly; but there were some significant differences in the style of the running. As observers of train running in later years came to appreciate, it was not characteristic of the day-to-day work of these engines when the drivers were not under special instructions. The engine was worked very hard at the start, sustaining 47 mph up the 1 in 200 climb to Potters Bar. This would have involved an equivalent drawbar horsepower of about 700 and to do this the lever would have had to have been 'well down in the corner', as the saying goes, and those balanced slide valves exhausting very freely. On the racing descent from Stevenage through Hitchin, speed did not exceed 70 mph and yet a distance of 56½ miles was covered in the first hour out of

Up Anglo-Scottish express near Potters Bar: note the mixture of clerestory, elliptical and flat-roofed stock, hauled by engine No 990 Henry Oakley (C. Laundy).

Kings Cross. The shorter incline of 1 in 200 gradient from Huntingdon up to the Leys signal box was rushed at a minimum speed of 54¾ mph and the maximum speed of the whole journey, 73 mph, was briefly attained descending from Abbots Ripton to the Fens, near Holme. The 100th milepost out of London, near the Stoke signal-box and at the conclusion of the long adverse stretch from Peterborough, was passed in 108½ minutes, the train having averaged 55½ mph from the start; being well ahead of time the train was stopped ½ mile short of the entrance to Grantham station, 105 miles, in 2 seconds under 114 minutes.

Considerably more detail is available of another early run of No 990, also in 1898, on an up express which one finds Rous-Marten referring to as '. . . the so-called "Flying Scotsman"' (!), which it actually was, pulling the 10:00 am from Edinburgh to Kings Cross, though the name was rarely used at that time. The train then ran non-stop from York to Grantham, but slipped a coach at Doncaster. The engine must have been worked very hard from the start to make such good time to Naburn, with a load of 315 tons. In the early 1930s, when the Gresley non-streamlined 'Pacifics' were at their zenith it was rare to cover that first 4.2 miles in much less than 7¼ minutes; and then the trailing load in relation to the tractive effort of the locomotive was 36½, as compared to 45½ in the case of No

GNR 'The Flying Scotsman' in 1898 York–Grantham

Load, to Doncaster; 293 tons tare, 315 tons full
Load, to Grantham; 271 tons tare, 290 tons full
Engine (4-4-2) No: 990

Distance Miles		Actual m s	Average speed mph
0.0	YORK	0 00	—
4.2	Naburn	6 34	38.4
7.1	Escrick	9 24	61.4
9.7	Riccall	11 57	61.2
13.8	SELBY	16 37	52.7
18.4	Templehirst	22 55	43.8
22.2	Balne	27 01	55.6
25.2	Moss	29 51	63.6
28.0	*Shaftholme Junction*	32 36	61.0
30.1	Arksey	34 42	60.0
32.2	DONCASTER	36 44	61.8
36.9	Rossington	41 54	54.5
40.5	Bawtry	46 21	48.6
42.4	Scrooby	48 08	63.8
44.3	Ranskill	49 54	64.6
46.5	Sutton	52 03	61.5
49.6	RETFORD	55 12	59.0
56.3	Tuxford	63 01	51.5
60.8	Crow Park	67 02	67.2
61.8	Carlton	67 54	69.2
—	troughs		slack
68.1	NEWARK	75 17	51.4
72.8	Claypole	80 44	51.7
76.7	Hougham	86 00	44.4
78.5	Bàrkston	88 28	43.8
82.7	GRANTHAM	94 26	42.2

Down Sheffield and Manchester express near Hadley Wood, hauled by 4-4-2 No 949 (C. Laundy).

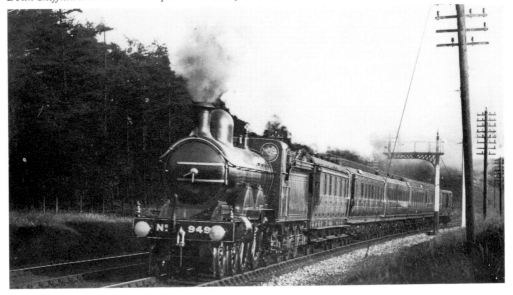

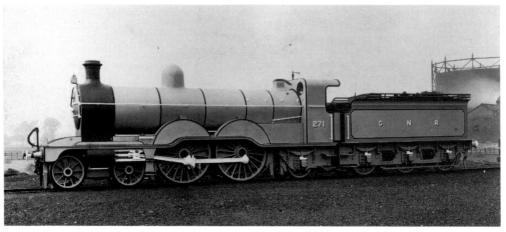

Ivatt's experimental 4-cylinder 'Atlantic', No 271, as originally built (British Railways).

990 on this 1898 occasion. As will be seen from the tabulated log of the journey, speed did not much exceed 60 mph on the level stretches from Templehirst to Doncaster and between Scrooby and Retford. Rous-Marten stated that '. . . directly after Carlton station, the driver, finding he would be at Newark before his booked time, promptly eased down to 50 miles an hour and went under easy steam all the rest of the way'. At that time however it was customary — indeed mandatory, I believe — to reduce speed to 40 mph when picking up water. The reduction over Muskham troughs, just before the bridge over the Trent, was probably, therefore, the cause of the sudden drop in average speed, even though the line between Carlton and Newark is level. There can have been little in the way of easing afterwards, for such average speeds to be maintained up the climb past Barkston to Peascliffe Tunnel, again on 1 in 200. This was, indeed, a very fine run.

The next developments came in 1902. The first was the building at Doncaster of the experimental four-cylinder 'Atlantic' engine No 271. As originally built and fitted with the Stephenson-link motion, all four cylinders drove on to the leading pair of coupled wheels; so, to provide for an adequate length of connecting rods, the spacing between the rear pair of bogie wheels and the leading coupled wheels was increased from the 5 ft 3 in on No 990 to 6 ft 1½ in. To avoid lengthening the engine unduly, the distance between the rear pair of coupled wheels and the trailing axle was reduced from 8 ft 0 in to 7 ft 6 in. The total engine wheelbase was increased

from 26 ft 4 in to 26 ft 9 in. The four cylinders were 15 in in diameter with the very short stroke of 20 in and, with a boiler pressure of 175 lb per sq in, the nominal tractive effort was 10 per cent higher than that of No 990, though for all that only reached the still modest figure of 17,200 lb. On this engine, also, some changes were made in the boiler proportions. Its centre was pitched 2 in higher, and the following difference from that of No 990 are to be noted.

'Atlantic' Boilers

Engine No	990	271
Length of barrel, ft-ins	14-8⅝	15-4¼
Outside diameter, smallest ring, ft-ins	4-8	4-6⅞
Distance between tube-plates, ft-ins	13-0	14-0
Tubes		
number	191	141
outside diameter, ins	2	2¼
Total heating surface, sq ft		
tubes	1302	1162¾
firebox	140	140¼
total	1442	1303
Grate area, sq ft	26.75	24.5
Boiler pressure psi	175	175

With all the motion inside, No 271 looked a very neat and handsome locomotive, though little is known of her performance in this first condition. That she was soon rebuilt with a considerable change in the valve gear may or may not have been significant. With such small cylinders it cannot be said that in her first state there was any risk of 'beating the boiler'.

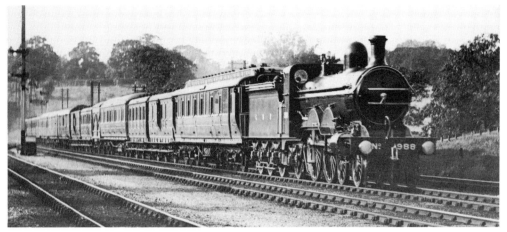

Up express, south of Hadley Wood tunnel, with an extraordinary mixture of stock, hauled by 'Klondike' No 988, the first (later) to be superheated (C. Laundy).

Later in 1902 and through the early months of 1903 came more 'Atlantic' engines from Doncaster. They were numbered 250 to 260, but were not 'outshopped' in numerical order. The first one out, No 251, differed from all the rest and, although having the same engine machinery, was fitted with an enormously large boiler. It was, of course, the prototype of the large-boilered 'Atlantics' that in later years won such undying fame for the locomotive department of the GNR and its successor. At this stage in the present book, however, I am leaving consideration of this notable prototype for a later chapter. The ten additional 'Klondikes' were all in service by the summer of 1903 and, by that time, the allocation of the 21 locomotives of this class was as follows: Doncaster, 982, 983, 984, 985, 986, 989, 250, 260; Grantham, 990, 949, 950, 257, 258, 259; Kings Cross, 252, 253, 254; and Peter-

borough, 987, 988, 255, 256. For the record, the pioneer large-boilered engine No 251, and the experimental four-cylindered No 271 were stationed at Doncaster.

Some new and accelerated services were introduced in the summer of 1902. Although the Great Central had developed some very fast services over the London extension, the Great Northern had not relinquished its interest in the London-Manchester business and this was reflected in non-stop runs between Kings Cross and Nottingham via Grantham. Another interesting service at the time provided for several expresses to make non-stop runs between Kings Cross and Newark, no doubt to give good connections to and from Lincoln. In the summer of 1902, the Great Northern had the non-stop runs of over 100 miles shown in the table below.

Distance miles		Time minutes	Speed mph	No of trains daily
156	Kings Cross-Doncaster	181	51.7	1
128½	Nottingham (Victoria)–Kings Cross	146	52.9	1
127¾	Nottingham (London Rd)–Kings Cross	145	52.9	1
120	Kings Cross–Newark	137	52.5	1
120	Newark–Kings Cross	141	51.0	1
117½	Newark–Finsbury Park	143	49.3	1
105½	Kings Cross–Grantham	115*	55.1	10
105½	Grantham–Kings Cross	114*	55.5	4
103	Finsbury Park–Grantham	126	49.0	1
103	Grantham–Finsbury Park	120	51.5	2

* Fastest train

Top *'Klondike' No 983, fitted with outside-framed bogie, the only one to be so equipped* (British Railways).

Above *The four-cylinder 'Atlantic', as first rebuilt, with outside Walschaerts valve gear for the outside cylinders* (W.J. Reynolds).

The Nottingham non-stops were very light trains and were worked by the Stirling 7 ft 6 in 2-2-2s, while the fastest of the Grantham–Kings Cross runs were also lightly loaded expresses to and from Manchester via Retford and Sheffield. The East Coast expresses running non-stop between Kings Cross and Grantham were timed in much more leisurely style. The down 'Flying Scotsman' was allowed 120 minutes for the run and the 2:20 pm down from Kings Cross 124 minutes, average speeds of 52.7 and 51.0

mph respectively. Start-to-stop average speeds of 50 to 53 mph were usual for the heavy Anglo-Scottish and Yorkshire expresses. It was on these trains, rather than the competitive Manchester 'flyers' that the 'Atlantics' were mostly employed.

When the question came up, early in 1903, of accelerating certain of the Leeds and Bradford trains in competition with the Midland, a special run was arranged on which the 9:45 am down from Kings Cross was to be worked ahead of normal time where possible and engine No 990 *Henry Oakley* was used as far as Grantham. With no more than a moderate load, estimated at 212 tons gross behind the tender, the uphill running was as near 'all-out' as I have ever seen reported with a 'Klondike'. For going up to Potters Bar, a speed of 53½ mph was sustained on the 1 in 200 gradient and this would represent an equivalent drawbar horsepower of about 900. For cylinders of only 18¾ in diameter by 24 in stroke, this was a terrific effort and must be borne in mind when maximum efforts of the large-boilered 'Atlantics' are analysed in later chapters of this book. This was no flash in the pan so far as No 990 was concerned, as the summary log of the run shows.

Distance miles		Actual m s	Average speed mph
0.0	Kings Cross	0 00	—
—		pws	—
12.7	Potters Bar	17 58	42.4
31.9	Hitchin	36 04	63.7
58.9	Huntingdon	59 19	69.8
70.0	*Milepost 70*	69 00	68.2
76.4	Peterborough	76 24	51.9
95.2	Swayfield Box		
		96 20	57.2
		99 21	signal stop
105.5	Grantham	112 43	
Net time, min		104	

The bank from Huntingdon to the Leys Box was rushed at a minimum speed of 60 mph and there was some easing prior to the regulation slack through Peterborough station, to 10 mph, because of temporary injector trouble on the locomotive. Although a special occasion, it was the finest-ever performance with one of these engines on a medium-load train.

Before the beautiful new, vestibuled-car trains were put on to the London-Leeds service on New Years Day 1903, a trial trip was run, two days earlier; it was of interest that, on the return journey, the four-cylinder 'Atlantic' No 271 was used. This, though, is the only reference I have ever seen to the working of this engine in its original condition. It had been reported as on test between Doncaster, Lincoln and Boston, and Rous-Marten once remarked that he was making some experimental trips with it and would have much to say about it later. But whatever he had to say never seems to have got into print and in 1905 the engine was extensively rebuilt using the Walschaerts valve gear outside, and slide valves on top of the cylinders. In its original form it had piston valves, though of what type I cannot say. Ivatt was a close friend of Wilson Worsdell, Chief Mechanical Engineer of the North Eastern Railway, and that company was making extensive use of W.M. Smith's segmental type of valve. It could well be that No 271 was fitted experimentally with these.

The promised acceleration of the Leeds service was made in July 1903, with the 9:45 am down run non-stop to Doncaster and the 2:00 pm up non-stop from Wakefield to Kings Cross (176 miles). The latter, although timed fast, was a light train, and when it first ran consisted of no more than three of the new, vestibuled, 12-wheeled coaches from Leeds and a fourth, from Bradford, attached at Wakefield. The gross trailing load was then no more than 145 tons. Interestingly, Rous-Marten logged one of the newest 'Klondikes', No 253, soon after the train had been put on. It was an easy task for the locomotive and a number of incidental checks did not prevent overall time being kept. Perhaps the most significant feature of the run was the ease and rapidity with which it was worked up to 85 mph on the descent from Stoke Tunnel towards Peterborough, further evidence of the freedom of exhaust from the balanced slide valves. The following is a summary log of the run.

Distance Miles		Actual m s	Remarks
0.0	Wakefield	0 00	—
19.9	Doncaster	20 25	—
—	Muskham troughs	slack	40 mph
70.4	Grantham	72 54	
—	Monkswood Box	signal stop	73 sec
99.5	Peterborough	106 16	10 mph
—	Stukeley Box	signal check	
—	Hatfield	signal check	
—	Finsbury Park	pws	
179.9	Kings Cross	181 40	
Net time, min		173	
Booked time, min		190	

Although the formation of the train remained very light, up to the time of withdrawal of the Wakefield–London non-stop run, in World War I, it was generally worked by one of the large-boilered 'Atlantics', when plenty of these became available.

The weakness of the 'Klondikes', if one may presume to call it so, was shown in the regular haulage of the heavy East Coast trains and another journey, also made in 1903 by Rous-Marten, makes this clear, despite his enthusiasm for the overall result. One of the 250–260 series, number not specified, had to haul a gross trailing load of 380 tons, on a timing of 184 minutes non-stop over the 156 miles from Doncaster to Kings Cross. Apart from the slacks over the Muskham and Werrington water troughs and the usual 'dead-slowing' through Peterborough, the train was unchecked and clocked up a start-to-stop time of 182 minutes 2 seconds, with an average speed of 51.4 mph. Rous-Marten commented, 'Such a performance by one engine would have been deemed quite incredible, even at a date long subsequent to the Aberdeen Race, and it is exceedingly gratifying to realise what valuable progress has been made since that period in respect of the most important phase of locomotive engineering'. Fair enough, up to a point; but the only details of intermediate uphill speeds that were reported were minima of 36 mph from Retford up to Askham Tunnel and 37½ mph up Abbots Ripton bank — both relatively

short inclines. There was, however, a long sustained burst of speed downhill from Stoke Tunnel, with a maximum of 85 mph. From the viewpoint of locomotive effort it would have been almost as easy to do this with the 380-ton load, as to do it with 145 tons of the Wakefield non-stop. The Rev W.J. Scott, a lifelong East Coast enthusiast, was not impressed with the 1903 service and concluded his summary article in *The Railway Magazine* with the words, 'Cockshott; thou should'st be living at this hour'.

One can understand how Scott, with vivid memories of the Aberdeen race and events leading up to it, yearned for a return to the day when Cockshott, that most enterprising of traffic managers fairly set the heather on fire, with his timetabling innovations; but after the race the dead hand of the Anglo-Scottish agreement on minimum times hung over all the Scottish express service, and the 'Flying Scotsman' itself and the popular 2:20 pm down from Kings Cross were leisurely trains. Even when many large-boilered 'Atlantics' had been built, the 'Klondikes' continued to work regularly on the heaviest trains, particu-

Up summer express, Scarborough and Whitby to Kings Cross, made up of North Eastern Railway stock, approaching Peterborough, hauled by 'Klondike' No 984 (C. Laundy).

larly north of Grantham. But coming to ana-
lyse some of the hardest work on these trains,
reference must be made to another on the 2:00
pm up from Leeds, after the load had been
increased by one extra vehicle from Leeds and
a through carriage from Huddersfield added
to the section attached at Wakefield, making
up a gross trailing load of 180 tons. The same
London-based 'Klondike' as on the previous
run was involved, No 253, but on this
occasion there were no checks, other than
slowing over water troughs and the usual 10
mph crawl through Peterborough. The times
were: 22 min 52 sec to Doncaster; 74 min 58
sec to Grantham; and 102 min 27 sec to
Peterborough, by which time 5 min had been
gained on the schedule. An easy and un-
delayed run up to Town brought the train into
Kings Cross in 186¾ minutes from Wakefield. Maximum speed down the Stoke bank
was 82 mph.

The notable accelerations of the Sheffield
trains in the summer service of 1905, which
gave the Great Northern some start-to-stop
bookings at nearly 58 mph, were made with
quite light trains that were usually worked by
single-wheelers, rather than 'Klondikes'; and
it may or may not have been significant that it
was the Stirling 7 ft 6 in 2-2-2s and the Ivatt
'263' class 4-2-2s that were used, rather than
the famous bogie 8-footers. The new 6:10 pm
down from Kings Cross ran non-stop to Sheffield via Retford, 162 miles in 170 minutes,
and when it was first put on it consisted of no
more than three coaches, albeit of the heavy,
12-wheeled, vestibuled stock and a little less
than 120 tons behind the tender. On the up
train, hauled by a 2-2-2 rebuilt with a domed
boiler, Rous-Marten recorded a net time of
160 minutes from Sheffield to Kings Cross.
North of Sheffield the Great Central continued the fast work, having to run the 48½
miles to Manchester Central, non-stop, in just
over the hour.

The 'Sheffield Special', as it was known on
the GNR, did not last long in its original form
and, with the addition of through carriages for
other destinations and an increasing load, the
'Klondikes' came to take a hand in its haulage.
The restaurant-car section was transferred to
Hull, instead of Manchester, and through
carriages for Newcastle were attached to the
rear. Its working then became a rather extraordinary locomotive proposition. A stop was
inserted at Grantham and from there onwards
the Great Central Railway took over the haulage, but only to Retford. The through

carriages for Manchester were marshalled
next to the engine and with these the GCR
locomotive continued on its own line to Sheffield. Another Great Northern engine, usually
a 4-4-0, took the rest of the train on to Doncaster but, before proceeding direct to Hull,
detached the two rear coaches, which were
bound for Newcastle. These were then taken
on to York by a Great Eastern train, with a
GER engine working through. This train was
the 4:30 pm from Liverpool Street to York,
which had thus left London 1 hour 35
minutes before the Great Northern 'flyer'.
Finally, to complete singularity, so far as
those through Newcastle coaches were concerned, they were attached at York to a train
of Lancashire and Yorkshire Railway stock, a
through express from Liverpool, though now
hauled by a North Eastern engine. Could one
now imagine greater complexity in locomotives and rolling stock on a single journey from
Kings Cross to Newcastle!

The Great Central 3:40 pm from Manchester to London at that time carried through
carriages for both Kings Cross and Marylebone, and the former going forward at 4:48
pm from Sheffield were taken non-stop to
Grantham by the same Great Central engine
that took over haulage of the 6:05 pm from
Kings Cross on the northbound run. The up
Manchester train made a very fast run up to
London, being booked to cover the 105.5
miles from Grantham to Kings Cross in no
more than 110 minutes. It often had however
no more than four coaches, about 150 tons
behind the tender, and, with an 'Atlantic' to
haul it, there were no difficulties in keeping
time provided the line was kept clear. All too
frequently, the fast expresses were checked by
bad traffic regulation. The one train that
seemed assured of a good road was the 2:00
pm from Leeds, with its non-stop run from
Wakefield to Kings Cross.

An interesting record exists, from the
writings of Cecil J. Allen, of the running of
the up morning 'flyer' from Nottingham
which was allowed only 113 minutes from
Grantham to Kings Cross, inclusive of a
2-minute stop at Peterborough. The log was
taken in 1909, when the load was no more
than three 12-wheeled coaches, making 115
tons behind the tender. For once there were
no checks, other than the slowing over
Werrington water troughs. For those who
knew the East Coast main line in later days, I
should add that the additional set of troughs,
south of Stevenage, were not laid in until after

World War I. The log of the run is set out below.

Distance miles		Schedule min	Actual m s	Average speed mph
0.0	GRANTHAM	0	0 00	—
8.4	Corby		11 50	42.6
16.9	Essendine		19 05	70.3
29.1	PETERBOROUGH	32	32 20	55.2
7.0	Holme		9 00	46.6
17.5	HUNTINGDON	19	19 20	61.1
24.7	St Neots		25 25	70.9
35.3	Biggleswade		35 05	65.9
44.5	HITCHIN	46	43 50	63.1
51.4	Knebworth		51 05	57.1
58.7	HATFIELD	60	58 05	62.6
63.7	Potters Bar		63 35	54.5
67.2	New Barnet		67 10	58.5
73.8	Finsbury Park		73 35	61.8
76.4	KINGS CROSS	79	78 30	—

The engine was 'Klondike' No 252 and, although the train left Peterborough 3 minutes late, time was thrown away at the finish by a very slow and unenterprising run downhill from Potters Bar, and an absolute crawl from Finsbury Park down into Kings Cross.

With the heavy East Coast trains, details of a run with the down 'Flying Scotsman' were taken by Mr J.F. Gairns, for many years editor of *The Railway Magazine* and also a qualified locomotive engineer. The engine as far as Grantham was a 'Klondike', No 257, with a gross trailing load of 290 tons. Gairns quoted few intermediate times, but it was good work with this load to pass Peterborough (76.4 miles) in 80¾ minutes from the start. It is evident that the engine was worked very hard up the initial climb to Potters Bar for, after falling to 38 mph on the 1 in 200, there was an acceleration, still on the gradient, to 42 mph. The equivalent drawbar horsepower would have been between 780 and 800. After passing Potters Bar (12.7 miles) in 21¾ minutes, there came some fast running with a maximum of 80 mph down the bank from Stevenage to Three Counties; but having passed Peterborough in such good time, the engine was not pressed so hard on the ascent to Stoke and the speed fell to 36 mph. The 100th milepost was passed in 112½ minutes and Grantham was reached a minute early, in 119 minutes from Kings Cross.

Two reasonably good runs north of Grantham on the 2:20 pm 'Scotsman' from Kings Cross were logged by Cecil J. Allen, the first of which features the same engine that gave J.F. Gairns the good run on the 10:00 am down. Both these East Coast expresses, both north and south of Grantham, were worked by engines and men from Grantham shed. The first of the two runs began quite brilliantly

GNR 2:20 pm Grantham–York ex-Kings Cross

Distance Miles		Schedule min	Actual m s	Average Speed mph	Actual m s	Average Speed mph
Load, tons gross			350		355	
Engine (small 4-4-2) No:			257		949	
0.0	GRANTHAM	0	0 00	—	0 00	—
6.0	Hougham		8 55	40.3	9 45	37.0
14.6	NEWARK	17	16 10	71.2 troughs	pws 19 05 signal stop	55.5
—			— pws			—
20.9	Carlton		21 55	65.7	35 15	—
26.4	Tuxford		30 30	38.5	42 50	43.5
33.1	RETFORD	39	38 10	52.4	50 40	51.2
42.2	Bawtry		46 40	64.3	60 05	57.7
—			pws	—	—	
50.5	DONCASTER	58	56 00	53.3	69 30	52.9
52.6	Arksey		59 50	32.9	71 45	56.0
60.5	Balne		68 30	54.9	80 10	56.3
68.9	SELBY	79	77 40	55.1	89 10	56.0
75.6	Escrick		86 55	43.6	97 45	47.0
—			signals	—	—	—
82.7	YORK	97	97 00	—	106 25	49.1
	Net times, min		90½		93½	

with a sustained 73 mph down to the Trent valley and, although the check near Carlton and that through Doncaster station took their toll, there was plenty of time in this leisurely schedule. No faster speed than 55 mph was needed on the level north of Doncaster, and, despite a relatively slow recovery from the Selby regular restriction, the train was able to clock into York on time. On the second run the stop north of Newark was due to the breaking away of a freight train on the up line; the express was kept waiting until it was ascertained that no derailment had taken place. In consequence Retford was passed nearly 12 minutes late and it was not until after Doncaster that a modest attempt was made to regain something of the lost time. Even so, the sustained speed on the lengthy level stretches before Selby was not more than 56–57 mph. The net average speeds of 55 and 53¼ mph on these two runs, over an easy road, with a very favourable downhill start from Grantham are a reflection of the relatively easy demands made upon locomotive power by the crack trains of the East Coast service.

At the same time a study of many contemporary records of running between Kings Cross and York, made available to me by courtesy of the late E.L. Bell, suggests that with trains of 300 tons or more the driving was not very enterprising. This is also borne out by the experience of Cecil J. Allen, who as an inspector of materials for the Great Eastern Railway had to travel at least once a week from London to the steel works on Tees-side. While most of the data came later to concern the larger-boilered 'Atlantics', the working of the 'Klondikes' followed the same general pattern. On the lighter trains, like the 'Man-chesters', via Retford, and the special 2:00 pm up from Leeds there was plenty of fast running; but it was only on special occasions, when Mr Ivatt himself or other high dignitaries of the GNR were travelling, that the engines of both varieties were exerted uphill. It was still a time when drivers had their own engines and they took pride, not only in immaculate appearance but in reliable mechanical performance; and while not out of balance to the same extent as the larger-boilered class, so far as disparity between boiler and cylinder power was concerned, the 'Klondikes' were not powerful engines by the standards of the early 1900s. Cecil J. Allen summed them up, in 1914, as 'curiously variable engines, as far as performance goes; at times they can be record-breakers of the first water, but on other occasions they are unaccountably sluggish'.

Sluggish is perhaps not quite the correct term to use for these engines, because it might suggest some inherent weakness, such as a restriction in the steam circuit that induced unduly high back pressure. This was certainly not the case with any of Ivatt's engines. Instances when they seemed to be 'dragging their feet' would almost certainly be due to the temperament of the driver, who was disinclined to hurry. It would equally not be due to any shortage of steam, for the 'Klondikes' were excellent in this respect. It was frequently stated in their early days that they were so designed as to be readily fitted with the larger boilers of the '251' class, if the latter proved successful. But this was never done. All the 'Klondikes' retained small boilers throughout their long lives, even though later, with superheating, they were fitted with extended smoke-boxes. The details of these

One of the second production batch of 'Klondikes', No 254: note that part of the firebox shielding has been removed (C. Laundy).

changes in design are dealt with in a later chapter. Ivatt's own experiments with super-heating began with the fitting of the Schmidt apparatus to one of the 'Long Tom' 0-8-0 mineral engines of the '401' class and to a 'Klondike', No 988. Both classes had the same design of boiler, and the recessing of the boiler proper rearwards from the blast-pipe and chimney gave the necessary space for accom-modation of the superheater without any outward change in the appearance of the engine, other than the fitting of piston valves above the cylinders and the use of a mechani-cal lubricator.

Reverting to driving practice, however, one can quite imagine that a careful engineman would be disinclined to thrash a locomotive along, with a wide-open regulator and the lever well forward towards the corner, making the noise once aptly described as 'peppering along' even though it did not involve excessive coal consumption. The Great Northern men had grown up in the Stirling tradition, and with relatively large cylinders and small boilers one just had to work the engines on a light rein, or quickly run short of steam. There was a very heavy East Coast train then due to arrive at Kings Cross at 4:12 pm, which had made connections from many parts of the North-East and was then booked to run the 79.6 miles from Doncaster to Peter-borough in 93 minutes and the concluding 76.4 miles to Kings Cross in 90 minutes, involving start-to-stop average speeds of 51.4 and 50.9 mph, respectively. In 1912, Cecil J. Allen was using it on occasions; its timekeep-ing, even with no delays was not exactly heroic, and even he forebore to give the numbers of the engines. On one run a 'Klon-dike' with a 420-ton loading and no checks managed to stagger through from Doncaster to Peterborough in 104¼ minutes. Another engine of the class took 101¾ minutes to get the same train through to Kings Cross, though on a later occasion yet another 'Klon-dike' did much better in taking a load of 405 tons through to Kings Cross in 92½ minutes. On the longer stretches of 1 in 200 rising gradient, speed fell to about 30 mph and it must be added that the large-boilered engines did very little better.

Intermediate between the very light Manchester 'flyers' worked in conjunction with the Great Central Railway and the heavy East Coast trains was the 5:30 pm from Kings Cross, which began as a fast competitive special for Nottingham, with a through carriage for Newcastle, and was quickly trans-formed into the principal evening dining-car express for Newcastle with one through coach for Nottingham! North of Grantham its usual load was about 200 tons, regularly hauled by the Ivatt 4-2-2 singles of the '263' class. It was allowed 94 minutes for the run of 82.7 miles to York, but for some reason it became tradi-tional to run hard over the Great Northern part of the line to Doncaster and to take it easy afterwards. Then one night a 'Klondike', No 983, was put on instead of the usual single-wheeler, incidentally the one engine of the class that had outside frames on the bogie. Whether this was a regular working or an *ad hoc* substitution I do not know; but whatever it was, No 983 made the fastest start ever on record with that train to passing Doncaster. It was all done in the opening stages with a time of 14 min 50 sec to passing Newark (14.7 miles). After that, the average speed over the ensuring 35.8 miles to Doncaster was no more than 60 mph. Even so, this took the train through Doncaster in 50 min 40 sec, leaving the driver more than 43 minutes to cover the remaining 32.7 miles on to York.

In the period before World War I, with rela-tively few enthusiasts taking detailed notes of train running, the meticulously compiled logs that we have grown accustomed to in recent years, with complete details of the rise and fall of the speed throughout the journey were rare. While I can believe that certain observers like C. Rous-Marten and Cecil J. Allen did take a good deal of intermediate detail, they did not often include it in their published work, most of which was in the nature of summary reports, unless something exceptional trans-pired. Present-day enthusiasts who may be anxious to compare their own observations with what happened in the first decades of this century could well be disappointed in the paucity of fine detail. Nevertheless, the notebooks made available to me by Mr Bell do contain a good deal more and, to conclude this chapter, I have set out, in the full details in which it was recorded, a run from Grantham to York on the down 'Flying Scotsman' made in March 1909. It does not reveal any particu-lar enterprise or merit — if anything, rather the reverse; but I have included it here as a detailed example of daily work of the time. The train had been worked down from Kings Cross by a large-boilered 'Atlantic' and arrived at Grantham a minute early, in 119 minutes.

The train left Grantham a minute late, but

the start was not particularly brisk and, from the maximum of 67 mph descending to Newark, speed fell away rather poorly on the level across the Trent valley to Crow Park. Seeing also that the permanent-way check came before Dukeries Junction the subsequent recovery was slow and an average of only 60 mph the best that could be done on the slightly favourable stretch from Retford to Scrooby. They were not doing much better on the level from Shaftholme Junction, and the the signal check before Templehirst proved disastrous, eventually making the train more than 5 minutes late into York. A speed of 60 mph on the level with this load would have involved more than about 600 horsepower, which is a long way below those vigorous uphill efforts on special runs when Ivatt himself was, metaphorically speaking, looking over the driver's shoulder!

GNR 'The Flying Scotsman', March 8 1909

Load: 314 tons tare, 330 tons full
Engine (small 4-4-2) No: 989

Distance Miles		Schedule min	Actual m s	Average speed mph
0.0	GRANTHAM	0	0 00	—
4.2	Barkston		7 42	32.7
6.1	Hougham		9 31	62.8
9.9	Claypole		12 55	67.0
14.6	NEWARK	17	17 07	67.1
20.9	Carlton		23 23	60.5
21.9	Crow Park		24 28	55.5
—			pws*	
25.8	Dukeries Junction		31 07	35.2
26.45	Tuxford		32 31	29.4
33.1	RETFORD	39	40 07	43.8
36.3	Sutton		43 16	60.3
38.5	Ranskill		45 31	58.7
40.35	Scrooby		47 20	61.2
42.2	Bawtry		49 18	56.5
43.9	*Pipers Wood Box*		51 17	51.6
45.85	Rossington		53 37	50.3
50.5	DONCASTER	58	58 24	58.7
52.6	Arksey		61 12	45.0[†]
54.7	*Shaftholme Junction*	63	63.40	51.1
57.5	Moss		66 44	54.6
60.5	Balne		69 48	58.5
—			signals severe*	
64.3	Templehirst		77 42	28.8
68.9	SELBY	79	83 31	47.3[†]
73.1	Riccall		90 02	38.6
75.7	Escrick		93 01	52.3
78.55	Naburn		96 11	54.0
82.7	YORK	97	102 15	41.0
	Net time, min		96¼	

* Cost of checks: Dukeries Junction, 2 min; Templehirst, 4 min.
[†]Speed restrictions, Doncaster and Selby.

Chapter 3

Engine 251 and after

In October 1937, my friend and fellow graduate at Imperial College, A.F. Webber, read a paper before the Institution of Locomotive Engineers with the title *The Proportions of Locomotive Boilers.* He opened with these words: 'The Stephenson locomotive boiler is one of the marvels of our age. There is no single invention of the whole of the Industrial Revolution and its aftermath which was so nearly perfect at the moment of its inception and which has been so little altered in principle through a century of development.' While this is true enough, it is not to say that the boiler ceased to give locomotive men cause for concern in later years and that there were no boiler designs produced that did not steam freely. On the Great Western Railway in the early 1900s, G.J. Churchward went so far as

to say that his principal problem was that of the boiler, while H.A. Ivatt, with an eye always upon the running, said that the power of a locomotive could be gauged by its capacity to boil water. And yet, in the ever-famous GNR No 251, he fathered an engine the performance of which in its original form was the very negation of his own truism.

From the details of the working of the 'Klondikes' given in the preceding chapter, it is fairly evident that in heavy, express-passenger work they were deficient in cylinder power and that to produce haulage efforts in any way commensurate with their boiler capacity they had to be worked at expansion rates in their cylinders that were well beyond the economic ideal. That they produced the power in such circumstances and were not

Above *The first large-boilered 'Atlantic', No 251, with experimental stove-pipe chimney* (British Railways).

Opposite *Reproduction of a portrait of H.A. Ivatt by Lance Calkin* (British Railways).

Below *Cross-sections through boiler of No 251 : (a) through driving axle and through first boiler ring; and (b) through smoke-box: front elevation*

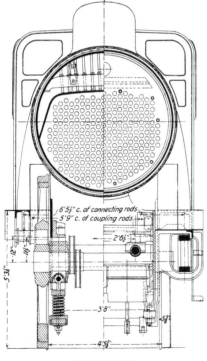

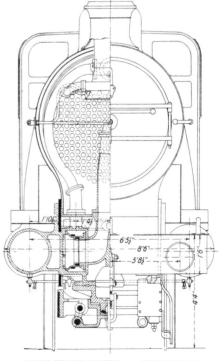

CROSS SECTIONS.
THROUGH DRIVING AXLE.   THROUGH FIRST BOILER RING.

SECTION THROUGH SMOKEBOX.   FRONT ELEVATION.

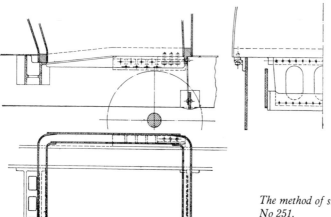

The method of support for the wide fire-box on engine No 251.

choked on the exhaust side was undoubtedly due to the excellent design of the Richardson-type balanced slide valves, which exhausted the relatively large volume of steam from the cylinders directly through the back of the valves. The next step in 'Atlantic' design on the GNR seems inexplicable in retrospect. One can hardly believe that Ivatt, with his interest in running, was unaware of the way the 'Klondikes' had to be thrashed when a big effort was required from them; and yet on engine No 251 he put a boiler with a total heating surface 65 per cent greater, with the engine layout, cylinders, valves and valve-gear design completely unchanged. One could understand it if that huge boiler had been no more than a prototype — a prelude to a new design of locomotive with enlarged proportions all round. But this did not prove to be the case. No fewer than 78 'Atlantic' engines of identical design to No 251 were built at Doncaster between 1904 and 1908.

Before attempting to review design policy, however, it is necessary to study the details of that remarkable boiler. The distance between the tube-plates was increased to 16 ft 0 in and the diameter of tubes increased from the 2 in of the 'Klondikes' to 2¼ in. Because of this increase in length there was no recessing rearward of the smoke-box and to provide adequate volume the smoke-box itself was notably extended ahead of the chimney. There were 248 tubes and their spacing can be seen from the accompanying cross-sectional drawings. That showing the smoke-box emphasises the extremely simple and direct arrangement for exhaust of the steam, through the back of the slide valves. Exceptional interest was shown in the design of the firebox, which was fre-

quently quoted as being of the Wootten type, extensively used in America at the time. The eminent engineer-historian E.L. Ahrons, who had his ears very close to the ground on all matters concerning locomotive design in that era, does not agree with this view. He believed that the origin of the wide firebox on the GNR 'Atlantics' lay in the broad-gauge boilers of the Great Western 8 ft 4-2-2s. Those engines had grates 5 ft 5 in wide between the frames, because the width of the gauge permitted this. Ivatt was aware of the excellent steaming qualities of the broad-gauge engines and the contour of the firebox of the '251' class GN 'Atlantics' bore a strong resemblance to that of the Gooch 8-footers.

The support for the wide firebox of these engines as a standard-gauge design had to be something special. As the firebox was wider than the distance between the frames, the usual type of expansion bracket could not be used and the design adopted is shown in the accompanying drawing. A cast-steel angle-bracket was attached to the outside frame, on which the rear part of the foundation ring rested for about half its length. About one third, in length and width, of the top flange of the bracket was cut away in order to make room for a clip, which was cut out to receive the reduced web of the angle and which was secured to the foundation ring by 1¼ in studs. The front of the foundation ring rested, for the greater part of its length, on a steel casting extending between the inside of the frames. The boiler was further held down by a thin plate, the top edge of which was rivetted to a projection on the bottom of the back portion of the foundation ring. The lower edge of this plate was rivetted to a frame cross-stay and the

A standard non-superheated, large-boilered 'Atlantic', No 300 (C. Laundy).

flexibility of the plate allowed the boiler to expand without hindrance. Constructionally the boiler and its wide firebox were outstandingly successful.

The details of these remarkable boilers may be summarised as follows:

Diameter of barrel (max)	5 ft 6 in
Tubes	
Number	248
Outside diameter, ins	2¼
Length between tubeplates, ft-in	16-0
Heating surfaces, sq ft	
Tubes	2,359
Firebox	141
Total	2,500
Grate, sq ft	30.9
Working pressure psi	175

Two other points that affected the free steaming of these locomotives were the proportions of the blast pipe and the chimney. The blast pipe tapered from 11½ in diameter, at the outlet from the valve chests, to 5¼ in at the orifice, which was exactly at the height of the centre line of the boiler. The chimney was 1 ft 3 in diameter at the choke. The wheel spacing and the engine machinery was the same as on the 'Klondikes'.

While it could be said that the building of engine No 251 started the fashion for large 'Atlantics' in Great Britain, the influences were not by any means entirely from Doncaster. Nor did the four other railways that followed adopt the rather extraordinary relationship between total heating surface and cylinder volume. In the comparison that follows, I am leaving out of consideration the Churchward development at Swindon, which was something that stood quite apart. Furthermore, the North Eastern locomotive of 1903 had its origin in a visit Wilson Worsdell paid to the USA with a party of NER officers when he became impressed with the work currently been done by 'Atlantic' engines between

Railway	GNR	NER	GCR	LBSCR	NBR
Cylinders					
diameter, ins	18¾	20	19½	18½	20
stroke, ins	24	26	26	26	28
Total heating surface, sq ft	2,500	2,456	1,911	2,459	2,256
Grate Area, sq ft	30.9	27	26	30.9	28.5
Boiler pressure psi	175	200	180	200	180
Ratio					
Total heating surface to cylinder					
volume, cu ft	326	259	212	304	222
Nominal tractive effort, lb	15,670	23,250	18,750	18,930	21,170
Ratio					
Tractive effort to cylinder volume,					
cu ft	2,040	2,475	2,075	2,340	2,080
Ratio					
Total heating surface to TE to tons	357	237	228	291	223

Philadelphia and Atlantic City. The basic dimensions of five varieties of British 'Atlantic' engines, all with two outside cylinders, are set out in the table on the previous page.

It is the last row in this table of comparisons that is the most arresting, especially when one adds that the ratio of total heating surface to tractive effort in tons was no more than 194 on the Great Western 'Saint' class. No one would be likely to suggest that the boilers of these latter engines failed to produce steam for their maximum haulage efforts, which at times bordered upon the phenomenal.

As to the other engines in the table of comparisons, when Wilson Worsdell returned from the USA and was anxious to build a large 'Atlantic' for the North Eastern, his very able and forthright chief draughtsman, Walter M. Smith, was seriously ill and away from the works for many months. The story goes that on his return he did not approve, though work was too far advanced for any alterations to be made. The Brighton engine was a close copy of the Great Northern design, in looks at any rate, and was a natural result of Douglas Earle-Marsh's recent move from his former appointment as works manager at Doncaster. The Great Central engine, by J.G. Robinson, was aesthetically one of the most beautiful express locomotives that have ever run the rails in Great Britain; but in their early days they were very lightly loaded and seem to have been built more for prestige than for actual traffic requirements. It was not until after World War I when running conditions became far more onerous that one came to appreciate their sterling worth. The fine North British 'Atlantics' were at first under something of a cloud due to the antagonism of the civil engineer, who did his best to get them banned, because of the alleged damage they were doing to the track. After his retirement, purchase of further engines of the class was authorised and they became established as a successful design.

The table makes it amply evident how deficient in cylinder capacity the '251' class of the Great Northern Railway was. A study of much contemporary running makes this clear also from the practical operating viewpoint. But before quoting a number of performance details one must give credit to No 251 and her sisters for the prestige they brought to the Great Northern in another direction, that of publicity. The poster artists were suitably impressed by the seemingly immense girth of

that boiler, and, admittedly in caricature, it got bigger and bigger until it attained a diameter of about *ten feet*. The results prompted a railway *littérateur* of the day to remark, 'No 251, bigger boilered than ever, leers at us from every hoarding'! In other respects too the design provided material for the less direct, more subtle means of publicity. It quickly became one of the most popular prototypes for the growing hobby of running model railways. In those early years, while clockwork and electricity were alternative forms of motive power, the attraction for most devotees of the hobby was live steam, from Gauge One upwards, and that huge boiler, which was not an unmixed blessing on the real engines, was a godsend in miniature. More models were made of these engines perhaps than of any other prototype among pre-grouping designs, not forgetting the 10¼ in gauge example that made a lot of the running at the British Empire Exhibition at Wembley in 1924 and had the honour of hauling King George V and Queen Mary on one of their visits. So far as putting outsize boilers on 'Atlantics' of the generic Great Northern design went, Messrs Bassett-Lowke out-Ivatted Ivatt himself with the magnificent *Synolda* built for the Sand Hutton Railway in 1913, which is 15 in gauge and which I saw still at work at Carnforth in the early summer of 1983.

Reverting to the 'real things' rather than the miniatures, one can well imagine how impressive the railway enthusiasts of those days found the '251' class, with their massive appearance and always immaculate turn-out. This interest was well reflected in the number of colour plates that distinguished the railway press in the years 1903–08. *The Railway Magazine* had no fewer than three, in the lithographed style, showing engines 271, in her original form with inside valve gear, 251 herself and the compound 292, of which there is much to be said later. *The Locomotive Magazine* had a large reproduction of a very striking F. Moore painting showing an East Coast express pounding up through the woods towards Hadley Wood South tunnel, hauled by engine No 279, while in 1908, after the second Doncaster-built compound started service, there was a beautiful F. Moore portrait of her. In the famous series of coloured postcards issued by the Locomotive Publishing Company there are many examples and, although the tone of the green is not always accurate, they are delightful collectors' pieces nevertheless. I do not think it would be going much too far to suggest that they were the most popular locomotive type in Great Britain in that era, using the word popular in its broadest sense.

In the chronology of the class it must be noted that the first production batch of 251s was built at Doncaster in the summer of 1904, comprising the twenty engines 272 to 291, and they took over many of the principal East Coast duties. The following year saw a further 20 added to the stock, Nos 293 to 301 and 1400 to 1410. Also in 1905, Ivatt began his experiments with compound locomotives. The four-cylindered 292 was interposed in the regular series, while at the same time the unusual step was taken by Mr Ivatt of inviting tenders from the leading outside firms of locomotive manufacturers for the construction of a compound 'Atlantic' engine of the same general size and tractive power as that of his own standard express-passenger locomotives. The firms invited to tender were given complete freedom in design, while conforming, of course, to the weight and structural limits already in force on the Great Northern Railway. The design accepted was that from the Vulcan Foundry and was one closely based on the current practice of Alfred de Glehn. Except that it used a somewhat lower boiler pressure, its basic dimensions bore a striking correspondence to the compound 'Atlantics' recently built for the Paris-Orleans Railway, as is shown by the following table:

4-cylinder De Glehn Compound 4-4-2s

Railway	PO	GNR
Cylinders HP diameter, ins	14	14
stroke, ins	25.2	26
LP diameter, ins	23.6	23
stroke, ins	25.2	26
Total heating surface, sq ft	2,609	2,514
Grate area, sq ft	33.4	31
Working pressure, psi	228	200

The trials arranged between this Vulcan engine, Mr Ivatt's own compound, No 292, and standard engines of the large-boilered 'Atlantic' type are discussed in some detail later. In the meantime, construction of the standard engines continued until, by the end of 1908, a total of 80 of the class was in service, the later series from 1411 to 1451 being interrupted by another 4-cylinder compound, No 1421. The popularity of the large-boilered 'Atlantics' was further evidenced when the Rev J.R. Howden published the first edition

of his *Locomotives of the World* in 1909, illustrated entirely in colour, which included a front view of No 1414 on the cover and an extensive description and beautiful F. Moore plate of the compound No 292 in the text.

Coming now to actual running, the serial articles of Charles Rous-Marten in *The Railway Magazine* include, in the year 1906, some intriguing data. From time to time, in connection with a variety of British locomotives, he refers to 'making experiments' with them, frequently resulting in the securing of a very fine performance. That his 'experiments' did so was often the result of some special arrangements being made, such as the presence of a locomotive inspector riding on the footplate or even the attendance of the locomotive superintendent himself. But from whatever cause or circumstance, I have come to regard occasions when Rous-Marten said he was 'making experiments' as ones unlikely to yield an ordinary run-of-the-mill performance from the locomotive. It certainly seemed to be the case with the large-boilered 'Atlantics' of the Great Northern, when he made a series of runs on the 1:30 pm Leeds express from Kings Cross to Doncaster. This was the fastest of the ordinary expresses, booked to run the 76.4 miles to Peterborough in 83 minutes and the ensuing 79.6 miles on to Doncaster in 88 minutes. The usual load was a beautifully uniform rake of eight clerestory-roofed 12-wheelers, which, to use Rous-Marten's favourite expression, 'together with passengers, luggage, staff and stores', would make a gross load of about 300 tons behind the tender.

The working book times made very uneven demands upon the locomotives, with times and corresponding average speeds as follows:

Distance Miles		Time minutes	Average speed mph
0.0	Kings Cross	0	—
17.7	Hatfield	23	46.2
31.9	Hitchin	37	60.8
58.9	Huntingdon	63	62.3
76.4	Peterborough	83	52.5
29.1	Grantham	35	49.9
43.7	Newark	50	58.4
62.2	Retford	69	58.4
79.6	Doncaster	88	54.9

Those of my readers who were familiar with customary running over this route in the last years of steam will realise at once the unrealistic nature of the above sectional timings. To pass Hatfield in 23 minutes would have involved passing Potters Bar, 12.7 miles out of Kings Cross, in no more than 18 minutes and drivers, as practical men, would not pound their engines to such an extent when they could, with perfect ease, cut 2 or even 3 minutes from the leisurely Hitchin-Huntingdon allowance. But when Rous-Marten made his 'experiments', instructions were evidently given, probably by Ivatt himself, that strict sectional time was to be kept. He logged the running of four different engines, Nos 251, 275, the compound No 292 and 294. By contemporary standards the climbs to Potters Bar were little short of phenomenal, with times from the four engines, in the same order, of 18 min 0 sec, 17 min 53 sec, 19 min 02 sec and 16 min 23 sec. The work of No 294 was indeed extraordinary, but at the time she differed from the rest of the class in having a boiler pressure of 200 lb per sq in, instead of 175, for comparison with the compounds, as will be discussed in detail in a later chapter.

After these extremely vigorous starts, the average speeds made by the four engines over the ensuing 63.7 miles to the stop at Peterborough were 61, 60.8, 60.7 and 59.7 mph, all arriving between one and 2½ minutes early. All four engines were then worked extremely hard up to Stoke box. To pass Grantham in 35 minutes from the standing start at Peterborough would mean covering the 23.7 miles up to Stoke in the level half-hour at most; but the four engines, flailed to their utmost, as between Kings Cross and Potters Bar, made times of 26 min 46 sec 26 min 51 sec, 27 min 10 sec and 26 min 14 sec. After that, Nos 251 and 292 were run easily, though still arriving at Doncaster comfortably ahead of time; but 275 and 294 went on to make quite record times of 81 min 43 sec and 83 min 3 sec, with start-to-stop average speeds of 58.5 and 57.5 mph. In the course of these runs engines 251 and 294 are both credited with sustained minimum speeds of 52¾ mph on the 1 in 200 banks, which would indicate an equivalent drawbar horsepower of about 1,050 and a drawbar pull (related to level track) of about 3 tons equal to a pull of rather more than 40 per cent of the nominal tractive effort of the locomotive. The engines concerned must have been driven something very near to 'all-out' to achieve such performance.

While having every admiration for a display of such capacity, which is in itself a remarkable tribute to the design of the cylinders and valves that could pass such volumes of steam freely, the working was the very antithesis of the more modern principles of efficient locomotive working. In the last 20 years of steam on British Railways, when so much study was given to scientific train timing, it was generally established that locomotives would be working at their most efficient and with minimum coal consumption if the rate of steam production in the boiler was kept approximately constant. These 'experimental' runs of Rous-Marten's were the very reverse, requiring a tremendous initial effort, and then very light steaming for the succeeding hour. At that time however the preparation of working times and the intermediate allowances were usually the work of non-technical timetable clerks; and not only on the Great Northern but on most British main lines, the point-to-point bookings were fixed to show as little as possible excess of speeds over 60 mph even though the start-to-stop averages might be 55 mph or more. The famous 3-hour Paddington-Exeter schedule of the Great Western for example, although requiring an overall speed of 57.9 mph had no faster point-to-point average than 63.7 mph.

Particularly on the Great Northern, when there was no inspector, or locomotive superintendent at their elbow, drivers worked in a more logical and efficient way, steaming their engines at a more nearly constant rate of evaporation in the boiler, and so avoiding the risk of tearing the fire to pieces by an unduly vigorous climb to Potters Bar and having steaming troubles for the rest of the run. About a year after the conclusion of his 'experiments', Rous-Marten went down to York on the 'Flying Scotsman', presumably without any prior arrangement. It was at the height of the summer holiday traffic and a relief train was running at 9:55 am non-stop to Doncaster. There a North Eastern engine took over and continued non-stop to Newcastle. Despite the running of a relief train the 'Scotsman' itself was loaded to nearly 400 tons, and one of the large 'Atlantics' did no better than a sustained 36 mph on the 1 in 200 to Potters Bar, taking 28½ minutes to pass Hatfield. But there was some fast downhill to follow, with a maximum of 80½ mph near Three Counties. Each adverse stretch took its toll however, with minimum speeds of 40½ mph up the rise to Abbots Ripton and 36 mph on Stoke bank, and the train was 2 minutes late on arrival at Grantham, in 125 minutes from Kings Cross. The equivalent drawbar horsepower on the Potters Bar climb, of 800, was a long way below the spectacular 1050 on the experi-

Top *Anglo-Scottish express climbing the bank out of Kings Cross, hauled by 4-4-2 engine No 289* (Loco Publishing Co Ltd).

Above *Up East Coast express near Werrington Junction, Peterborough, hauled by non-superheater 4-4-2 No 1412* (C. Laundy).

mental runs of Rous-Marten. There seemed to be a shortage of engines on this later occasion, for the best that Grantham could turn out for the 400-ton 'Flying Scotsman' was a 4-4-0, No 1338; and on the 97 minute timing for the 82.7 mile run to York she lost 7 minutes making an average of no more than 47½ mph.

Despite the introduction of many new 'Atlantics', however, it is surprising how use of the smaller engines persisted, not only on the very light Manchester trains but on the heavier East Coast expresses. In preparing a table of runs on the 10:00 am and 10:10 am departures from Kings Cross, both non-stop to Grantham, I have arranged them in chronological order, rather than the more usual way of ascending loads to show the use of the eight-wheeled engines, both of the 4-2-2 and 4-4-0 types. It is often thought that Ivatt's earlier 4-4-0s, as distinct from the superheater

The last but one of the non-superheater 'Atlantics', No 1450. See also note about this photograph in Chapter 6 (British Railways).

engines of the '51' class were intended for no more than intermediate passenger work; but contemporary recordings show a considerable use of them on fast express trains, where they put up good performances. The use of an Ivatt 4-2-2 on the 10:10 am as late as 1906, by which time there were 50 large-boilered 'Atlantics', not to mention the 21 'Klondikes', was remarkable. The last run in the table, on the 10:10 am in 1910, took place after that train had an additional stop inserted, at Peterborough, but was still booked to reach Grantham in 121 minutes. In contrast to the summary details of his runs published by Rous-Marten, these tabulated journeys were taken from a collection of logs in which the time was recorded to the nearest second at every passing station.

On the first of the tabulated runs the Ivatt 'single', No 269, made heavy weather of the start out of Kings Cross, though the load of 275 tons could be regarded as something bordering on the excessive for an engine of this type; and on the long 1 in 200 rise from Wood Green to Potters Bar one could not really expect much better speed than the final average, from New Barnet, of 36.4 mph. The initial working book time of 23 minutes out of Hatfield was a counsel of perfection. It was significant that in the later years of Pacific engines working from Kings Cross it was not revived until the days of the streamlined trains. In any case the 4-2-2 engine was 7¼ minutes 'down' on schedule as early as Hatfield. Although more than 4 minutes had been won back by Peterborough, on the very easy subsequent point-to-point bookings, the

maximum speed had not exceeded 72 mph, near Three Counties. On the climb to Stoke box, culminating with nearly 3 miles at 1 in 178 from Corby, the speed fell to just under 36 mph and there was a loss of 5¾ minutes to Grantham, without any signal or permanent-way checks.

On the second run, made in 1904, with the 4-4-0 engine, No 1388, there was a very good start for an engine having cylinders no larger than 17½ in by 26 in, 2½ minutes being gained on the time of the previous run by New Southgate. But after that there was some pretty level pegging between the two runs right on to Grantham. The 4-4-0 reached a maximum of 76 mph descending from Hitchin, but otherwise there was very little in it and its arrival was 3 minutes late. On the third run, again with an Ivatt 4-2-2, but a lighter load of 190 tons, there was an excellent start out to Finsbury Park and, with good climbing out to Potters Bar, the time through Hatfield was very near to the standard post-war norm of 25 minutes. Furthermore, with a maximum of 80 mph near Three Counties and fast running for some while thereafter, this train was well ahead of all others in the table at Tempsford. But then the engine seemed to go to pieces — metaphorically, I must add. By Peterborough, from leading the 4-4-0, No 1388, by 2½ minutes, she had dropped a minute behind and a clear 7 minutes were lost on schedule between Peterborough and Grantham. In the very complete details of passing times contained in the records made available to me there is not a hint of the cause of the obvious distress that developed on the

			1903		1904		1906		1909		1909		1910		1911	
Year:																
Train (ex-Kings Cross):			10:10 am		10:10 am		10:10 am		10:00 am		10:00 am		10:10 am		6:05 pm	
Load, tons gross:			275		280		190				365		275		325	
Engine no:			269		1388		264		1426		300		1414		287	
Engine type:			4-2-2		4-4-0		4-2-2		4-4-2		4-4-2		4-4-2		4-4-2	
Distance Miles		**Schedule min**	**Actual m s**	**Average speed mph**	**Actual m s**	**Average speed mph**	**Actual m s**	**Average speed mph**	**Actual m s**	**Average speed mph**	**Actual m s**	**Average speed mph**	**Actual m s**	**Average speed mph**	**Actual m s**	**Average speed mph**
0.0	KINGS CROSS	0	0 00	—	0 00	—	0 00	—	0 00	—	0 00	—	0 00	—	0 00	—
2.6	Finsbury Park		8 50	17.6	6 55	22.6	6 16	24.9	7 17	21.4	6 51	22.8	6 19	24.7	6 16	25.0
5.0	Wood Green		12 38	37.9	10 20	42.2	9 34	43.6	10 40	42.6	10 40	37.8	9 23	45.2	9 40	42.3
6.5	New Southgate		14 50	40.9	12 16	46.5	11 21	50.5	12 29	49.6	12 34	47.4	11 05	53.0	11 31	45.3
9.2	New Barnet		18 56	39.5	16 32	38.1	14 57	45.0	16 16	42.8	16 34	40.5	14 38	45.7	15 10	44.3
12.7	Potters Bar		24 42	36.4	22 22	36.0	20 08	40.5	21 43	38.5	22 09	37.6	19 36	42.3	20 06	42.3
17.7	HATFIELD	23	30 18	53.5	27 49	55.0	25 30	55.9	27 05	55.9	27 47	53.2	24 56	56.3	25 06	60.0
22.0	Welwyn		34 26	62.3	31 59	62.0	29 48	60.0	31 36	57.2	32 03	60.5	28 56	64.5	29 04	65.0
25.0	Knebworth		37 55	51.7	35 32	50.8	33 40	46.6	35 16	49.1	35 37	50.3	32 09	56.0	32 10	58.1
28.6	Stevenage		41 31	60.0	39 09	59.7	37 19	59.2	38 44	62.3	39 17	59.0	36 07 pws	54.6	35 25	66.4
31.9	HITCHIN	38	44 37	64.0	42 14	64.3	40 22	65.0	41 49	64.3	42 20	65.0	42 29	31.3	38 29	64.5
35.7	Three Counties		47 55	69.1	45 19	73.8	43 20	76.5	44 47	76.5	45 20	76.0	46 58	50.7	41 25	77.7
41.1	Biggleswade		52 40	68.2	50 46	68.2	47 51	73.2	49 04	75.5	49 59	69.7	52 02	64.0	45 37	77.1
44.1	Sandy		55 25	65.5	52 50	65.1	50 25	70.2	51 35	71.8	52 50	67.0	54 42	67.5	48 25	64.2
47.5	Tempsford		58 38	63.6	56 02	63.8	53 33	65.1	54 35	68.0	55 50	64.4	57 49	65.7	51 20	69.2
51.7	St Neots		62 48	60.6	60 14	60.0	57 58	57.1	58 36	62.8	60 19	56.2	61 53	62.0	55 19	68.3
56.0	Offord		66 46	64.9	64 18	63.5	62 10	61.6	62 31	65.9	64 39	59.5	65 47	66.2	59 10	67.1
58.9	HUNTINGDON	66	69 35	61.8	67 07	61.8	65 25	53.5	65 15	63.6	67 44	56.4	68 29	64.5	61 55	63.4
63.5	Abbots Ripton		74 59	51.1	72 39	48.9	71 49	43.1	70 29	52.8	73 47	45.6	73 43	51.1	67 09	52.7
69.4	Holme		80 25	65.2	77 54	67.5	77 58	57.6	75 11	75.3	79 03	67.3	78 43	70.8	72 16	69.2
76.4	PETERBOROUGH	85	87 55	56.0	85 04	58.7	86 06	51.6	82 04	61.0	87 03	52.5	85 58	58.0	79 25	58.8
84.8	Tallington		98 17	48.6	95 22	48.8	97 33	43.9	92 35	49.5	97 58	46.2	97 41	43.0	90 15	46.5
88.6	Essendine		102 46	50.7	99 40	53.0	102 20	47.6	96 27	59.0	101 58	57.0	101 44	56.2	94 25	55.4
92.2	Little Bytham		107 15	47.8	104 07	48.5	107 11	44.5	100 22	55.1	106 02	53.1	105 41	54.7	98 24	54.0
97.1	Corby		114 30	40.6	111 32	39.6	115 26	35.6	106 59	44.4	113 02	39.5	111 44	48.6	104 28	54.0
100.1	Stoke Box		119 15	37.9	116 28	36.5	121 07	31.7	111 22	41.0	117 42	38.3	115 39	46.0	108 25	45.7
102.0	Great Ponton		121 41	46.9	118 56	46.2	123 48	42.5	113 55	44.7	120 09	46.5	117 48	53.1	110 38	51.5
105.5	GRANTHAM	120	125 44	51.8	120 59	51.8	127 58	50.4	118 40	44.2	124 17	50.8	121 47	52.5	114 28	54.8

locomotive after so fine a start. It was most likely poor steaming. The pioneer 'Klondike', No 990 *Henry Oakley*, took on at Grantham and leaving there 7 minutes late with this light load had actually regained all the lost time by Selby (68.9 miles in 72 min 7 sec), but was badly delayed by signals thence into York.

The work of the large 'Atlantics' on the 'Flying Scotsman', revealed in all its detail, provides a very interesting study. There was the customary loss of time on the optimistic initial booking out to Hatfield, with both engines falling to around 36 mph at Potters Bar and both recovering well on the undulating stretch to Stevenage. Then engine No 1426, on the first of the two runs, put on a splendid spurt that recovered the early arrears by Huntingdon and took the train through Peterborough all but 3 minutes early. Note should be taken of the fine speed maintained up the bank from Huntingdon followed by a maximum of 80 mph descending to the Fens, at Holme. With the heavier load of 365 tons, engine No 300 came down the bank from Stevenage pretty smartly, but the speed fell off sadly afterwards and, from being only 31 seconds behind No 1426 at Hitchin, No 300 was 5 minutes in the rear on passing Peterborough and still 2 minutes late. The long uphill section took its toll on both runs, but while No 1426 had time in hand and did not need to be pressed unduly hard, No 300 fell still further behind and finished at Grantham 3¼ minutes late. The last-mentioned run was of a kind all too common with the large-boilered 'Atlantics' in their non-superheated condition. It was not often, on other than special occasions, that one could note running of the quality put up by No 1426 on the first of these two trips.

The third of the 'Atlantic' runs, on the 10:10 am Anglo-Scottish express, after an additional stop had been inserted at Peterborough, was also a good performance, though with a considerably lighter load. The start was vigorous, the climbing to Potters Bar excellent and the time to Knebworth — by one second — the fastest of the whole series. But the permanent-way slowing between Stevenage and Hitchin was very severe and cost a full 5 minutes in running. The recovery from it was rather slow, seeing that the gradients are so very favourable from Hitchin, and it was not until Sandy that something like normal speed had been regained. Even then the going seemed to lack enterprise, seeing that the load was not unduly heavy and the

train running behind time. The point-to-point times from Sandy were no better than those made by the more heavily loaded 1426 on the 'Flying Scotsman'. After getting away from the Peterborough stop, good work was done up to Stoke box, with an average speed of 51 mph from Tallington to the summit. There was also a very smart finish into Grantham on this trip.

The last of the tabulated runs comes from the records of Mr R.E. Charlewood, who took over writing the monthly feature 'British Locomotive Practice and Performance' in *The Railway Magazine* for a short time after Rous-Marten's sudden death in 1908. In later years, I had the pleasure of meeting Charlewood on a number of occasions and of appreciating his skill and experience as a recorder of train running. It is important to mention this because this run on the fast evening express to Sheffield and Manchester, with an exceptional load for that train, is the finest all-round performance I have ever seen with on of these engines in its non-superheated condition. The hill climbing, both to Potters Bar and between Essendine and Stoke box was not so fast as on Rous-Marten's 'experimental' trips, but it was a much more balanced performance, with really fast running between Hitchin and Huntingdon, where the average speed for 27 miles was 69.3 mph. This train, which normally carried a load of no more than about 200 tons had a sharp timing of 116 minutes to Grantham, and this was improved upon by 1½ minutes with a load of 325 tons. Whether any communication was made previously to the driver that he was being logged in full detail I do not know; but from my acquaintance with Mr Charlewood in more recent years I would think it unlikely.

One cannot refer to these early days of the large-boilered 'Atlantics' without mentioning the unlucky engine of the class, No 276, and the misfortune she and her crew sustained on September 9 1906, when working the 8:45 pm express from Kings Cross to Scotland. Among major accidents on the British railways this, tragic derailment at Grantham will always remain one for which no definite explanation has been forthcoming. The facts are simple enough. The junction points for the Nottingham line at the north end of Grantham station were set for the branch. A mineral train from that line had just passed through and the signalman in the North Box, expecting to be offered another shortly, left the points set for the branch. Although the down express had

Down Newcastle express leaving Hadley Wood Tunnel, hauled by 4-4-2 No 1415 (C. Laundy).

been accepted, it was due to stop in the station and, with heavy mail traffic, was usually at the platform for many minutes longer than for an ordinary day-time passenger stop. The junction ahead was fully protected by all the signals leading up to it being in the danger position. But the express instead of stopping at the platform ran clean through at a speed estimated variously at between 40 and 50 mph, and took the curve on to the Nottingham branch. The derailment however did not take place at that first turn-out but on a reverse curve just where the line crossed a highway; and it was the *tender* of No 276 that came off first. Derailing to the left it hit and demolished the parapet of the bridge; the engine slewed to the right and turned over, and such vehicles of the train that did not pitch down the embankment piled up against the wrecked engine and caught fire. The driver and fireman were both killed; so were many of the passengers.

The inquiry on behalf on the Board of Trade was conducted by that celebrated Inspecting Officer, Colonel P.G. Von Donop, who, despite his name, was a thoroughgoing English Officer of the Royal Engineers. But while he pursued a great variety of lines of investigation, everything centred ultimately upon the one simple and unanswerable question, as to why the driver appears to have made no attempt to stop in Grantham station, as he was scheduled to do. His and the fireman's instantaneous deaths in the accident effectually closed any avenues of inquiry in that direction. The backplate of the firebox and the fittings mounted on it were all so smashed up that it was impossible to tell afterwards if the brake had been applied, what the position of the regulator handle had been, or to discover any other clues. The engine itself should have been in first-class condition. It was one of the first production batch of large-boilered 'Atlantics' built in 1904 and had been outshopped from Doncaster after its first general repair only two months previously. She was Driver Fleetwood's regular engine. There was one unusual circumstance, in that his mate, Ralph Talbot, was not a regular fireman. It was not unusual at that time for the best pupils of the Locomotive Superintendent to function occasionally as fireman, to

gain experience. In most cases, as on other railways, they went as a third man to help the regular fireman and only from time to time. But, on that fatal night, Talbot was on his own on No 276.

There was an added poignancy to the affair because Talbot, in the course of his pupillage at Doncaster, had become a close personal friend of another pupil, none other than O.V.S. Bulleid, who completed his practical training not long before the Grantham accident. He was then appointed as personal assistant to the Locomotive Running Superintendent. In that capacity, Bulleid had the sad task of stripping down the wrecked 276, on the footplate of which his friend had been killed. There was a slender hope that stripping the engine down might lead to some clue as to why her driver and fireman had acted or, more likely, failed to act as they did when their train was approaching Grantham; but although the engine was very much knocked about there was no evidence of anything fundamentally wrong with it. In any case it was the tender and not the engine that initiated the actual crash.

The mystery surrounding the accident persisted for many years on the GNR. Among the older enginemen, No 276 became looked upon in the same way as are unlucky ships among sailors — an ill-starred engine. This reputation did not die out with the coming of the LNER. Although it is taking the story nearly 20 years on, a friend of mine was travelling from Leeds to Kings Cross by one of the fast Pullman Limited trains and was interested to see that the engine was No 276, or 3276 as she was in LNER days. They made a rather poor run and, on arrival at Kings Cross, my friend, himself a locomotive man, stopped for a chat with the driver. He was an elderly man who had been in the railway service for many years and in response to my friend's enquiries he said: 'She's not a good engine. Never has been since the accident at Grantham. You know, sir, yesterday was the anniversary of the smash, and as I took her down to Leeds I just wondered whether she might take the wrong turning at the north end of the station!' I have a personal story of a different kind to tell of No 3276 towards the end of this book.

Chapter 4

Compounds and trial runs

The ever-increasing cost of coal, even as long ago as the early 1900s, was making all railway administrations conscious of the need to economise and locomotive engineers on several British lines began experimenting with newer forms of compound expansion. The two principal protagonists of the system in the latter part of the nineteenth century, the London and North Western Railway and the North Eastern Railway, had both of them abandoned the forms they had been following, though at the turn of the century two new systems were coming into prominence; the French, propounded by Alfred de Glehn, and that of W.M. Smith, then Chief Locomotive Draughtsman of the North Eastern Railway. The four-cylinder, two-crank systems, using cylinders in tandem, or one above the other that were at one time quite popular in the USA found no favour in Great Britain; but the Smith and the de Glehn systems were subjected to extensive trial. Reference has been made in the preceding chapter to the experimental compound locomotive purchased from the Vulcan Foundry and the similarity of its basic dimensions to those of the compound to those of the compound 'Atlantics' built by Mr de Glehn's firm for the Paris–Orleans Railway; and of exceptional interest are the two compound 'Atlantics' of Mr Ivatt's own design built at Doncaster.

The first of these, engine No 292, was completed in March 1905 and had the standard boiler of the '251' class, except that the working pressure was 200 lb per sq in, instead of the usual 175. But it was the control system of this engine that was unusual; and although a considerable amount of data was published concerning the running of this engine, and of its fuel and operating costs, there is not a word about the technicalities of driving what was, at the time, a uniquely interesting compound locomotive. The high-pressure cylinders, outside, were very small, having a diameter of no more than 13 in with a stroke of 20 in, with balanced slide valves actuated by outside Walschaerts valve gear; the low-pressure cylinders had a diameter of 16 in with a 26 in stroke, with valve movements controlled by Stephenson's link motion. When working 'compound' the calculated tractive effort of the engine was no

more than 8994 lb, which would have been useless for climbing the banks of the Great Northern main line with the heavy East Coast expresses, and so the controls permitted the engine to be worked as a 'simple', not merely when starting, but for as long as the driver found it necessary. Furthermore, when working simple, the controls allowed the use of full boiler pressure in all four cylinders, unlike most other compounds which had the option of alternative working and provided for no more than a reduced pressure in all four cylinders when working simple. The calculated tractive effort when working simple with No 292 was 20,070 lb, considerably more than that of a standard '251' class engine.

Having regard to the uneven demands of the express train schedules of the day, with the point-to-point timings, if strictly maintained, requiring a very hard effort uphill, and very light steaming elsewhere one can appreciate that, in designing No 292, Ivatt had in mind the use of simple working continuously from Kings Cross up to Potters Bar, from Tallington up to Stoke box and similarly on the other adverse stretches of line, and the improved economy of compound working elsewhere. In the absence of any details of the footplate techniques used, it is not possible say definitely how this worked out in practice, except that it is tolerably certain that such hill-climbing performances as were recorded by Charles Rous-Marten, to be referred to in detail later, could not have been achieved with the engine working compound and having no more than 8994 lb of tractive effort, at maximum, available. The engine had separate reversing levers, side by side for adjusting the valve gear of the high- and low-pressure cylinders. The Vulcan compound purchased for comparison had the usual de Glehn features, except that the driver's lever for controlling non-compound working was so arranged that it changed automatically to compound as soon as the driver let go of the lever. There was clearly no intention to work non-compound in the ordinary course of running, only when starting from rest. To provide close comparison between the two types of compound and the ordinary 'Atlantics', one of the latter, No 294, was arranged

Above *The first Doncaster-built 4-cylinder compound 'Atlantic', No 292* (British Railways).

Below *The Vulcan-built 'de Glehn' type 4-cylinder compound, No 1300, on down local train near New Barnet* (C. Laundy).

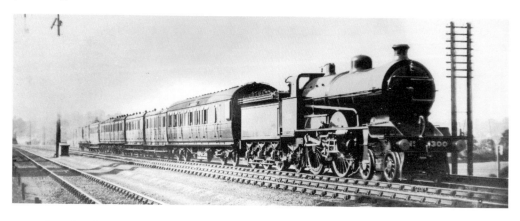

to work at 200 lb per sq in.

Before the very comprehensive series of tests between the three locomotives were commenced, three special runs were made from Leeds to Kings Cross in October 1905. Very little is known about these runs and such information is not entirely convincing. It was reported in *The Locomotive Magazine* that the trials were conducted, 'between Leeds and London, with the customary stop at Wakefield, the scheduled times of departure and arrival between 1:45 and 5:02 pm respectively'. Whether these were the overall times between Leeds and Kings Cross, inclusive of the Wakefield stop was not made clear; but as, when the fast 2:00 pm up from Leeds was put

on, with its strictly limited load, the overall time to Kings Cross was 3 hr 27 min, one can presume that the 3 hr 17 min, referred to in the published report, was from Wakefield only. Even this, with a load of eight 12-wheelers, would have required a start-to-stop average speed of 53.6 mph. The first engine to be tested was the Vulcan compound, on October 17, which made the run in 3 hr 21 min, or at an average speed of 52.3 mph. On the following day one of the standard 'Atlantics', No 296, was put on — not the high-pressure one — and it made the journey in 3¼ hours, travelling at 54.1 mph. The Doncaster compound No 292 was not tried until 9 days later and took 3 hr 25½ min, which gives an average speed of 51.5 mph. It was not stated whether any incidental delays were experienced but, in any case, little in the way of reliable conclusions can be drawn from the details published. With a load of at least 280 tons behind the tender, however, some fairly hard running would have been involved.

Rous-Marten reported on his experiments in *The Railway Magazine* for May 1906 and, with the 300-ton 1:30 pm from Kings Cross, the 12.7 miles out to Potters Bar took 19 min 2 sec, with a sustained speed of 45 mph on the 1 in 200. After that, the ensuing 63.7 miles to the stop at Peterborough took 62 min 56 sec, to arrive one minute early. From the restart, the 23.7 miles up to Stoke box took 27 min 10 sec, an excellent time, and the minimum speed on the final 3 miles at 1 in 178 was 48¼ mph. Subsequent minimum speeds, at Markham summit and Pipers Wood box (north of Bawtry), after considerably shorter inclines, were 53, and 52¾ mph and the total

time from Peterborough to Doncaster, travelling 79.6 miles, was 85 min 49 sec, which gives an average speed of 55.6 mph. Assuming that the speed approaching Stoke box was sustained, or very nearly so at the conclusion of this long incline, the equivalent drawbar horsepower would have been about 950, clearly indicating that the engine was being worked 'simple'. Even so this engine made consistently *slower* uphill times than those of the ordinary 'Atlantics' against which Rous-Marten tested her. At the time, he was not able to get a run with the Vulcan compound No 1300, which had sustained a slight mishap to her machinery and was in the shops for repairs.

Some very hard running was made with 292, ostensibly for Rous-Marten's benefit, on the 6:20 pm express from Doncaster to Kings Cross, with a load of 330 tons. The start, on level track, was exceptionally vigorous, passing Rossington, 4.8 miles, in 5 mins 57 sec,

	Engine No 1300	Engine No 292	Engine No 294
Makers	Vulcan Co	GNR	GNR
Date first into service	July 1905	March 1905	May 1905
General			
weight, in working order, lbs.	159,040	153,440	152,990
on drivers, lbs	82,880	80,640	80,640
engine and tender, in working order, lbs	250,660	245,060	244,610
Wheelbase,			
driving	8 ft 6 in	6 ft 10 in	6 ft 10 in
total engine	28 ft 3 in	26 ft 4 in	26 ft 4 in
total engine and tender	49 ft 6 in	48 ft 5½ in	48 ft 5½ in
Tractive power, lbs	14,869	8,994	16,875
Tractive power, No 292, working simple	—	20,070	—
Cylinders,			
number	4	4	2
type	Compound	Compound or simple	Simple
Diameter and stroke, high-pressure, ins	14 × 26	13 × 20	18¾ × 24
Diameter and stroke, low-pressure, ins	23 × 26	16 × 26	—
Valves			
high-pressure (HP)	6½ in Piston	Balanced slide	Balanced slide
low-pressure (LP)	Balanced slide	Balanced slide	—
greatest travel, ins	5⅜	4⅜	4⅛
outside lap, ins	⅞	HP 1, LP ¹⁵⁄₁₆	1³⁄₂₆
inside clearance, ins	—	⅛	⅛
lead in full gear, ins	¼	HP ¼, LP ¹⁄₁₆	¹⁄₁₆
Wheels,			
arrangement	4-4-2	4-4-2	4-4-2
driving diameter, ins	80	80	80
driving journals, diameter and length, ins	8½ × 9	7½ × 7	8½ × 9
bogie diameter, ins	38	44	44
bogie journals diameter and length, ins	5¾ × 9	5¾ × 9	5¾ × 9
trailing diameter, ins	44	44	44
trailing journals diameter and length, ins	5½ × 10	5½ × 10	5½ × 10

	Engine No 1300	Engine No 292	Engine 294
Boiler			
Working pressure, lbs per sq in	200	200	200
Outside diameter, ins	63	66	66
Firebox, type	Narrow	Wide	Wide
Firebox, length and width outside, ins	120×48½	71×81	71×81
Firebox, plates,			
thickness, ins	$\frac{5}{8}$	$\frac{9}{16}$	$\frac{9}{16}$
water space, ins	3 and 3½	3 and 3½	3 and 3½
Tubes, number, and outside diameter, ins	149-2¾ Serve	248-2¼	248-2¼
Tubes, length	12 ft 4 in	16 ft 0 in	16 ft 0 in
Heating surface*			
tubes, sq ft	2,344	2,359	2,359
firebox, sq ft	170	141	141
total sq ft	2,514	2,500	2,500
Grate area, sq ft	31	31	31
Ratios			
Cylinders	1:2.70	1:1.96	—
Weight on drivers — tractive effort	5.5	8.96	4.78
Weight on drivers — tractive effort, No 292			
as simple	—	4.02	—
Total weight — tractive effort, No 292	10.69	17.06	9.07
as simple	—	7.65	—
Tractive effort×diameter of drivers — heating			
surface	473.15	287.8	540.00
Tractive effort×diameter of drivers — heating			
surface, No 292 as simple	—	642.24	—
Total heating surface — grate area	81.1	80.64	80.64
Tube heating surface — firebox heating surface	13.79	16.73	16.73
Weight on drivers — total heating surface	32.96	32.26	32.26
Total weight — total heating surface	63.26	61.38	61.2
Volume of cylinders in cubic ft	17.14	9.12	7.67
Total heating surface — Volume of cylinders	146.6	274.12	325.94
Grate area — volume of cylinders	1.8	3.39	4.04

*Heating surface tubes: in the case of the 'serve' tubes, the heating surface equals the actual area, including the ribs, exposed to the heated gases. In the case of the plain tubes, the area on the water side is used.

The second Doncaster-built 4-cylinder compound 'Atlantic', No 1421 of 1907 (British Railways).

Results of trials

	Engine No 1300	Engine No 292	Engine No 294
Miles run, engine	11,286	11,670	11,673
Miles run, train	11,405	11,415	11,415
Speed, average, mph	49.02	49.9	49.58
Weight of train, average, tons	229.98	238.03	234.29
Ton-miles			
Total train	2,540,130	2,717,112.5	2,674,420
Including engine and tender	3,803,030	3,993,812	3,949,110
Per hour, engine and tender	16,759	17,337	17,030
Coal used			
per engine-mile, lbs	44.86	43.02	44.31
per train-mile, lbs	45.84	43.98	45.31
per ton-mile, lbs	0.133	0.126	0.131
Oil used			
per 100 engine-miles, pints	7.34	7.18	6.22
per 100 ton-miles, pints	0.022	0.021	0.0184
Costs			
Coal			
per engine-mile, pence	2.4	2.3	2.37
per ton-mile, pence	0.0071	0.0067	0.007
Oil			
per engine-mile, pence	1.165	0.16	0.14
per ton-mile, pence	0.00049	0.00047	0.00041
Repairs			
per engine-mile, pence	0.56	0.45	0.37
per ton-mile, pence	0.0017	0.0013	0.0011
Total			
per engine-mile, pence	3.125	2.91	2.88
per ton-mile, pence	0.0092	0.0085	0.0085

and Retford, 17.5 miles in 20 min 20 sec. The engine was much eased after passing Markham summit, and severely checked by signal in the approach to Grantham; but a good run up to Kings Cross, in 117 min 21 sec, for the remaining 105.5 miles, brought the train in a minute early. For once, on Rous-Marten's experimental trips there was some fast downhill running. The 3.6 miles from Little Bytham to Essendine were covered at an average speed of 81.6 mph, which probably indicated a maximum of 83 or 84 mph. These runs suggest that No 292 was a successful engine and it is significant that it was the last of the Great Northern compounds to survive as a compound.

It was in 1906 that Ivatt arranged for a very interesting and exhaustive set of trials, not in the way of measuring maximum power, or speed, but of overall performance, in which engine No 292 was set against the Vulcan compound, No 1300, and the 2-cylinder simple 'Atlantic' No 294, which had the higher boiler pressure of 200 lb per sq in. Each of the three engines was under close examination for 9 weeks and, to eliminate as far as possible the human factor during that period, it was arranged that each engine should be worked by three different sets of men. Three sets of men from the Doncaster top link were selected and each of these crews had each of the three engines for three weeks continuously, on all their normal link workings. These, throughout the trials were on the same group of trains, mostly express passenger. Before commencing the actual trials, during which coal and oil consumption was measured, records of the timekeeping and of the general conditions that might affect the running, such as adverse weather, each crew was given a week's running on each engine, so as to familiarise themselves with its characteristics. The results, entirely without comment, were communicated to the Institution of Mechanical Engineers in a brief paper by Mr Ivatt himself, from which the numerical details shown in the table above have been taken.

To these figures it only needs to be added that no engine lost any time during the 9 weeks of trials and that the coal consumption quoted in the table of results included that used for lighting up.

From this very extensive series of observa-

The compound 'Atlantic', No 292, on an up express near Peterborough (C. Laundy).

tions, made in the fairest and most impartial set of conditions, it would seem that the result was as near as possible a dead heat. The only appreciable difference lay in the cost of the running repairs, which made the total cost, per engine mile, heavier in the case of the Vulcan than that of the two Doncaster-built engines. It would have been interesting to have had included a standard engine of the '251' class, with 175 lb per sq in pressure; but, of course, Doncaster would have had ample data already from the regular working of these engines. One outcome was that a second 4-cylinder compound 'Atlantic' was built at Doncaster, differing somewhat from No 292. The control arrangements were the same, with a change valve permitting the use of simple working continuously for as long as necessary and not just for starting as in the de Glehn system. But an important change from No 292 was the use of larger low-pressure cylinders, which made the tractive effort when working simple considerably greater. The low-pressure cylinders were, indeed, 18 in (diameter) by 26 in (stroke), almost exactly equal in volume to the two 18¾ in by 24 in cylinders of the standard '251' class. This new engine, No 1421, had a tractive effort of 23,620 lb when working simple, as compared to the 20,070 lb of No 292 and the 14,800 lb of the '251' class, as calculated by the formula Ivatt used in his paper to the Institution of Mechanical Engineers, in 1907. On this reckoning, No 1421 was by far the most

powerful express-passenger engine that had yet been used on the Great Northern Railway. Unlike No 292, the valve gear for the inside cylinders was Walschaert's.

Against this notable increase in tractive effort, Ivatt made a rather extraordinary change in the design of the boilers. He reverted, first, to the recessed form of smoke-box tube-plate used on the small-boilered 'Atlantics', though not to the same extent, and abandoned the impressive-looking forward extension of the smoke-box ahead of the chimney. The distance between the tube-plates was reduced from the 16 ft 0 in of the standard boiler used on the '251' class, including the compound No 292, to 14 ft 6 in, with a reduction in outside diameter of the tubes from 2¼ to 2 in and an increase in their number from 248 to 293. Thus despite the considerable reduction in their length, the heating surface of the tubes was reduced only from a total of 2,359 sq ft to 2,208 sq ft. The firebox heating surface was slightly greater than that of the standard, large 'Atlantics', at 143.6 sq ft against 141 sq ft. The boiler pressure was 200 lb per sq in, as on No 292. Both these Doncaster-designed compound 'Atlantics' were unique in allowing for continuous working as simples when so required and they had an unusual composite form of blast pipe, the construction of which is shown in the accompanying drawing. When the engine was working compound, the entire exhaust to atmosphere passed through the oval pipes, 10½ in wide at

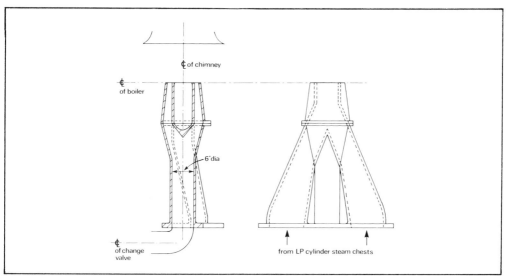

Top *The Vulcan compound, No 1300, on down express near Potters Bar* (C. Laundy).

Above *The composite blast-pipe.*

their connection to the valve chests, and ejected into the smoke-box, through the inner jet of the blast pipe which had a diameter of 5 in. When working simple, the exhaust from the high-pressure cylinders went up the central 6 in diameter pipe, which was splayed out at the top to admit the entry of the oval pipes from the low-pressure cylinders.

It was a complicated arrangement and, because the separate and independently controlled valve gear for the high- and low-

pressure valve motions would govern the amount of steam passing through the respective sections of the blast pipe, it would obviously need considerable experience on the part of the driver to ascertain the ideal settings of the two separate reversing levers to avoid getting the exhaust starved of steam or, alternatively, being choked. That the men found the way to adjust successfully was amply shown by the running performances of No 292 already quoted. So far as driving technique is concerned it is important to recall at this point that the Vulcan-built engine No 1300 did not have *all* the special features included in the de Glehn compounds, with which those of us who had the privilege of riding some of those engines in France later became familiar. For instance, when working 'full compound' the French engines had a valve which admitted additional live steam from the boiler direct into the low-pressure cylinders, initiating what was sometimes termed 'reinforced compound' working. One could not keep it up for long, but while in progress it gave terrific results. The Vulcan engine supplied to the Great Northern Railway had that company's patent starting valve and their patent compound reversing gear. Unlike the Doncaster arrangement, the gear was operated by a screw mechanism, that provided fine adjustment of the cut-off in the cylinders.

I have not been able to trace any contemporary reports of the ordinary running performance of the compound engine No 1421. Rous-Marten died in April 1908 and his immediate successors in the authorship of the 'British Locomotive Practice and Performance' feature in *The Railway Magazine* did not seem to have the personal *entrée* to the 'corridors of power' in the railway world to get locomotives specially allocated for them to make experimental runs. Although the ace photographers of the day like C. Laundy and W.J. Reynolds recorded the comings and goings of both 1421 and the Vulcan No 1300, these locomotives eluded the men with the stop-watches. Very many years later, however, when I was engaged on some literary work about North Eastern locomotives, the late K.J. Cook, then Chief Mechanical and Electrical Engineer of the Eastern and North Eastern Regions of British Railways, very kindly allowed me to browse through some of the old records obtained with the former North Eastern Railway dynamometer car. Almost accidentally, I came across records of a trial run with the new East Coast Joint Stock Royal Train, which had been built for the convenience of King Edward VII, many of whose journeys to Scotland commenced from the homes of his sporting friends in the Dukeries. The object of the test run made on February 18 1909 was apparently to measure the rolling resistance of the sumptuous new 12-wheeled saloons built for the King and Queen, marshalled in a train of beautiful, standard ECJS coaches and making up, with the dynamometer car, a tare load of 302 tons. As when the King would be travelling, real express running began at Doncaster and to my great interest I found that the Great Northern had worked the train to York with the compound 'Atlantic' No 1421.

The North Eastern engineers in the dynamometer car, though taking much detail as to the working of their own engines, northward from York, unfortunately recorded no corresponding data for the Great Northern engine. This was a great pity because from the charts that I was able to examine at Darlington it is evident that No 1421 put up a magnificent performance. With the heavy East Coast express trains of the day, the large-boilered GNR 'Atlantics' used to sustain speeds of around 55 to 60 mph on the level stretches north of Doncaster. Anything over sixty was considered quite exceptional, with a load of anything much more than about 275 tons. Yet here was No 1421 doing 60 mph, less than 4¾ miles out of Doncaster; by Moss, 7 miles from the dead start, the speed was 68 mph, and it finally reached a sustained 73 mph on level track, before easing down for the severe speed restriction through Selby, which station, 18.4 miles from Doncaster, was passed through slowly in 19½ minutes from the start. A drawbar pull of 1½ tons was registered in the dynamometer car at 70 mph, which is equivalent to about 700 drawbar horsepower, and one would dearly have liked to know how the engine was being worked to manage this and how the boiler stood up to the demands upon it for steam. The maximum output, approaching Selby at 73 mph would have been equivalent to about 850 drawbar horsepower. It is of interest by way of comparison, that haulage of the train was taken over at York by one of the, then, brand-new 4-4-0s of the 'R1' class, which carried a boiler pressure of 225 lb per sq in. She took 21 minutes to cover the first 18, almost level, miles from York and speed had not then exceeded 65 mph, working with 27 per cent cut-off and steam-chest pressure averaging about 150 lb per sq in. The honours were quite clearly with the Great Northern engine.

Later that same year came the locomotive interchange trials with the London and North Western Railway, in which one of the latest of the large-boilered 'Atlantics', No 1449 worked for a time between Euston and Crewe, in exchange for a 4-4-0 of the 'Precursor' class, No 412 *Marquis*, which ran between Kings Cross and Doncaster at the same time. This

The 1909 Interchange Trials: the GNR 4-4-2, No 1449, on down Sunday LNWR express on Bushey troughs (C. Laundy).

friendly exchange was made at the instigation of C.J. Bowen Cooke, the recently appointed Chief Mechanical Engineer of the LNWR, with the full approbation and co-operation of Mr Ivatt. The trials were much more extensive than some of the interchanges conducted in later years, notably those organised by British Railways, in 1948. Then, the various competing locomotives made no more than two return trips from Kings Cross to Leeds and back, 740 miles in all, and 1,200 miles on the West Coast main line between Euston and Carlisle. In 1909, on the Great Northern, the competing engines each ran 4,992 miles, that is sixteen return trips from Doncaster to Kings Cross and back while, on the LNWR, the aggregate mileage run by both engines was 4,113. On the Great Northern, the tasks set to the rival engines bore a very close resemblance to those of 1906 set for the three varieties of 'Atlantic' and the mileage run was roughly half. The average loads were slightly heavier,

but the speeds were also considerably higher. At a time when I was writing some articles for *The Railway Magazine* on the subject of interchange trials, Sir Nigel Gresley, then Chief Mechanical Engineer of the LNER gave me the following overall figures:

Engine	GNR No 1451	LNWR No 412
Average load (16 trips Doncaster to Kings Cross and back 312 miles)	237¾ tons	236½ tons
Coal consumed (ex-Houghton Colliery) Per train mile	34.6 lb	36.5 lb
Per ton mile (excluding engine and tender)	0.145 lb	0.154 lb
Oil and tallow per 100 train miles	4.12 lb	4.53 lb
Speed	53.12 mph	52.73 mph

In comparing the above results with those of

the 'Atlantic' trials of 1906, which show a considerably higher coal consumption per train mile and a very much lower consumption per ton mile, the higher figures for the earlier set of runs not only included the coal used in lighting up, but also the results of routine link working, not all of it on express trains. One of the Doncaster turns that was actually being worked by the ill-fated No 276 on the night of the Grantham accident involved working a slow train from Doncaster to York, then an express to Peterborough and finally back to Doncaster on the train that 'took the wrong turn' at Grantham. Such a duty would involve considerable stand-by usage of fuel. In the 1906 results, the figures for coal consumption per ton mile included the weight of the engine and tender in the train; so as to make a true comparison with those of the 1909 Interchange Trial with the LNWR, the coal per train mile for the three engines involved in 1906 should be quoted as 32.0 (No 1300), 30.1 (No 292), and 30.9 (No 294), thus corresponding more closely with the 34.6 lb per train mile of No 1451 in 1909 and giving a logical result for the higher average speeds run on the later set of trials. The higher consumptions per train mile in 1909 also account for the differences in coal per ton mile.

For the trials on the LNWR, Sir William Stanier, then Chief Mechanical Engineer of the LMS, very kindly had the old Crewe dynamometer car records looked up and furnished me with some very interesting information. In all, 26 runs were made by each engine, but it was only at the conclusion of the trial period that the dynamometer car was used. The trains principally worked were the 10:00 am Scottish express from Euston to Crewe, and the heavy up Liverpool and Manchester express due to arrive in Euston at 8:10 pm. The maximum load for an LNWR 'Precursor' class 4-4-0 on these turns was 'equal to 19½'. The system of load reckoning at that time rated a six-wheeled coach as '1', an eight-wheeled bogie coach as '1½' and a 12-wheeler, either dining or sleeping car, as '2'; but so far as actual tonnage was concerned there was considerable difference between some of the 8-wheelers then in use on express trains, varying from 22 to 24 tons for the older flat-roofed corridor coaches to just over 30 tons for the latest. A train including nine of these latter and three 12-wheeled dining cars 'equal to 19½', could weigh little short of 400 tons tare. The overall results on the LNWR were:

Engine	LNWR No 510	GNR No 1449
Average load per trip	290 tons	320 tons
Total number of trips	26	26
Train miles run	4,113	4,113
Ton miles run (excluding engine & tender)	1,194,250	1,317,448
Coal burned per train mile	40.73 lb	41.08 lb
Coal burned per ton mile	0.140 lb	0.128 lb

The above figures for coal consumption, good for both engines, cannot be exactly pinpointed because the record unfortunately does not give the average speed of the trains worked. It would most likely have been around 53–54 mph.

The results of the dynamometer car tests on the 10:00 am from Euston to Crewe are illuminating, thus:

Engine	LNWR No 510 Albatross	GNR No 1449
Date	25 June 1909	26 June 1909
Train	10:00 am ex-Euston	10:00 am ex-Euston
Maximum drawbar pull on starting	8½ tons	9⅛ tons
Length of trip	158.1 miles	158.1 miles
Total running time (including stops)	186 min	185¾ min
Total running time (excluding stops)	179½ min	180¾ min
Average Speed	52.9 mph	52.5 mph
Maximum Speed	70 mph	73 mph
Load, tare, behind tender	399 tons	398 tons

Here again there was very little in it between the two engines, but apart from the technical information made available to me, I learned more recently of some interesting sidelights on the trials. H.G. Ivatt, the last Chief Mechanical Engineer of the LMS, was, like his father, a Crewe man by training and at the time of the trials he was a junior engineer on the staff of C.J. Bowen Cooke. From the time when he was Principal Assistant to the CME of the LMS, I had a good deal of pleasant correspondence with him and later used to meet him on occasion. One day, when he came to see me and spent an hour or so in my office at Chippenham, he began to reminisce about the 1909 Interchange, in which of course he was more than usually interested. He told me how his father bet the driver of the visiting LNWR 4-4-0, *Marquis*, that he could

Leeds express passing the long-dismantled Holloway Road station, hauled by LNWR 4-4-0 No 412, Marquis (C. Laundy).

The 1909 Interchange Trials: an up Liverpool express just south of Crewe, hauled by GNR 4-4-2 No 1449 (Loco Publishing Co Ltd).

GNR 'Atlantic' working in 1910

Non-superheater engines '251' class

Run no	Train	From	To	Load, tons	Distance, miles	Booked time, min	Started late, min	Actual time, min	Net time, min	Net gain or loss, min	Booked average speed, mph	Net average speed, mph
1	5:30 pm	Kings Cross	Grantham	235	105.5	117	—	118¼	116¼	+¾	54.0	54.5
2	5:30 pm	Kings Cross	Grantham	235	105.5	117	—	118½	118	−1	54.0	53.7
3	2:32 pm	York	Grantham	330*	82.7	97	—	98¼	98¼	−1¼	51.2	50.5
4	5:30 pm	Kings Cross	Grantham	235	105.5	117	—	118¼	117½	−½	54.0	53.9
5	1:30 pm	Kings Cross	Peterborough	300	76.4	83	—	84	80	+3	55.1	57.2
6	2:56 pm	Peterborough	Doncaster	300	79.6	88	1¾	86	86	+2	54.4	55.5
7	10:40 am	Doncaster	Kings Cross	290	156.0	180	8¾	181½	179½	+½	52.0	52.2
8	1:03 pm	Doncaster	Peterborough	335	79.6	93	3¼	93½	93½	−½	51.6	51.1
9	2:40 pm	Peterborough	Kings Cross	335	76.4	90	3½	88½	88½	+1½	50.8	51.8
10	10:40 am	Doncaster	Kings Cross	260	156.0	180	4½	182¼	182¼	−2¼	52.0	51.4
11	2:32 pm	York	Grantham	290*	82.7	97	67¾	113½	106½	−9½	51.2	46.5
12	4:13 pm	Grantham	Kings Cross	290	105.5	122	84½	126	126	−4	51.8	50.3
13	2:32 pm	York	Grantham	330*	82.7	97	1¼	95	95	+2	51.2	52.2
14	4:13 pm	Grantham	Kings Cross	330	105.5	122	—	123¼	120	+2	51.8	52.7
15	6:05 pm	Kings Cross	Grantham	200	105.5	112	—	114	114	−2	56.4	55.5
16	10:00 am	Kings Cross	Grantham	290	105.5	120	—	123½	123½	−3½	52.6	51.2
17	2:32 pm	York	Grantham	290*	82.7	97	1½	96½	96½	+½	51.2	51.3
18	4:13 pm	Grantham	Kings Cross	290	105.5	122	¾	122¾	122¾	−¾	51.8	51.6
19	5:30 pm	Kings Cross	Grantham	235	105.5	117	—	117¾	117¾	+2¼	54.0	55.2
20	1:03 pm	Doncaster	Peterborough	325	79.6	93	5½	103¼	103¼	−10¼	51.5	46.3
21	2.40 pm	Peterborough	Kings Cross	325	76.4	90	15¾	95	95	−5	50.8	48.2
22	10:00 am	Kings Cross	Grantham	290	105.5	120	—	122	119	+1	52.6	53.2
23	12:04 pm	Grantham	York	290	82.7	98	2	98¾	96¾	+1¼	50.7	51.2
24	10:00 am	Kings Cross	Grantham	290	105.5	120	—	119¾	119¾	+¼	52.6	52.9
25	12:04 pm	Grantham	York	290	82.7	98	½	96¾	94¾	+3¼	50.7	52.4

*Load 25 tons more from York to Doncaster (slip coach).

not pass Potters Bar in less than 20 minutes from Kings Cross and promised him a new hat if he did so! But as a Crewe man 'H.G.' was naturally more interested in the work of his father's engine on the LNWR. He told me that on the first day the 'Atlantic', No 1449, was on the 10:00 am Scotsman there was immense satisfaction on Crewe platform when the train was wired 2 minutes late on passing Nuneaton. Many of the lesser lights in the locomotive department firmly believed that no engines other than their own could work the West Coast expresses to time. On hearing the news from Nuneaton, 'She'll never make that up' was the unanimous verdict, and an arrival in Crewe about 5 minutes late was confidently predicted; but to the chagrin of the bowler-hatted fraternity gathered on the platform to welcome her No 1449 sailed into Crewe dead on time!

For most of the trial period, both on the GNR and the LNWR, the rival engines had been working service trains and no one except a road pilotman had been allowed on the footplate. But on the last two days, when first the 4-4-0, *Albatross*, and then the 'Atlantic', No 1449, were on the 10:00 am from Euston to Crewe, the LNWR dynamometer car was attached and Bowen Cooke himself travelled in it. H.G. Ivatt told me how pleased he was that 'Bowen' deputed him to ride on the footplate of his father's engine. With a load of practically 400 tons tare behind the tender, at least 425 tons full, the Great Northern driver faced his toughest task. While they waited for the 'right-away' at Euston, David Button, the pilotman, an 'ace' Camden driver with a record of many Royal Train workings to his credit, said cheerily, 'If you stick on Camden bank you won't be the first to do it!' But they did not stick and although a little time was lost going up to Tring, there was nothing more to slow them, and they were on time at Rugby. Passing Nuneaton they were, as usual about 2 minutes late; but the engine ran well across the Trent Valley, and Crewe was reached on time. The speed restriction on the Trent Valley Junction curve, approaching Stafford was, however, interpreted somewhat liberally, and on arrival at Crewe, Bowen Cooke came up to the engine and made to reprimand both the driver and the pilotman, although of course speed was left entirely to their judgement. There were no such refinements as speedometers on British locomotives in those days. Anyway the Great Northern driver, smiling broadly, cut Bowen Cooke

short by saying, 'It's a beautiful curve'.

'Never mind about beautiful curves,' rapped out Bowen Cooke, 'You went round at 50, when you should have done only 30'.

Ivatt told me with a chuckle, how the Great Northern driver smiled even more broadly, and said once again, 'It's a beautiful curve!'

Unfortunately no detailed logs were taken of the working of the GN 'Atlantic', No 1449, during her stay on the North Western, but I am glad to include here one splendid photograph of her, leaving Crewe on the heavy up Liverpool and Manchester express, when the load appears to have been 'equal to 23' — ten 8-wheelers, many of them of the latest 30-ton stock, and *four* 12-wheeled dining cars — about 440 tons tare! It would have been interesting to know how she wheeled that lot up to Euston. It was evidently something of an occasion, because both driver and fireman are looking out to greet the official LNWR photographer.

In concluding what could be termed the non-superheater era of the Great Northern 'Atlantics' it must nevertheless be admitted that while the '251' class was capable of excellent work when under special observation, the general standard of performance left much to be desired. The late Cecil J. Allen, as a regular traveller between London and Teesside, and a meticulous recorder of train running, presented in *The Railway Magazine* in 1910, an analysis of his most recent 25 journeys on Great Northern expresses, all made in the first 3 months of that year. It is a most absorbing document, which shows not only failures to keep time when the start of the journey was punctual, but a disinclination to make up time when the starts were late. It made a distinctly unfavourable comparison with a similar analysis that he presented at the same time covering his experiences when travelling behind the 'Precursor' class 4-4-0s of the LNWR over the same period. The chief point for emphasis in studying this analysis is that it was not the experience of a privileged observer, making 'experiments', with the blessing of the locomotive department, but that of an ordinary traveller, having no conversation with drivers, certainly not before the runs and, in the majority of cases, not afterwards either. In certain cases, the actual number of the locomotive was not obtained, though they were all uniformly of the non-superheated '251' class. The average load on the 25 runs was 249 tons, length of run 93.7 miles and the net average speed 53 mph.

Chapter 5

Superheating—the first stages

Ever since the basic steam locomotive had been 'made to go' by George and Robert Stephenson and their friends, successive generations of engineers sought to improve its efficiency. I am not thinking now of means to increase the durability and dependability of the machinery, but of what is known technically as the heat-balance sheet: the overall ratio between the latent energy potential in the coal fired, and the power made available at the drawbar for haulage of a train. To the very last days of the steam locomotive it remained astonishingly low, but at the turn of the century it was a great deal worse, little more than about 4 or 5 per cent. Means were sought of improving this, by increasing the range of expansion of the steam by two-stage or compound working; some engineers tried to reduce the heat loss through radiation by providing their cylinders with steam jackets, but by far the most promising development around 1900 was that of the Prussian engineer Wilhelm Schmidt in his work on superheating. By heating the steam beyond its temperature of formation in the boiler, its volume was increased and the capacity of the locomotive increased accordingly. To take an actual example, at a boiler pressure of 175 lb per sq in, as on the Great Northern 'Atlantics', the temperature of formation is 377°(F), but if it was further heated — superheated — to a temperature of 527°(F), its volume would be increased by about 12 or 13 per cent.

In applying this basic principle to a locomotive, three broad alternatives were available, examples of which were to be seen in British practice in the years before World War I. Compared to the situation that arose in North America and on the continent of Europe, the railways of Britain were rather slow in adopting superheating. This could be attributed in part to an innate conservatism, with perhaps some reluctance to take up a foreign idea, but more on account of the high quality of coal available in Great Britain — far better then than anything used abroad, so much so that some of the French railways had fleets of colliers that came across and collected Welsh coal for their own use. The Great Northern was well placed in this respect in having the Yorkshire coalfields on their doorstep. On the Great Western, Churchward

sought to improve the thermal efficiency, without going to the complication of compounding, by increasing the range of expansion, using a high initial pressure, a very long piston stroke and cutting off very early in the stroke. With saturated steam there was a risk that the steam would be expanded to the extent of condensation at the end of the stroke and he aimed at providing just enough superheat to avoid this. It remained standard Great Western practice for nearly 40 years. Other engineers used the increased volume of superheated steam to give a more powerful engine, from roughly the same sized boiler, by using larger cylinders.

On the Great Northern, Ivatt followed neither of these practices. He did not consider that current traffic requirements demanded more powerful passenger engines than his 'Atlantics', but instead took advantage of the greater volume of superheated steam, not only to use larger cylinders, but also to reduce boiler pressure, hoping thereby to reduce his boiler maintenance charges. But, in enlarging the cylinders, he still further accentuated the difference between Churchward's practice and his own. In the non-superheated Great Northern 'Atlantics', the piston stroke was unusually short, for the 20th century, at 24 in; and when converting the first of these engines to superheating the cylinder diameter was increased from 18¾ to 20 in. The contrast between Churchward's 18½ in by 30 in and Ivatt's 20 in by 24 in was profound. This, so far as stroke was concerned, was understandable in the first experimental application, in that it involved the alteration of an existing engine and, naturally, the expense of rebuilding the machinery to accommodate a longer stroke would have been undesirable. But when he came to build new superheater 'Atlantic' engines Ivatt retained the 24 in stroke.

The first engine to be altered was one of the 'Long Tom' 0-8-0 mineral engines, but a 'Klondike', No 988, followed soon afterwards, in 1909. Both classes had the same boiler, and with the recessed front tube-plate there was plenty of room in the smoke-box to accommodate the superheater, without any extension in front. There was, in fact, little outward sign that a superheater had been fitted. Both the

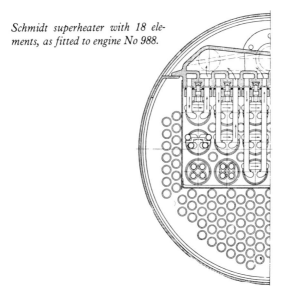

Schmidt superheater with 18 elements, as fitted to engine No 988.

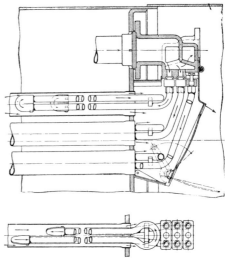

0-8-0 and the 4-4-2 were equipped with piston valves and the former, having inside cylinders, had the valves mounted directly above, with the front of the valve chests prominent, on the front of the smoke-box; but on the 'Klondike', the piston valves were below and in line with the cylinders, and the only outward sign of superheating was the mechanical lubricator mounted on the running plate on the right-hand side.

The form of the Schmidt superheater fitted to engine No 988 is shown in the accompanying drawing. There were 18 elements, but that shown has 130 small tubes, whereas that on No 988 had only 104. The smoke-box ends of the elements were enclosed in a box provided with a damper. This was arranged to open and shut automatically as the regulator was opened and shut, so that it was impossible to burn the elements when there was no steam in them. The damper was worked by a small cylinder placed on the left hand side of the outside of the smokebox, fed with steam through a small pipe connected to the superheater header. It was one of the special features of the Schmidt superheater design that the driver was given independent control of the damper, if it was necessary to use it and, by partially closing the damper door while steam was on, the degree of superheat could be regulated as desired. This was sometimes used to good effect if an engine was a little 'shy' for steam at the beginning of a run. With a partial closing of the damper the proportion of the amount of steam passing through the

small tubes was increased and the increased draught necessary for this livened up the fire. A pyrometer gauge, indicating the temperature of the steam was mounted on the right-hand side of the cab, just ahead of the driver's stance.

Dr Schmidt's development of the principle of superheating went a great deal farther than the designing of the superheater itself, as he applied his ingenuity to the entire 'front-end' of the engine. Great importance was attached to the design of the cylinders and valves. The piston heads, which were of cast steel, were floating in the cylinders, by having tail rods extending through the front covers. Thus the weight of the piston head was carried in the stuffing boxes in each cylinder cover and this reduced wear on the lower part of the cylinder walls. This was a significant change from the cylinder design of the original Doncaster 'Atlantic' engines. The piston valves, of 8 in diameter and of Schmidt's patented design, had his type of Trick ports and inside admission. By this means valve-spindle packings were rendered unnecessary and the exhaust steam passages were kept away from those of the live steam. The so-called Trick ports were derived from a very old idea ascribed to Alexander Allan and have been vividly described as having a supercharging effect in getting steam into the cylinders. On some British locomotives to which Schmidt's type of piston valve with Trick ports were applied, it has been suggested that their beneficial effect was nullified by provision of inadequate

Top *The first superheated large 'Atlantic', No 1452. The small cylinder for operating the damper of the Schmidt apparatus can be seen on the side of the smoke-box in line with the handrail* (British Railways).

Above *The 2:20 pm Scotsman north of Hadley Wood, hauled by No 1459, one of the 1910 batch of Schmidt superheater 'Atlantics'* (O.S. Nock Collection).

Below *One of the earliest of the small Atlantics to be superheated: No 950 on up Newcastle express near Potters Bar* (C. Laundy).

exhaust ports. But this was certainly not the case on the superheated 'Atlantics' of the Great Northern Railway.

One of the most important considerations with the use of superheated steam is the lubrication. Prior to its introduction, when locomotive cylinders were fed with what is kown technically as 'dry saturated steam' the steam itself was a natural lubricant and the parts exposed to it needed little in the way of special attention. But when superheated, with the steam becoming an intensely dry, searing gas, it was another matter. Lubrication became all important and much trouble was experienced in early days in finding a lubricant that would remain stable and function properly at the high temperatures involved. But, by the time the Great Northern was ready to begin its first trials with superheater engines, the firm of C.C. Wakefield & Co had found the answer and made available to locomotive engineers the first form of the famous Wakefield mechanical lubricator. This was used on the first 'Atlantic' engine to be superheated, No 988. On this engine the new cylinders, with tail rods and the Schmidt type of piston valve, were 20 in (diameter) by 24 in (stroke), and with the boiler pressure reduced from 175 to 165 lb per sq in, the nominal tractive effort was 16,260 lb instead of the original 15,670. It was of course, not merely a question of a slightly increased tractive effort. The increased fluidity of the superheated steam enabled it to flow more freely through the various ports and passages and would contribute to a free-running engine. In an article contributed to *The Railway Magazine* in February 1911, J.R. Bazin, then Assistant Works Manager at Doncaster and subsequently Chief Mechanical Engineer of the Great Southern Railway, in Ireland, stated that No 988 had been doing very fine work, on a much reduced coal consumption.

The improvement in performance was indeed such that when, in 1910, authority was given for the construction of more first-line express passenger locomotives, Ivatt decided on a further reduction of boiler pressure, to 150 lb per sq in, on nine new engines similar to the '251' class, but having 20 in by 24 in cylinders, piston valves and 18-element Schmidt superheaters. The tenth engine differed, in carrying a boiler pressure of 160 lb per sq in; this was No 1454. The other nine were 1452–3 and 1455–61. The engines with 150 lb boilers had a tractive effort of 15,250

lb. Apart from the tail rods and the small cylinder for actuating the superheater dampers on the left-hand side of the smoke-box, just above the handrail, the new engines could be readily distinguished from the '251' class by the setting forward of the chimney in order to clear the header of the superheater. The actual layout in the smoke-box can be seen from the accompanying drawing. There were some slight difference in dimensions from those of the '251' class. The blast-pipe orifice was increased from 5¼ to 5½ in diameter, thereby increasing the cross-sectional area by 9.6 per cent. In the non-superheater engines the tip of the orifice was exactly on the horizontal centre line of the boiler, while in the 1452–61 class it was ⅝ in higher. Clearly some very careful attention had been paid to the draughting on the new engines.

Much apparently conflicting information has been published over the years about the details of the superheaters fitted to the Great Northern 'Atlantics'. Engine No 988, with 18 elements, gave a superheater heating surface of 343 sq ft and at first the '1452–61' class had an identical apparatus, despite the greater length of the boiler barrel on the larger engines. It was then noticed from the pyrometer gauge in the cab that the 'Klondike' was obtaining a much higher degree of superheat, due no doubt to the return bends of the elements being much closer to the firebox. On the '1452–61' class, the elements were lengthened accordingly, increasing the heating surface to 428 sq ft. The fact that this surface area was almost exactly the same as that of the 24-element Robinson superheaters, fitted subsequently to many of the '251' class, led to the wrong conclusion that 1452–61 had 24-element superheaters when new. The lengthening of the elements evidently took place very early in the life of these engines because in the aforementioned article in *The Railway Magazine*, in 1911, J.R. Bazin quotes the heating surface as 428 sq ft. In later references to these engines and to the 'Klondikes', the superheater heating surfaces were quoted as 320 and 254 sq ft; this was due to a sudden change of mind in the Doncaster drawing office in calculating the inside, rather than the outside area of the elements. In addition it was originally the practice to include the portion of the elements in the smoke-box, while later it became the practice to include only that portion within the flue tubes. The relevant values quoted were as follows overleaf:

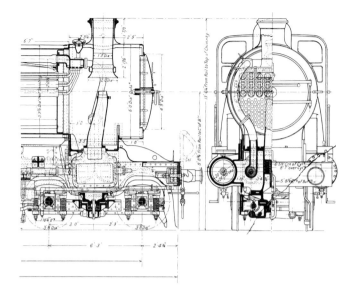

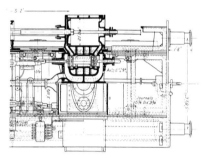

Smoke-box arrangement on 1452–61-class large 'Atlantics'.

Number of elements*	By old method, sq ft	By later method, sq ft	
18	343	254	original
18	428	320	later standard
24	570	427	later standard

*When the 32-element superheater was introduced in 1919, the heating surface, by the later standard method of calculation, was 568 sq ft.

The work of the new engines in ordinary service was soon being very fully documented. The late Cecil J. Allen, in his regular journeys to and from Tees-side, had many journeys behind them and he wrote enthusiastically of his experiences. In the light of the wonderful work they did in the years between the two World Wars, these earlier runs would not appear to be anything very special, but despite the use of no higher boiler pressure than 150 lb per sq in, on average they showed a marked superiority over those of the non-superheater engines. Summary details are tabulated on seven runs with the 1:03 pm express from Doncaster to Peterborough. It was a relatively heavy train for those days on the GNR and had what even then would have been considered a fairly liberal allowance of 93 minutes for the 79.6 mile run, calling for an average speed of only 51.3 mph. Not one of the engines concerned was unduly exerted, particularly on the 5 miles of 1 in 200 ascent between Grantham and the Stoke summit signal-box. In the years between the two world wars, minimum speeds of less than 40 mph at Stoke would have been considered poor, and yet the very best on these runs was 36 mph and the lowest no more than 30 mph. In setting out the details of these runs, I was reminded of the occasion in 1932 when I clocked one of these engines, admittedly then fitted with a 32-element superheater, to haul a load of 325 tons from Doncaster to Peterborough in 71 min 10 sec; pass-to-pass, with slow speed through both stations, when the minimum speed at Stoke was 48½ mph. Back in 1911, there was plenty of fast running

GNR 1:03 pm Doncaster–Peterborough

Engine (superheater 4-4-2) No:	1453	1454	1456	1456	1452	1456	1456
Load, tons gross:	330	360	365	375	375	400	405

Distance miles		Actual m s	Actual m s	Actual m s	Actual m s	Actual m s	Actual m s	Actual m s
0.0	Doncaster	0 00	0 00	0 00	0 00	0 00	0 00	0 00
17.4	Retford	21 15	21 00	21 40	20 55	22 00	21 30	22 10
35.9	Newark	41 35	40 30	42 55	41 10	42 20	40 45	42 35
50.5	Grantham	59 20	58 55	60 00	59 05	60 05	58 55	62 25
55.9	Stoke Box	67 15	68 05	67 55	68 20	68 10	67 55	71 20
79.6	Peterborough	91 15	90 35	91 20	90 35	91 10	90 20	93 25
	Minimum speed at Stoke, mph	30	31	36	32	35	33	33

GNR 2:20 pm Wakefield–Kings Cross

Run no:			1		2		3	
Engine No:			1459		278		1461	
Load, tons gross:			165		175		190	

Distance miles		Schedule min	Actual m s	Speed mph	Actual m s	Speed mph	Actual m s	Speed mph
0.0	WAKEFIELD		0 00		0 00		0 00	
5.5	Nostell		8 20	—	8 22	—	7 15	—
13.3	Hampole		15 49	77	15 47	79	14 08	77½
19.9	DONCASTER	21	21 39	—	21 49		19 56	—
24.6	Rossington		26 38	63/60	26 47		24 52	
28.2	Bawtry		30 29		30 26		28 16	
32.0	Ranskill		33 55	69	33 55	67	31 35	69
37.3	RETFORD	39	39 01	—	39 07	—	36 46	—
44.0	Tuxford		46 10	—	46 22	—	44 09	53
49.5	Carlton		50 27	83	51 11	70	48 44	75
55.8	NEWARK	59	57 11		57 15		54 30	—
66.2	Barkston		67 57		67 49		65 23	56
70.4	GRANTHAM	75	72 36		73 40		70 25	—
75.8	*Stoke Box*		79 07	42	80 22	44	76 46	41
83.7	Little Bytham		86 15	—	87 26	79	84 04	77½
—			signals	—	—	—	signals	
91.1	Tallington		94 04	—	93 28	—	90 43	—
99.5	PETERBOROUGH	105	104 52	—	102 49	—	100 59	—
—			pws		—		—	—
106.5	Holme		112 46		111 31		109 20	—
112.4	Abbots Ripton		119 35		117 13		115 03	59
117.0	HUNTINGDON	124	124 12	77	121 50	75	119 52	69
124.2	St Neots		130 05	68	127 56		126 43	—
134.8	Biggleswade		139 08	72	138 24	eased	137 19	—
140.2	Three Counties		144 02	—	144 27		142 48	—
144.0	HITCHIN	152	147 34	—	148 44		146 44	45
147.3	Stevenage		151 14	40	152 56	45	150 55	—
158.2	HATFIELD	167	162 14	—	163 42	—	161 49	68
163.2	Potters Bar		167 45	—	168 56	—	167 05	—
—			—	—	signals		Fog	—
170.9	Wood Green		176 29	—	—	—	signals	—
173.3	Finsbury Park		179 35	—	179 20		179 08	
—								
175.9	KINGS CROSS	187	184 18		182 50		183 03	

Leeds and Bradford express climbing the bank out of Kings Cross, past Belle Isle signal-box, hauled by superheater 4-4-2 No 1460 (F.E. Mackay).

on the down gradients and Allen's records include frequent speeds of 75 to 79 mph downhill.

Another interesting record of those early days of the superheater 'Atlantics' is tabulated, this time on the down 'Flying Scotsman', which was then allowed the level two hours for the run of 105.5 miles from Kings Cross to Grantham. It began badly, with the engine slipping so continuously as to take 8¼ minutes to cover the first 2.6 miles out to Finsbury Park and the ensuing 10.1 miles up to Potters Bar took another 14½ minutes. After that, however, they went like the wind. From a maximum of 75 mph north of Hatfield, the climb to Woolmer Green summit was rushed at no lower speed than 60 mph and the 27 miles from Hitchin to Huntingdon took no more than 22 min 40 sec, an average of 71.5 mph and including a sustained maximum of 85 mph near Three Counties. The Stukeley bank, beyond Huntingdon, was taken at a lowest speed of 50 mph while a maximum of 77½ mph descending to the fringe of the Fens, near Holme, took the train through Peterborough in 80 min 25 sec, with the lateness of 4¾ minutes at Hatfield changed to a passage 3½ minutes early at Peterborough. As in the case of the up journeys previously referred to, the hill climbing to Stoke was very slow, not that anything faster was needed in the circumstances, to reach Grantham 2½ minutes early.

But a run like this certainly established the superheater 'Atlantics' of the 1452–61 series as very speedy machines.

So far as speed was concerned, the 2:00 pm up from Leeds was the star train of the service with its non-stop run of 187 minutes for the 175.9 miles from Wakefield to Kings Cross. The timing of that train included one of those timetabling inconsistences that simply defy logical explanation. The publicly advertised time of arrival in Kings Cross was 5:25 pm, yet the working time was 5:27 pm, so that the train could be 2 minutes late so far as the travelling public was concerned and yet the driver and guard could clock up an on time arrival! All records I have seen of the running of this train however consistently show arrivals ahead of the *public* time. The load was very light, not exceeding six coaches and, on two of the three examples of which tabulated details of the running are given, it was only five — on the heavier occasion three 'twelves' and two 'eights'. These runs were made available to me by the courtesy of the late E.L. Bell, compiled in the most minute detail. They date between January 1912 and March 1913. Although no actual records of maximum and minimum speeds were taken by stop-watch, the intermediate detail is such that the more significant speeds may be deduced with accuracy.

On the first run, with a very light load, the only feature of interest in the early stages was the fast descent from Tuxford to the Trent Valley, with a maximum speed of 83 mph. Then after the usual slowing over Muskham troughs the ascent to Stoke was taken under easy steam, with speed falling to 42 mph at the summit. Then, after the checks before Tallington and Holme had taken their toll and resulted in the train passing Huntingdon barely on time, the driver put on something of a spurt and gained 4¾ minutes on the easy allowance of 28 minutes from Huntingdon to Hitchin. After that, all was plain sailing and, after relatively slow running in from Hatfield, the train arrived in Kings Cross just ahead of the public time of 5:25 pm. On the second run, with non-superheater engine No 278, the train ran ahead of time all the way from Newark and, except between Tuxford and Carlton, there was no appreciable difference in the times and speeds, as one would expect with these light loads. On passing Hunting-

don well ahead of time, the engine was very much eased down and the arrival in Kings Cross would have been even earlier but for a signal check near New Barnet, which cost about a minute in running. The third journey included much the fastest start out of Wakefield and, with the effort continuing, Grantham was passed 4½ minutes early. Despite the signal check before Tallington and very easy running southwards from Huntingdon the driver had enough time in hand at Hatfield to offset the effects of fog in the London approaches and still to arrive at 5:23 pm.

There is really not much to be deduced from the running on this, the show train of the Great Northern express service. The ten superheater engines of the large-boilered 'Atlantic' type were not extended in their ordinary duties, and there was no Rous-Marten to make 'experiments' and urge the

Above *A reminder of the long 1912 coal strike: a 'Klondike' No 259, fitted for oil firing* (British Railways).

Below *The previously 4-cylinder, simple 'Klondike', No 271, as rebuilt in 1911, with 2 inside cylinders and Schmidt superheater* (W.J. Reynolds).

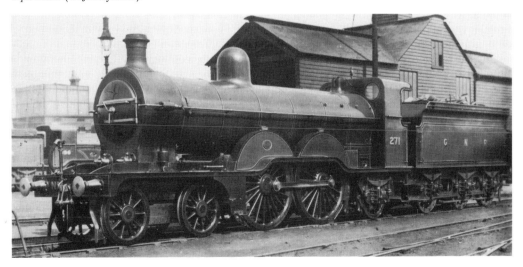

authorities to make exceptional hill-climbing efforts for his benefit. Comparisons may be odious but, having in mind the age-old rivalry between the East and West coast routes to Scotland, there was at that time no comparison between the work of the Ivatt superheater 'Atlantics' and the superheater 4-4-0 express engines of the London and North Western Railway. The honours were heavily on the side of Crewe. Nevertheless it must be emphasised that the all-round superiority, great though it was, proved to be transitory, and the locomotives Ivatt built at Doncaster between 1898 and 1910 were eventually to achieve a lasting fame unexcelled by any other British steam locomotive type. Ivatt himself retired in the summer of 1911 and it was the development carried out by his successor that enabled his engines to reach the heights.

When the news of Ivatt's impending retirement became known, there was considerable speculation in the locomotive world as to his possible successor. Hitherto, the directors of the Great Northern Railway had never promoted one of their own staff to the post of the Locomotive Engineer, which office also included responsibility for carriages and wagons. Archibald Sturrock, Patrick Stirling and Ivatt himself had all come from other railways. At the time, a likely successor was thought to be Stirling's son, Matthew, who had been a Great Northern man himself until he was appointed Locomotive, Carriage and Wagon Superintendent of the Hull and Barnsley Railway in 1885. He had held that post with distinction ever since and in 1911 he was 55 years of age. The most senior of the Doncaster men was F. Wintour, the Works Manager, but the choice, generally understood to have been unanimous round the Board Table, was for Herbert Nigel Gresley, who had been Carriage and Wagon Superintendent, since he came from the Lancashire and Yorkshire Railway in 1905. Gresley, who was then no more than 36 years of age, had, like Ivatt, begun his engineering career at Crewe, and after 5 years there had become a pupil of J.A.F. Aspinall, at Horwich. On the L&YR he became Assistant Carriage and Wagon Engineer.

On succeeding to the supreme command at Doncaster it was not long before he showed his hand; and, although the immediate developments did not at first directly concern the 'Atlantic' story, a reference to them is necessary at this stage because some features of his early work were to have a profound effect later. In his first entirely new design, the 'H2' 'Mogul' of 1912 (LNER Class 'K1'), although using a large 18-element Schmidt superheater capable of producing high steam temperatures, he used a higher pressure than Ivatt in his 1452–61 series of 'Atlantics', the Walschaerts radial valve gear and a 26-inch piston stroke. All the usual Schmidt features were included, such as piston valves with Trick ports and the superheater damper gear in the smoke-box; but at the same time, in another direction, the first breakaway from the Schmidt ring of patents associated with the superheater had been made. On the 'Long Tom' 0-8-0 mineral engines it had been found that with careful application of the Wakefield mechanical lubricator, the Richardson-type balanced slide valves could be made to work efficiently with high-temperature superheated steam and this, avoiding their replacement, would lessen the cost of fitting superheating equipment to existing locomotives.

At the same time, Gresley, like several other British railway locomotive engineers was anxious to get away from constraints inevitably connected with the Schmidt apparatus and, just as Churchward, Robinson and Urie did, in 1913, he designed a superheater of his own. One of the disadvantages of the Schmidt type, from the maintenance point of view was that difficulty was sometimes experienced in removing one element for examination or replacement without disturbing a number of others. Gresley's apparatus was of the twin-tube type, as shown in the accompanying drawing using separate top and bottom headers respectively for the saturated and superheated steam. The upper one was connected with the main steam pipe from the dome, while the lower connected directly to the steam pipes leading to the cylinders. There were 34 superheater flues in all, but of only 4 in diameter, instead of 5¼ in in the Schmidt, and with only 17 complete superheater elements. The accompanying drawing shows the apparatus fitted in the smoke-box of one of the 'H2' class 'Moguls', but it was later applied to three small-boilered and ten large-boilered 'Atlantics'. It will be noticed that in this apparatus the smoke-box damper gear had been dispensed with and that an anti-vacuum, 'snifting', valve has been included on the saturated steam side. This later became standard practice.

The next development in superheating came in 1914, when ten new engines of the

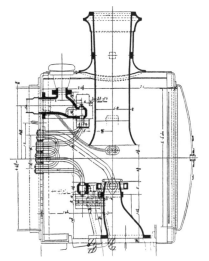

The Gresley twin-tube superheater, as fitted to the 'H2' class 2-6-0s.

'Mogul' type (GNR Class 'H3') with larger boilers were fitted with Robinson apparatus. These engines, Nos 1640–9, were the first of the subsequently numerous LNER Class 'K2'. The superheaters had 24 elements, providing a heating surface of 403 sq ft and they could be accommodated conveniently, because the boilers themselves were of 5 ft 6 in diameter, as on the large 'Atlantics'. The Robinson superheater, though very similar, was sufficiently different from the Schmidt as not to infringe the latter's patents, and on being taken up commercially it was advertised as 'a sound running-shed job'. I remember this claim once invoking strong criticism from a Great Western man, when an engineer from Darlington was in a party being conducted round the sheds at Old Oak Common, and our guide asserted that the Robinson superheater was not a 'running-shed job', but a works job! Be that as it may, the Robinson remained Gresley's standard for the rest of his career, apart from the few engines fitted with his own twin-tube type.

Returning now to the 'Atlantic' history proper, by 1911 Ivatt was sufficiently disenchanted with his one four-cylinder simple engine, the small-boilered 'Atlantic' No 271, with Walschaerts valve gear, to have it completely rebuilt, with two inside cylinders 18½ in by 26 in, an 18-element Schmidt superheater of the same dimensions as on the otherwise standard small 'Atlantic' No 988 and piston valves. Both these engines as originally rebuilt retained the non-extended smoke-box.

No records of any runs with engine No 271 in her 2-cylinder condition seem to have been preserved. In view of this conversion it is interesting that, in 1915, Gresley rebuilt one of the large 'Atlantics', No 279, with four cylinders, though there was a notable difference in the machinery from Ivatt's first rebuild of No 271 in 1904. From the beginning of his chieftainship, Gresley took a close personal interest in the locomotive running and spent much time studying the working arrangements to see if more efficient utilisation of the stock could be obtained. The enterprise of the traffic department in running an increasing number of fast, fully fitted freight trains was making it necessary to use express-passenger 'Atlantics' on some of these duties. The marked disparity between the boiler and cylinder capacity, reflected in slow uphill running, would have been familiar enough to him.

Engine No 279 was very extensively rebuilt, with four cylinders, 15 in diameter by 26 in stroke, and a boiler fitted with 24-element Robinson superheater and a working pressure of 170 lb per sq in, increasing the nominal tractive effort by nearly 40 per cent above that of the '1452' class. That the boiler would be able to support such an increase did not seem to be in much doubt, if one compared the heating surface and grate area with that of contemporary four-cylinder simple engines. The arrangement of the machinery was quite different from that of No 271 in her second state. The latter had Walschaerts gear for the outside cylinders and ordinary link motion inside, four sets in all, whereas on No 279 there were only two sets, with the valves of the inside cylinders driven off the outside Walschaerts gear through an arrangement of rocking shafts. At the time some emphasis was laid upon the novelty of the arrangement, which is shown in detail in the accompanying drawings; however, apart from using rocking shafts instead of levers, it was no different in its essentials from the system of derived valve gear used on the four-cylinder express locomotives of the London and South Western ('Paddleboats') and the London and North Western (Claughton class).

The piston valves, of 8 in diameter, were large in relation to the cylinder volume and should have contributed to a free-running engine; but in contrast to those of the standard large-boilered 'Atlantics', whether with balanced slide or piston valves, the steam passages were rather long and tortuous. Two

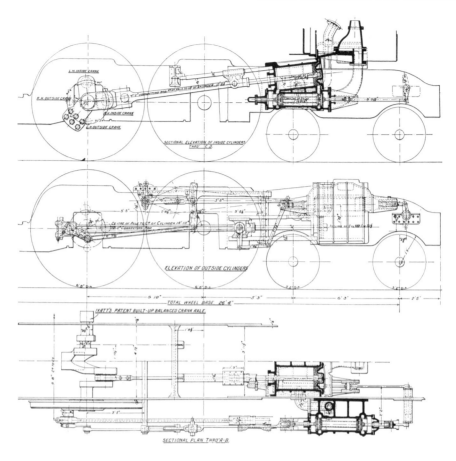

Above *The 4-cylinder 'Atlantic', No 279: plan and cross-sectional views showing the arrangement of valves, cylinders and gear.*

Below *The 'Royal' Atlantic No 1442, on a down East Coast express near Potters Bar just prior to superheating* (C. Laundy).

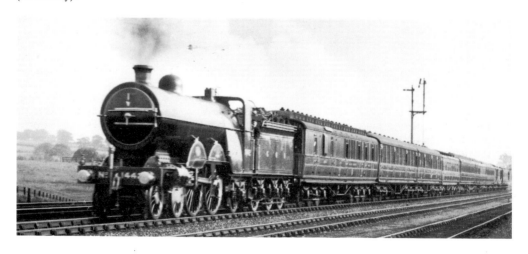

Engine No 1442, just after being fitted with a 24-element superheater in 1914, on a down Leeds and Bradford express near Hadley Wood (C. Laundy).

other detailed features may be noted from the drawing, namely the Ivatt patent built-up, balanced-crank axle, which had been used on the four-cylinder compound 'Atlantics', and the single slide-bar cross-head of the inside cylinders, first used on this engine and later to become a Gresley standard. The Robinson superheater fitted to this engine was the same as that being currently used in the modernising of the standard engines of the '251' class which, by the year 1915, were already distinguishing themselves by work definitely superior to that of the 1452–61 series, as might be expected in any case from the higher boiler pressure of 170 lb per sq in. From this stage onwards in the story of the development of the original engines, I do not have details of which individual units, when superheating was applied, retained their original cylinders and balanced slide valves, and which received new 20 in diameter cylinders and piston valves. The general consensus of opinion among the running staff was that it did not make a great deal of difference to the performance. What did make a difference was the higher boiler pressure and, ultimately, the further change to 32-element superheaters.

Two runs made in the early months of the First World War on the heavy and popular 2:20 pm Scotsman from Kings Cross to Grantham, with the same engine and the same driver, show a significantly improved standard of performance, particularly in the uphill work. The details are tabulated on page 67; at the outset, following good starts up the Holloway Bank, both trains were slackened for permanent-way work in Wood Green tunnels. It was noteworthy that, on each occasion, the substantial loads were afterwards accelerated on the continuous 1 in 200 gradient to a sustained speed of 45 mph up to Potters Bar summit; and although the unrealistic working time of 23 minutes to Hatfield was not kept, the time of 25 min 40 sec on both runs was excellent, with loads of 350 and 355 tons. At that time construction of the Hertford loop line was in progress with the burrowing junction from the down loop line at Langley, between Knebworth and Stevenage; both trains had to reduce speed severely over the constructional works. From the checks experienced thus far the trains were 5 and 7 minutes late on passing Hitchin. On the first of the two, a clear road was obtained almost to Grantham; but this particular driver did not indulge in such high downhill speeds as some of his colleagues and the gain in time on the easy point-to-point bookings between Hitchin and Peterborough was not so great as might have been expected in the circumstances; but very good work was done on the long, rising stretch to Stoke, although the speed was allowed to fall off appreciably on the last 3 miles at 1 in 178 to the summit. With the train running late on both occasions, the final speed of 37½ mph was poor, compared to what had been done between Wood Green and Potters Bar. A later chapter of this book will relate how this same engine, No 1404, became one of the immortals of the British steam-locomotive world.

A very interesting event, in the early history of superheating on the Great Northern Railway, was the first rebuilding of the 4-cylinder compound No 1421, in 1914, making it the only superheated compound the company ever possessed. In its original form, as evidenced earlier in this book from the dynamometer test run with the Royal Train, the locomotive was capable of extremely fine work, but I have not been able to trace any details of performance when superheated. Because of the shorter distance between the tube-plates retaining the original boiler with its recessed front tube-plate, the heating surfaces, as rebuilt, differed from both the '1452–61' series and from the rebuilds of the '251' class, which had 24-element Robinson superheaters. That fitted to the compound 1421 had the following dimensions:

Engine No 1421 4-cylinder compound

Heating surfaces
Small tubes	
number	165
outside diameter, ins	2
Large tubes	
number	22
outside diameters, ins	5¼
Heating surfaces, sq ft	
Small tubes	1,252.5
Large tubes	438.5
Firebox	140.5
Superheater elements	352.5
Total	2,184.0

Although it is stepping out of strict chronological order, it is convenient at this stage to mention the important alteration made, in 1917, to another of the experimental compound 'Atlantics' introduced by Ivatt, the Vulcan engine No 1300, which until then had been in the 'Atlantic' link at New England shed, Peterborough. At that time the bulk of the more important express duties were performed by engines based either at Grantham or Doncaster. Many of the smaller-boilered 'Atlantics' were at Peterborough and photographic evidence of the working of No 1300, as a compound, shows her frequently on trains of lesser importance. The fact that No 1300 was a non-standard engine led Gresley to

rebuild her with his own two-cylinder simple engine layout, with outside Walschaerts valve gear. The boiler was still in excellent condition and, as part of the rebuilding, it was fitted with a 22-element superheater. It is interesting to set alongside the proportions of the four varieties of single-expansion superheated 'Atlantics' of the GNR. Although the ratio of tractive effort to heating surface was much larger than in the standard 2-cylinder 'Atlantics', it was almost exactly the same as on the larger-boilered Gresley 'Moguls' of the '1640' class.

In studying the proportions of the rebuilt Vulcan engine No 1300, the relatively small amount of heating surface furnished by the superheater elements will be noticed. But this engine had a much smaller boiler, of only 5 ft 3 in diameter, permitting a superheater of only 22 elements, while the length of the barrel was no more than 11 ft 11 in, as compared with the 16 ft between the tube-plates of the superheated '251' class. The firebox, on the other hand, was very long, narrow and sloping, with a grate area of 31 sq ft. By comparison with the ordinary 'Atlantics', it cannot have been a very easy engine to fire. In my own lineside observations, from 1921 onwards I saw the engine occasionally but always on secondary duties. Before rebuilding, it had been stationed at New England and, from the trains I saw it working, I should imagine that it returned there afterwards.

GNR Kings Cross–Grantham 'The Flying Scotsman' in 1911

Load: 320 tons gross
Engine (4-4-2) No: 1461

Distance miles		Actual m s	Speed mph
0.0	Kings Cross	0 00	—
2.6	Finsbury Park	8 15	—
12.7	Potters Bar	22 45	—
17.7	Hatfield	27 45	75/60
31.9	Hitchin	40 25	85
44.1	Sandy	49 50	—
58.9	Huntingdon	63 05	—
—		—	50/77½
76.4	Peterborough	80 25	—
88.6	Essendine	95 45	—
101.1	Stoke Box	109 50	—
105.5	Grantham	117 30	—

GNR 2:20 pm 'Scotsman' 1915

Engine: (superheated 4-4-2) No 1404
Load, tons gross: 330–5

Distance miles		Schedule min	Actual m s	Average speed mph	Actual m s	Average speed mph
0.0	KINGS CROSS	0	0 00	—	0 00	—
2.6	Finsbury Park		6 40	—	6 50	—
—			pws		pws	
12.7	Potters Bar		20 55	—	20 45	—
17.7	HATFIELD	23	25 40	63.1	25.40	61.0
—			—	—	signals	—
25.0	Knebworth		33 00	59.2	35.05	—
—			pws		pws	
31.9	HITCHIN	38	43 00	—	45 00	—
37.0	Arlesey		47 25	67.8	49 10	73.5
—			—		signals	—
44.1	Sandy		53 55	65.5	56 25	—
51.7	St Neots		61 30	60.8	64 25	57.0
—			—		pws	
58.9	HUNTINGDON	66	68 45	59.6	72 35	—
63.5	Abbots Ripton		74 25	48.7	78 50	44.1
72.6	Yaxley		82 40	66.2	86 35	70.6
76.4	PETERBOROUGH	85	86 50	54.8	90 30	58.0
81.9	*Helpston Box*		94 45	41.7	98 20	42.1
88.6	Essendine		101 25	60.3	105 00	60.3
97.1	Corby		111 45	49.3	115 10	50.2
110.1	*Stoke Box*		116 05	41.5	119 20	43.2
—			pws	—	—	—
105.5	GRANTHAM	122	123 35	—	125 30	—
	Net times		118		116½	
	Max & min speeds			mph		mph
	Potters Bar			45		45
	Hatfield			76½		74
	Arlesey			—		75
	Abbots Ripton			45		42½
	Essendine			64½		63¾
	Stoke Box			37½		37½

GNR Superheated simple 'Atlantics' (large boiler)

	1910	1914	1915	1917
Date introduced:				
Engine No:	1452	1404	279	1300
Cylinders,				
number	2	2	4	2
diameter, ins	20	20	15	20
stroke, ins	24	24	26	26
Cylinder volume, cu in	15,080	15,080	18,400	16,330
Valve gear, type	Stephenson	Stephenson	Walschaerts	Walschaerts
Heating surfaces, sq ft				
Small tubes	} 1,909.5	1,355.5	1,355.5	993
Large tubes		526.5	526.5	373
Firebox	141	141	138	167
Elements	343	427	427	280
Total	2,396	2,450	2,447	1,814
Boiler pressure psi	150	170	170	170
Nominal tractive effort, lb	15,300	17,340	21,150	18,800
Ratio				
Tractive effort to total heating surface	6.38	7.09	8.64	10.37

Chapter 6

The war years

The month of August 1914 marked the beginning of one of the most profound changes in locomotive and train operating practice, not only on the Great Northern but throughout the British railways. The 'Atlantic' engines of the GNR came eventually to be more fundamentally affected than most, although at first the changes were almost imperceptible. This reflected the attitude of the country towards the war in its early days, when, for example, *The Railway Magazine* in its issue of October 1914 carried a lengthy article under the heading of 'Railway Business as Usual'. After the intense and largely clandestine task of getting the British Expeditionary Force to France, in which the Great Northern played an important part, things settled down again to an uneasy normality. To appreciate the full the difference between the line conditions in 1914 and 1919, and the tasks the 'Atlantic' engines were called upon to perform, one must look back briefly to the early summer of 1914 and to the express-train service from Kings Cross then provided. The 'Atlantics' were, of course, essentially main-line engines, and while they worked the famous Skegness excursions they had no other regular duties other than on the East Coast main line and between Doncaster and Leeds.

Not counting the duplication of the more popular expresses at the busiest holiday times, there were between 25 and 30 regular long-distance expresses leaving Kings Cross every weekday in the summer. The majority of these would be loaded to less than 300 tons and some of them to less than 200. Even an important and popular train like the 2:20 pm Scotsman would sometimes carry no more than 8 coaches, albeit of the heavy, 12-wheeled, ECJS type. Except in the case of a few trains of very light formation, the speeds were not heroic, and, in the case of the heavier East Coast trains were around 50–52 mph average; also, as mentioned in a previous chapter of this book, the running was not particularly enterprising in the matter of making up lost time. In addition to the expresses, there were many main-line semi-fasts, such as the 1:45 and 4:20 pm down from Kings Cross which were 'Atlantic'-hauled; when it is recalled that few of the regular passenger workings involved longer runs than

the 105½ miles between Kings Cross and Grantham it will be realised that the stud of 92 large-boilered 'Atlantics' plus the Vulcan compound No 1300 had quite a busy time of it.

Their activities were considerably inhibited by the traditions of single manning then in force on the Great Northern Railway and the mileage run by an engine was governed by the maximum that its driver could work within the 10-hour day, then the maximum for footplatemen. There were no lodging turns for express-train enginemen. The longest was the 'crack' Kings Cross duty of the 7:15 am breakfast-car express to Leeds, returning with the 2:00 pm up, non-stop from Wakefield, a mileage of 372 and an overall time of 10 hr 10 min from departure to arrival at Kings Cross. When the time came for 'Atlantics' to go to Doncaster Plant for general overhaul their own drivers would take them down personally, working 'light engine'. After overhaul was completed the driver would go to Doncaster and bring *his* engine back to base, whether it was Grantham, Peterborough or Kings Cross. Then, with its own driver, the engine would work sufficient light, running-in turns until he was satisfied it was ready for main-line express work.

Statistics compiled by that indefatigable notetaker, the late R.A.H. Weight, showed that the weekly mileages of some of the large-boilered 'Atlantics' in 1914 varied from 116 up to 1,942, all with their regular drivers. An extraordinary 'top link' duty at that time was to work the 9:20 am train from Kings Cross to Dunstable, as far as Hatfield, then to continue light engine to Hitchin. There the engine turned and stood up-side main-line pilot all day, until 5:23 pm when it worked the slow train arriving at Kings Cross at 6:47 pm. Mr Weight claims that the maximum mileage he noted in a week with one of the Kings Cross 'Atlantics' was 2,306, by engine No 301; but on a long-term basis most of these engines averaged around 1,350 miles per week. Grantham engines were responsible for most of the East Coast express workings, with one engine and its crew relieving the other at their home shed. There were no Great Northern engines shedded at York, while Doncaster was responsible for most of the London–Leeds

One of the first of the '251' class to be superheated: engine No 1401 (Rail Archive Stephenson).

expresses, except the celebrated 2:00 pm up 'flyer', which was worked by Kings Cross.

From the outbreak of war, 'Atlantics' were requisitioned at short notice for troop trains and other specials, while the Great Northern connection to the South Eastern and Chatham system, via the widened City lines of the Metropolitan Railway and the junction from Farringdon Street to Ludgate Hill, was used for many through specials bound for the Channel Ports. 'Atlantic' engines on such duties did not, however, proceed beyond their own main line. August 1914 brought immediate cancellation of two regular Anglo-Scottish services run during the summer months, namely the 11:20 am down Edinburgh express which ran via Harrogate and the separate 7:55 pm Highland sleeping-car express. The former ran direct from Doncaster via Knottingley, Church Fenton, Tadcaster and Wetherby, passing through Crimple Tunnel. It was usually worked by an 'Atlantic' and involved some hard climbing from Wetherby with a continuous ascent of 5 miles at 1 in 86–91 from Spofforth to Crimple Junction and beyond. This was the route taken for a short time in post-war years by the Edinburgh Pullman train, when it was running non-stop between Kings Cross and Harrogate, before it was named the 'Queen of Scots'. Other than these two and their corresponding up workings, there were not many alterations that affected the 'Atlantic' diagrams.

A welcome measure of relief, to those who had the responsibility for finding engine power for the increasing number of fast freights, was the building of more of the new 2-6-0 mixed-traffic engines. This avoided the kind of situation that R.A.H. Weight once noted in 1911, when Kings Cross shed found themselves without a suitable engine for a fast night goods to Peterborough and had to take the superheated 'Atlantic' that had just come in on the Wakefield non-stop, give it a 153-mile 'out-and-home' night run with a goods and then send it out on the 7:15 am express to Leeds, to return once more on the Wakefield non-stop, to complete 896 miles in 34½ hours with three sets of men! In the ordinary way, one engine and its men did not work the 7:15 am down, 2:00 pm up Leeds turn on two successive days, because in that era drivers and firemen were not expected to run such a daily mileage as 372 on two days running. Engines did this, regularly and continuously, but not on the Great Northern. At that time the London and North Western had one fast express duty of 384 miles daily, which was worked by one engine six days a week for about 3 months on end, by two regular crews on alternate days.

At first, in war conditions, there was no question of deceleration. The demand for travel facilities at first grew slowly, but the cancellation of some trains and the replacement of others by through carriages attached to other services, began a slow, but inexorable

Engine No 279, rebuilt by Gresley, with four cylinders and derived valve gear for the inside cylinders (British Railways).

increase in train loads; as in the hey-day of Patrick Stirling, piloting was not to be thought of. The trains that disappeared early in the war were the 10:35 am intermediate express to Scotland, the 1:40 pm to Harrogate, the 3:25 pm to York and the 6:05 pm to Hull and Sheffield. Lest I have cast aspersions on the enterprise of individual drivers in making up lost time I must tell a story about the 2:00 pm up from Leeds, just before it was withdrawn in 1915. There were times when alterations were made with little prior notice, and in this case it was announced that the train would call additionally at Grantham and Peterborough. No amended times were given and by then the Huddersfield through carriage, which was attached at Wakefield, had been withdrawn, leaving only the basic 5-coach set weighing about 175 tons. One of the star Kings Cross drivers, Tom Rowley, was on the job and no one told him of any revised schedule. So, with the superheater 'Atlantic' No 1458 he duly made the two extra stops and a signal stop before Grantham into the bargain, and arrived in Kings Cross at 5:25 pm, 2 minutes early by the working time. It is reported that the 76.4 miles up from Peterborough took only 72 minutes, start to stop.

So far as the work of the 'Atlantic' engines was concerned, with steadily increasing loads, but on pre-war schedules, the travelling records of the late Cecil J. Allen provide

valuable documentation. Nevertheless, it tells no more than a part of the story. Although he was travelling frequently, at times once a week from London to Tees-side, he was naturally making use of the principal express trains, which to some extent had preferential treatment, at any rate so far as locomotive power was concerned; thus the following analysis of running in 1915 and the first months of 1916 can be assumed to represent something of the cream of Great Northern 'Atlantic' performance. It shows also the weakness as well as the best work of the non-superheater engines. By the beginning of the year 1916, only a few of the '251' class had been rebuilt with superheaters and these had been allocated to Grantham shed, which was responsible for working the 2:20 pm Scotsman throughout from Kings Cross to York. The ten Ivatt superheater 'Atlantics', with 18-element Schmidt superheaters, were divided between Doncaster and Kings Cross sheds.

The first run (see page 79), with the non-superheated engine No 280 showed by far the fastest climb out of Kings Cross and, after two permanent-way checks, the driver did well to get through Peterborough on time; but the permanent-way check near Werrington Junction seemed to take heart out of the driver and all 'go' out of the engine. On the more gradual lengths of the long rise to Stoke summit, speed did not rise above 45 mph, though the concluding minimum speed of 38½ mph after 3 miles at

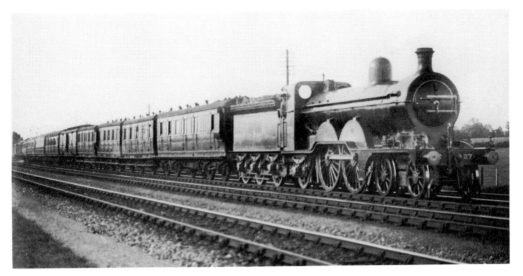

The rebuilt 'Klondike', No 271, on an up East Coast express near Potters Bar (C. Laundy).

1 in 178 was not too bad. On the second run, one of the newly superheated engines did not start too well and she was 4¾ minutes down at Hatfield; then a promising spurt up to 80½ mph was cut short by a dead stand for signals at Langford Bridge box, south of Biggleswade and this cost a full 6 minutes in running time. It took a little time to regain full speed after this hindrance, but some of the best times of the series were made between Peterborough and Stoke box, with an attained maximum speed of 60 mph before Essendine and a minimum of 41 mph at the summit.

Next are two runs with the non-superheater engine No 282, with one as bad as the other was good. On the first of the two, a characteristic start was made out to Potters Bar, with speed falling to 37½ mph, and then a good spurt to 71½ mph past Hatfield was cut short by a bad signal check at Digswell box, controlling the entry to the double-line section over the Welwyn viaduct and the two subsequent tunnels. The loss of running time was about 1¾ minutes. But from Hitchin onwards, a fine effort was made to recover the arrears with a maximum speed of 79 mph before Arlesey and the notable minimum, for a non-superheater engine, of 51½ mph before Abbots Ripton. The train was practically on time passing Peterborough, and with good work on the long climb to Stoke they would have been only a few seconds out at Grantham but for the final signal check. The second run

with the same engine was slower from the start and the maximum of 75 mph, below Hitchin, was cut short by a bad signal check. After that the driver seems to have given up trying. Of course something may have gone amiss on the footplate, of which a recorder in the train could not be aware; but the fact remains that between Arlesey and Stoke box, with no further checks, the second run fell to nearly 10 minutes behind the first and arrived at Grantham nearly 12 minutes late.

The next two runs, both with recently superheated engines of the '251' class are also in some contrast to each other. The first, with engine No 1406, got a bad start out to Potters Bar with signal checks and was 8 minutes late through Hatfield. All but a minute of this was subsequently made up, although this driver was not unduly pressing his engine uphill, seemingly choosing to run hard on the down-hill stretches, with the highest maximum speed of any in the table, of 82 mph near Arlesey. The recovery after the Peterborough service slowing was rather poor, to no more than 56 mph on the almost level stretches before Essendine. But if this run was mildly disappointing the next one, with No 1404, was really depressing, particularly as this particular engine had an excellent reputation. Without any checks, a total of 5¾ minutes was lost and there was no time on arrival at Grantham to enquire if there was anything wrong with the engine.

Top *An early morning picture of an up Scottish sleeping car express, south of Hadley Wood, hauled by 'Klondike' No 258* (C. Laundy).

Above *A down Scottish express near Hadley Wood, hauled by non-superheater 'Atlantic' No 1411* (O.S. Nock Collection).

Finally there are two runs with the non-superheater engine No 287, both with the same driver. The difference again was rather inexplicable. It is true that a load of 415 tons set a task, on a pre-war schedule, that was hardly foreseen when these engines were first introduced and the rather pedestrian rate of progress on the first run, with an overall average speed of 49.4 mph, might have been excused as a case of overloading, on a day when the weather was not too favourable. But then look at the truly splendid run made when the load was heavier still. Again there was a clear road throughout and, with some of the finest running I have ever seen with a non-superheater engine the arrival at Grantham

was a minute early. It is notable that the uphill work was as good as the free-running down-hill, especially in a minimum speed of 50 mph before Abbots Ripton and a vigorous recovery from the usual Peterborough slowing. Taken all round, these runs make a creditable showing, seeing that the engines were hauling heavier loads, in wartime conditions. From contemporary photographs however it would seem that engines were being well maintained and kept clean, though the days of having bevies of women cleaners at the major sheds had not yet arrived.

North of Grantham not only was the road less arduous but the schedule was easier, with an allowance of 97 minutes for the 82.7 mile run to York. The lighter working conditions were reflected in the frequent use of smaller engines, of the 'Klondikes' and even of 4-4-0s, on the heaviest of trains. From published records, it would seem that in those last months before the major deceleration of train timings it was the 'Klondikes' that were stealing the show and in the table on page 78 I have set out five runs with engines all in their original non-superheated condition. All showed net gains on schedule time, two indeed having net average speeds of 55 mph. In contrast to the first stage of the Anglo-Scottish run by the East Coast route, the northbound start from Grantham is excellent for speeding, though the advantage of the fine downhill run from Peascliffe Tunnel to the Trent valley was, at the time now under consideration, somewhat curtailed by the requirement to slow down to 40 mph north of Newark, over Muskham water troughs. Although the level stretch beyond gave some chance to work up speed again before tackling the climb through Tuxford to Markham, the 40 mph slack could take its toll with heavy trains. It was however not enforced when locomotives were not picking up water. The other severe hindrance was at Selby.

On the first three runs, speed was under, rather than over, 70 mph on the descent to the Trent valley and, not needing to take on water having come on fresh at Grantham, full speed could be continued from Newark to Carlton on the first run. On the lengthy levels north of Doncaster, speed was a little below 60 mph on all three runs, the work of the pioneer engine No 990 being the least distinguished of any. The honours rest with the last two runs, both of which showed commendable enterprise. On the fourth run, the storm delay north of Retford was due to what Allen described as 'a remarkable atmospheric disturbance in which the sky was so black in all directions as to make sighting of the signals difficult'. Presumably, at that time of day in the summer, the lamps were not lighted. After regaining normal conditions of visibility, speed was sustained at 60 mph on the level north of Doncaster. The five runs together certainly provide an interesting study of the work of the 'Klondikes' under almost maximum load conditions for the class.

Early in June 1916, only a week after the disturbing and inconclusive outcome of the great naval battle of Jutland, the cruiser HMS *Hampshire*, carrying Lord Kitchener to Russia, was sunk, and the famous Secretary of

State for War and all his staff perished. After the war it was learned that the Great Northern Railway had played no small part in conveying his Lordship on the first stage of that journey. The first special, of four coaches, left Kings Cross, as pre-arranged, at 5:45 pm on Sunday evening June 4, hauled by a 'Klondike', No 252. It ran to Grantham non-stop in 117 minutes, where engines were changed and a large 'Atlantic', No 284, took over. In the meantime, a representative from the Foreign Office had arrived at Kings Cross with important documents and stated that he must catch the special because it was necessary for him to sail with the party. An impromptu special train of two coaches was quickly arranged and the large 'Atlantic', No 1442, standing pilot at the time, was requisitioned and its driver was instructed to get through as quickly as possible.

They left Kings Cross at 6:56 pm and passed Hatfield in 20 minutes, Hitchin in 32, Huntingdon in 55, Peterborough in 70 and reached Grantham in 101 minutes, despite 4 minutes lost by slacks for relaying work. The net time of 97 minutes represented an average speed of 65.5 mph. From Grantham the train was taken forward by a 4-4-0 engine and made further fast time. The run of No 1442 from Kings Cross to Grantham was probably the fastest ever made in the history of the Great Northern Railway, because although its overall time was the same as that made on the last night of the 1895 'Race' by the Stirling 4-2-2 engine No 668, the latter had a clear road throughout. The upshot of this enterprising work was that although the second special left Kings Cross 71 minutes after the first, it arrived at York only 43 minutes after, where Lord Kitchener, advised by telephone of what had transpired, was waiting for the arrival of the Foreign Office representative and the dispatches he was carrying.

There was an amusing sidelight on this event, when details were published in 1919. Photographs were included of the two engines that made the record running with the second special, namely the 4-4-2, No 1442, and the 4-4-0. Both were clearly official pictures and I had not thought any more about the former, until I was checking up on the dates of when certain of the '251' class had been superheated and found that No 1442 received a 24-element superheater in 1914, two years before the record run! The engine illustrated in the 1919 Press Release was a non-superheater, and careful examination of the picture revealed that it was actually No 1450, on which the number had been photographically 'faked'. Engine No 1450 was not superheated until January 1920, and then she received a 21-element Gresley 'twin-tube'.

In May 1916, austerity began to strike harder at travellers on the Great Northern Railway, when all restaurant cars were withdrawn. For passengers going farther north, the North Eastern attached refreshment cars to some trains, but this drastic step was the prelude to the combining of services that had hitherto been run separately and the inclusion on some important expresses of non-corridor stock. With no longer any need to provide access to restaurant cars non-corridor coaches gave more seating accommodation for the same tare weight. On the trains that remained, there was, as yet, no appreciable deceleration and with some of the combined trains there were increasingly severe locomotive tasks. One of these was the 5:30 pm departure from Kings Cross, which combined the former 5:30 pm to Newcastle, the 5:45 pm to Leeds and the 6:05 pm to Hull, and it loaded up nightly never to less than 14 eight-wheeled coaches. The reduction in the aggregate express-train mileage was accompanied by some alteration in the drivers' links and the setting aside of superheater engines for the most onerous duties. While no new express-passenger locomotives had been built at Doncaster since 1910, the potentialities of the stud as a whole had been steadily increased by the equipping of more of the older engines with superheaters. Among these were a number of the 'Klondikes' and details of the work of three such engines between Kings Cross and Peterborough on the combined 1:30 and 1:40 pm express are especially interesting as they include the first 'Atlantic' to be superheated, No 988, and one of the first of those to have the 17-element Gresley twin-tube superheater, No 950 (see table on page 77).

This train was worked by Doncaster engines and men, in certain cases going through and in others with one engine and its crew relieved by another at Peterborough. Schedule time still remained the 'crack' 83-minutes (55.2 mph) throughout 1916. On the first run, engine No 950 did extremely well. The start out of Kings Cross was excellent and, after attaining 53 mph at Wood Green, the 7¾ miles at 1 in 200 up to Potters Bar did not bring the speed below 43 mph. Fast running followed, until interrupted by the permanent-way slack before Sandy but, with a good

recovery afterwards, Peterborough was reached just inside schedule time. The second run, with engine No 986 this time, was rather more traditional in its start out to Hatfield, but some very fast running followed, with a maximum of 82 mph near Arlesey. The check north of Sandy was no more than slight on this occasion, and the engine was driven with great vigour to top the rise to St Neots at 60 mph and to attain 69 between Offord and Huntingdon. But, because of the leisurely ascent to Potters Bar, this hard running afterwards was not enough to secure an absolutely punctual arrival in Peterborough.

The third run, with the pioneer superheater engine No 988, is an interesting example of the way the weather can affect running on the exposed stretches of the Great Northern main line. It was made not only in heavy rain, but with a strong and blustery west wind blowing. Out to Potters Bar in the shelter of the cuttings and tunnels the speed was much the same as on the previous run; but once on to the faster running sections of line, the weather began to take a more serious toll and from Hatfield onwards, particularly from Hitchin, No 988 fell steadily behind. I can well appreciate the difficulties on the exposed track through the relatively level country that extends almost without a break to Peterborough, having seen myself, from the footplate many years later, how similar weather conditions could affect a 'Pacific', even with so resolute a driver as John Duddington, he who later drove the 'A4' engine *Mallard* at 126 mph! So, reverting to 1916, No 988, without any checks other than the weather, brought her train into Peterborough 4¾ minutes late.

The running of this train, of the heavy, combined 5:30 pm ex-Kings Cross, and of the two surviving day Anglo-Scottish expresses during the remaining months of 1916, marked the final phases of pre-war speed with the Great Northern 'Atlantics' because, from January 1917, by Governmental decree, the so called 'Classified Train Services' were introduced at much reduced speed. All one-time competitive services were eliminated. From London, in the morning, one was allowed to travel to Perth and Aberdeen only from Euston; to Glasgow one had to go from St Pancras, and to Edinburgh and Dundee from Kings Cross. The 'Flying Scotsman', still leaving at 10:00 am took 9½ hours to Edinburgh, as did the much decelerated 2:20 pm, henceforth leaving at 2:00 pm. The fastest

The Vulcan compound No 1300, rebuilt as a 2-cylinder simple by Gresley in 1917 (British Railways).

Scottish train from Kings Cross was the 7:45 pm Aberdeen sleeper, which took 9 hours to Edinburgh. The restriction as to route thus imposed, with decelerated timings, was to produce train loads of unheard of magnitude on the East Coast route. At first only the 5:30 pm combined Newcastle, Leeds and Hull express retained a vestige of pre-war timings, with 125 minutes allowed for the 105.5 miles to Grantham, though, according to most reports, this timing existed on paper only. Drivers found such difficulty in lifting their huge trains out of Kings Cross and up the Holloway bank that their overall times to Grantham approximated more to the new timings of the day Scottish expresses which were at least 10 minutes longer than the 125-minute schedule.

With the change in timetabling philosophy, one could sense a lessening of care in the provision of clear roads for the most important and heavily loaded trains, and even though the passenger service was becoming severely restricted in volume the incidence of signal checks was very much on the increase. It could perhaps have been attributed to a deliberate change in priorities. Certainly the Great Northern main line was being very heavily used for freight and mineral traffic, and while in earlier years the fast express trains had been spread out through the timetable, it was now becoming imperative to run them in closely-spaced groups, so as to leave fairly lengthy periods between, in which the slow moving freights could have opportunities to make progress without the need for side-tracking to

clear the line for fast expresses. At the same time, wartime conditions were bringing so much extra traffic to intermediate stations that some of the secondary passenger trains were becoming notoriously bad timekeepers. There were slow trains leaving Kings Cross at 4:15 and 5:00 pm that seemed always to block the heavy 5:30 pm express on any occasion when the driver was making any attempt to keep the difficult 125-minute schedule to Grantham and, from the records handed down to us, it is clear that the majority of drivers grew to anticipate such trouble and to run easily in consequence.

Despite the greatly increasing loads, the old operating rule of 'one train, one engine' prevailed except in the one instance of Kings Cross. During the year 1917, when heavy loads and bad rail conditions frequently caused great difficulty to the drivers of the 'Atlantics' in getting their trains under way through the smoke-filled tunnels on gradients of 1 in 105, Cecil J. Allen several times suggested that recourse might be made to rear-end banking up to Holloway North box, providing that trains were not dispatched from the terminus unless the road was clear right out to Finsbury Park. This would mean no less than four block sections, then marked by the signal-boxes at Belle Isle, Holloway South and Holloway North. But, in 1918, the concession was at last made of allowing a pilot engine when the load exceeded 60 axles. This, during the war years, was always an Ivatt non-superheated 4-4-0, and it went to Potters Bar, where a stop was made to detach. But no pilots or rear-end bankers were ever provided at Grantham for southbound trains; and 'Atlantics' were left to struggle alone up the 5.4 miles to Stoke summit, even when the loads had grown to well over 500 tons! On one such occasion when the load was 590 tons engine No 1404 took no less than 16¼ minutes to pass the summit.

In the meantime, gradual, if slow, progress was being made with equipping the '251' class engines with superheaters and some of those newly modified in 1918 had the Gresley twin-tube type instead of the Robinson. The large-boilered engines had an appropriately larger version of the apparatus illustrated in Chapter 5 and had 21 elements, instead of 17, and a superheater heating surface of 410 sq ft against the 427 sq ft of the 24-element Robinson. It is not possible to form any opinion as to the comparative effectiveness of these two forms of apparatus. It was reported later that nine of the large-boilered 'Atlantics' at one time had the Gresley apparatus, but from the fact that the Robinson later became the LNER standard it can be inferred that the Gresley had not proved superior in maintenance charges or performance. The engines at one time fitted with Gresley apparatus were Nos 272, 273, 299, 1407, 1412, 1418, 1422, 1423 and 1450. There was a further engine, No 1417, fitted with a triplet-tube version of this superheater, presumably for comparison with the 32-element Robinson first used on No 1403 in 1919, but I have not seen any note of the working of No 1417, when so equipped.

The timing of 125 minutes from Kings Cross to Grantham, still existing on paper after the train itself had become a combined one for Newcastle, Leeds and Hull, seemed to have been so rarely observed, or even attempted to be, as to be non-existent. Since the combination of the former three trains, a stop at Doncaster was necessary; but although Doncaster engines and men worked the train as far as Grantham they were relieved there by Grantham men, who continued through to York, with a much reduced load from Doncaster. Details, in very abbreviated form, are tabulated of five runs on this train (see page 78), not because the locomotive performance was of any particular interest, but as an essential record of a not very distinguished period in Great Northern running. It is interesting that all five runs were made with engines of the original superheated batch of 1910, though whether any of them retained their 18-element Schmidt superheaters by that time I cannot say. One can be sure that all of them had by that time had their boiler pressure raised to 170 lb per sq in and, with an equal amount of superheater heating surface, their potentialities would be equal to those of the '251' class that had since been so equipped. The runs tabulated require no comment, except to draw attention to the losses in time and to the weather conditions, which probably had some effect upon the running.

It is rather remarkable that at that time in railway history that the continuation of four of these runs from Grantham to Doncaster included not a single check of any kind and the summary table (page 79) of the passing times features the running of two of the engines fitted with the Gresley twin-tube superheater, Nos 272 and 273. The latter, favoured by good weather, made quite a good run with the full load. Starting well from Grantham, speed was worked up to 70 mph on the falling gradients to the Trent valley and, through not taking water at Muskham, the speed was well maintained across the level to Carlton, passed at 64½ mph, and the rise past Tuxford to Markham summit was rushed at a minimum speed of 44 mph. After a slight reduction of speed at Retford, the train continued in excellent style, attaining 65 mph on marginally easier than level track before Scrooby troughs and again rushing the ascent to Pipers Wood summit at 48½ mph. Thus

The 4-cylinder 'Atlantic', No 279, on a very heavy down express, north of New Barnet (C. Laundy).

the good start-to-stop time of 55 min 10 sec was made from Grantham to Doncaster, a 55 mph average. The other three runs were slower by comparison, despite leaving Grantham well behind time on each occasion. On the fourth run, for example, the driver of No 272, after his good start to Newark with a maximum of 70 mph, allowed speed to fall to no more than 34 mph at Markham.

Lastly, to complete the picture of running conditions at the end of the war, there are tabulated summary details of three runs on which the train engines were piloted out to Potters Bar. The first was on the 2:00 pm Scotsman, before its withdrawal in 1918, and the other two were on the combined 1:30 plus 1:40 pm. The latter had a generous allowance of 103 minutes for the 76.4 miles to Peterborough, while the Scotsman had 138 minutes non-stop to Grantham, respective average speeds of 44.5 and 45.8 mph. While not very exciting by earlier standards these were eminently practical schedules in the prevailing conditions and ensured punctual running. For some reason the Great Northern Railway's distinguished partner retained, probably by oversight, some rather tight schedules north of York, which in the southbound direction led to very heavy trains being handed over to the Great Northern already well behind time; and at the end of 1918 and at the beginning of 1919, the record of main-line arrivals in Kings Cross was not very good, despite the generous time allowances in the Great Northern's own schedules.

In the accompanying table of runs on which the superheater 'Atlantics' were piloted out to Potters Bar, I have shown the times from the re-start there from a fresh zero, to emphasise the vigour with which the train-engine drivers got their huge loads under way again. Engine No 298, on the 2:00 pm Scotsman, made a fine start and the time of 49 min 35 sec to Huntingdon must have been exhilarating to record with such a load; but even before reaching Huntingdon, the train was getting so well ahead of time that easing down had begun and even after taking as much as 44 minutes from Peterborough to Grantham the arrival was just over a minute early. On the 1:30 pm, with 545 tons, engine No 1416 was not exerted once Woolmer Green summit was passed, but on the third occasion, No 1407, with a Gresley twin-tube superheater, did amazingly well, with 575 tons, until the drastic easing began around Huntingdon. It will be noticed that on this run, the 41.2 miles

from Hatfield to Huntingdon, by no means all downhill, were covered in 42¼ minutes at an average speed of 58½ mph. With this gargantuan feat of load haulage I can appropriately conclude this account of the GNR 'Atlantics' in the First World War.

GNR Kings Cross–Peterborough

Train:		2:00 pm	1:30 pm	1:30 pm
Engine No:		298	1416	1407
Pilot engine (4-4-0):		1314	1346	1314
Load, tons full:		500	545	575
Distance		**m s**	**m s**	**m s**
miles				
0.0	Kings Cross	0 00	0 00	0 00
2.6	Finsbury Park	6 20	6 45	8 05
12.7	Potters Bar	20 30	22 00	22 40
5.0	Hatfield	8 05	8 35	8 25
19.2	Hitchin	23 30	24 25	24 30
46.2	Huntingdon	49 35	54 55	50 40
63.7	Peterborough	70 15*	76 40	74 00
Total time from				
Kings Cross		92 55*	99 50	98 30
Speeds, mph				
	Hatfield	61½	62½	61
	Woolmer Green	46½	44	41
	Arlesey	74	67	75

*Passing time — 136 min 50 sec to Grantham.

GNR 1:30 pm Kings Cross–Peterborough

Run no:		1	2	3
Engine, (Small 4-4-2, superheated) No:		950	986	988
Load, tons full:		50	375	375
Distance				
miles		**m s**	**m s**	**m s**
0.0	KINGS CROSS	0.00	0.00	0.00
2.6	Finsbury Park	7 30	7 35	8 35
12.7	Potters Bar	21 00	23 05	23 40
17.7	HATFIELD	26 10	28 40	29 10
25.0	Knebworth	33 20	35 55	37 00
31.9	HITCHIN	39 35	42 10	43 40
37.0	Arlesey	43 35	46 00	47 50
—			pws	—
44.1	Sandy	50 05	51 35	54 25
—		—	pws	—
51.7	St Neots	58 40	59 30	61 55
58.9	HUNTINGDON	65 20	66 00	68 50
63.5	Abbots Ripton	70 30	71 00	74 30
69.4	Holme	75 30	76 05	79 50
76.4	PETERBOROUGH	82 40	83 30	87 50
	Net times, min	80½	82¾	87¾
Principal speeds, mph				
	Wood Green	53	—	50
	Potters Bar	43	37½	36
	Hatfield	72½	71½	70½
	Arlesey	77½	82	75
	Abbots Ripton	48½	51	45
	Holme	75	76	—

GNR 5:30 pm Kings Cross–Grantham in 1918

Engine No:		1454	1452	1455	1454	1454
Load, tons full:		425	430	440	460	475
Weather:		NE wind/rain	NE wind/rain	Fine	Fine	Very stormy

Distance miles		m s	m s	m s	m s	m s
0.0	Kings Cross	0 00	0 00	0 00	0 00	0 00
2.6	Finsury Park	7 40	8 05	7 40	8 10	10 75
—		—	—	pws	pws	—
12.7	Potters Bar	24 30	25 00	23 00	27 15	30 10
17.7	Hatfield	signals	signals	28 15	33 40	36 45
31.9	Hitchin	signals	signals	44 40	49 20	52 50
58.9	Huntingdon	76 10	79 05	69 20	74 00	78 05
76.4	Peterborough	97 05	99 05	89 30	92 20	98 05
—		signals	signals	122 05	125 30	135 35
100.1	Stoke Box	—				
105.5	Grantham	145 55	145 35	128 55	132 10	143 05
	Net times (schedule 125 min)	130	133	128	129	143

GNR 4:26 pm Grantham–York

Run no:			1	2	3	4	5
Engine No:*			258	990	949	257	258
Load, tons full:			345	355	360	360	375

Distance miles		Schedule min	Actual m s	Actual m s	Actual m s	Actual m s	Actual m s
0.0	GRANTHAM	0	0 00	0 00	0 00	0 00	0 00
6.0	Hougham		9 25	9 40	9 45	8 55	9 15
—			—	—	pws	—	—
14.6	NEWARK	17	17 20	17 05	19 05	16 10	16 35
—			—	pws	signal stop	pws	—
20.9	Carlton		23 25	25 55	35 15	21 55	22 10
26.4	Tuxford		30 05	33 45	42 50	30 30	28 20
33.1	RETFORD	39	37 55	41 35	50 40	38 10	35 55
—			pws	—	—	—	storm
42.2	Bawtry		47 25	50 20	60 05	46 40	46 10
—			—	—	—	pws	—
50.5	DONCASTER	58	57 20	59 10	69 30	56 00	55 30
54.7	*Shaftholme Junction*	63	62 05	64 20	74 05	62 20	59 55
60.5	Balne		68 15	70 45	80 10	68 30	65 55
68.9	SELBY	79	77 15	80 30	89 10	77 40	74 35
75.6	Escrick		86 05	89 55	97 45	86 55	83 15
—			—	—	—	pws	—
82.7	YORK	97	94 25	98 10†	106 25	97 00	91 55
	Net times		93	95	94	90½	90
Speeds							
	before Newark		—	69	—	72½	74
	after Tuxford		—	—	—	—	43
	near Balne		—	—	—	—	60

*Small-boilered type of engine
†To signal stop at Holgate Bridge box

GNR 5:30 pm Kings Cross–Grantham–Doncaster

Engine No:*		298	272	273	273
Load, tons full:		425	430	440	460
Weather:		NE wind/rain	NW wind/rain	Fine	Fine

Distance miles		m s	m s	m s	m s
0.0	Grantham	0 00	0 00	0 00	0 00
14.6	Newark	17 50	17 20	16 30	17 10
20.9	Carlton	24 00	23 35	22 00	23 00
28.0	Markham Box	33 30	33 05	30 25	32 35
33.1	Retford	38 55	38 25	35 45	38 40
50.5	Doncaster	57 40	57 35	55 10	59 20

*All superheater equipped: No 298, 'Robinson'; Nos 272–3, Gresley-twin.

GNR The 2:20 pm 'Scotsman' Kings Cross to Grantham

Run no:			1	2	3	4	5	6	7	8
Engine no:			280	1405*	282	282	1406*	1404*	287	287
Load, tons full:			345	365	385	390	400	415	415	425

Distance miles		Schedule min	Actual m s	Actual m s	Actual m s	Actual m s	Actual m s	Actual m s	Actual m s	Actual m s
0.0	KINGS CROSS	0	0 00	0 00	0 00	0 00	0 00	0 00	0 00	0 00
2.6	Finsbury Park		6 55	7 55	9 05	9 35	9 00	8 15	8 10	8 15
—			pws	—	—	—	signals	—	—	—
12.7	Potters Bar		21 10	22 35	23 55	24 50	25 30	24 25	24 10	23 20
17.7	HATFIELD	23	26 25	27 50	29 20	30 20	31 00	30 15	29 50	28 45
—			—	—	— signals	—	—	—	—	—
25.0	Knebworth		33 45	34 55	38 00	37 55	38 35	38 20	38 05	36 25
—			pws	—	—	—	—	—	—	—
31.9	HITCHIN	38	42 45	41 20	44 45	44 35	44 50	45 05	45 10	43 00
—			—	—	— signals	—	—	—	—
37.0	Arlesey		47 00	45 15	48 40	49 00	48 40	49 10	49 30	47 05
—			—	signal stop	—	—	—	—	—	—
44.1	Sandy		53 20	56 20	54 30	58 00	54 25	55 35	55 55	53 15
51.7	St Neots		60 30	64 15	61 20	66 30	61 20	63 15	63 35	60 20
58.9	HUNTINGDON	66	67 15	71 15	67 55	74 00	67 55	70 40	70 45	66 55
69.4	Holme		77 25	82 15	78 15	84 50	78 25	81 40	81 50	77 20
76.4	PETERBOROUGH	85	84 25	89 40	85 30	92 45	85 45	89 30	89 05	84 25
—			pws	—	—	—	—	—	—	—
88.6	Essendine		103 55	105 00	101 05	109 00	100 50	104 50	104 50	99 15
97.1	Corby		115 40	115 20	111 45	121 10	112 20	116 40	116 35	110 15
100.1	Stoke Box		120 00	119 40	116 15	126 10	116 40	121 20	121 10	114 40
—			—	— signals	signals	—	—	—	—
105.5	GRANTHAM	122	126 40	125 45	122 55	133 50	123 00	127 50	128 20	121 05
	Net times		118½	119¾	120½	129¼	121	127¾	128¼	121

Principal speeds, mph (at or near)								
Potters Bar	37½	40	37½	—	—	32½	36½	39
Hatfield	71½	72½	71½	69	69	66	64½	70½
Arlesey	74	80½	79	75	82	75	72½	77½
Abbots Ripton	50	43	51½	—	48	—	—	50
Holme	75	72½	71½	—	74	—	—	72½
Essendine (max)	45	60	60	—	56	—	—	61
Stoke Box	38½	41	37½	—	37	36	—	37½

*Engine fitted with 24-element superheater.

Chapter 7

Into the 'Grouping' era

Although the end of the war foreshadowed a time of great uncertainty for the future of British railways, with rival and vociferous projects for amalgamation of companies, nationalisation and such like, it was the great body of ordinary railwaymen who had to carry loyally on, despite the rantings of social reformers and politically activated idealists. By and large, the locomotive department of the Great Northern Railway had come through the four lean war years better than most. It had not been found necessary to adopt an austerity form of passenger-engine livery and the handsome and distinctive style that had remained unchanged since the early days of Patrick Stirling was for the most part as smartly turned out as ever. The mixed traffic and freight engines had been changed to 'battleship' grey, but all passenger classes, even down to the humblest of local train 'hacks' were still in green. Moreover it soon became evident, when post-war timetable revision began, that the 'Atlantics' had been maintained in good mechanical condition and were ready to resume a modicum of pre-war standards of running.

From the details of very many of his journeys published in *The Railway Magazine* by Cecil J. Allen, it would seem that no definite restraint on maximum speeds had been imposed on the Great Northern main line, as it had been on several other lines where high speed had previously been customary. With the limited nominal tractive power of the 'Atlantics', such restraint would have had a very hampering effect when advantage needed to be taken of the excellent alignment of the main line to run hard on favourable stretches — where a good speed could be readily attained with heavy trains to compensate for slow climbing of the banks. Although the entire British railway system remained under Government control for some time after the war, until, indeed, the broad outline of the 'Grouping' system had been established, the Great Northern was well to the fore in recasting its train services to suit the changing conditions and in restoring such amenities of travel as restaurant cars, on some trains, even though certain dishes had not yet become coupon-free!

In the higher echelons of railway mechanical engineering, certain pointers towards future development could have been discerned, even during the period of closest Government control under the Railway Executive Committee. In certain quarters it was thought likely that the railways would be nationalised after the war and it was also envisaged that once hostilities ended there would be a sudden, immediate crisis in engineering production in the country. Industry was geared up to a mighty output of war weapons and ammunition of all kinds, in an intense effort whose sudden cessation at the end of the war would leave a massive surplus of capacity, and railway managers, anticipating this situation, looked forward to an opportunity of replenishing their stocks of locomotives, normal replacement of which had been much curtailed during the war. With the prospect of nationalisation, a range of standard new designs was thought desirable and the REC asked the Association of Railway Locomotive Engineers — that rather exclusive club to which only Chief Mechanical Engineers and their principal assistants were admitted — to be ready with proposals for new designs.

As things turned out, only five of the 'big names' of the British locomotive world took any appreciable part in these discussions, which were abortive in any case. R.E.L. Maunsell of the SE & CR was Chief Mechanical Engineer to the REC, and it was his chief draughtsman, J. Clayton, who attended. The other four were Churchward, George Hughes of the L & YR, Fowler of the Midland, and Gresley. What they would have cooked up between them as a future British standard set of designs is wrapped in secrecy; but when it appeared that grouping of companies rather than nationalisation was to be the plan for the future, the project was dropped. After the Armistice of 1918, when Winston Churchill, as Minister of Munitions, wanted to order large numbers of locomotives to keep the arms factories going following the sudden end to the need for intense arms production, the locomotive engineers of the REC could not agree on any recommendation. Somewhat naturally, they all wanted their own designs! At the time it seemed as if Doncaster was wholly taken up, as far as design was concerned, with Gresley's new three-cylinder types, and the 'Atlantics' cast for little more than a caretaking role until new and more modern locomotives were available.

While nominal tractive effort has never been regarded as an infallible basis for assessing the capacity of locomotives, particularly those for express-passenger service, it is nevertheless revealing to set alongside each other the figures for the principal express-engine classes of eight leading British railways, in the year 1921, if only to emphasise the rather extraordinary position held by the Great Northern large-boilered superheated 'Atlantics', thus:

Railway	Engine class	Nominal TE, lbs
GWR	'Star' 4 cylinder 4-6-0	27,800
LSWR	Urie N15 2-cylinder 4-6-0	26,200
LB&SCR	Billinton 4-6-4 tank	22,400
GNR	Large superheater 4-4-2	17,340
LNWR	'Claughton' 4-cylinder 4-6-0	23,800
NER	Class 'Z' 3-cylinder 4-4-2	19,300
L&YR	Hughes rebuilt 4-cylinder 4-6-0	29,150
NBR	Reid superheater 4-4-2	23,324

The position is made still more singular in that the GNR 'Atlantics' had what would be considered in post-war years an old-fashioned valve gear and an adhesion weight of only 40 tons; and yet, with the exception of the Great Western 'Star' and on occasions the LNWR 'Claughton', the Doncaster engines came to outshine them all in the years between the wars.

The first time I personally saw the Great Northern 'Atlantics' at work was in 1919. My parents, then living at Barrow-in-Furness decided to spend the first post-war family holiday at Bridlington and, on our return, we travelled by a service that involved a change of trains at Selby. Where the first train went to afterwards I have no idea, but the change involved a long wait — to the displeasure of my parents and my delight. The main line was unusually busy at that time with Great Northern expresses in both directions. A very busy, up train stopped at Selby while we were waiting and on the down through line came none other than 'The Flying Scotsman', hauled by the superheated 'Atlantic' No 272. I fired off at it with my 'Box Brownie' but made a mess of it! In the following summer we repeated the trip and that time I was more successful. I still have today the snaps I took of the engines on the two portions of that up train; first, No 1449 (non-superheater), the engine that ran between Euston and Crewe in 1909 and then the superheated 1447. The 'Scotsman' came through hauled by No 1431, and the 'snap'

Engine No 1419, as first equipped, with booster and retaining original GNR boiler mountings (W.J. Reynolds).

Top *The inside-cylinder 'Klondike' on the GCR section: No 3271 photographed at Nottingham in 1928* (Rail Archive Stephenson).

Above *The first GNR compound 'Atlantic', as LNER No 3292, at New England, Peterborough, just before withdrawal for scrapping in 1927* (Rail Archive Stephenson).

was good enough for my friend, the late Jack Hill, to work up a magnificent painting which became the jacket illustration of my book *The Golden Age of Steam*.

By the spring of 1919, even the Great Northern had come to realise that the combined 5:30 plus 5:45 plus 6:05 evening train from Kings Cross was a somewhat unmanageable proposition, notwithstanding the provision of pilot engines out to Potters Bar; and the Newcastle section was once again run separately and accelerated. Not only so, but the unusual step was taken of omitting the stop at York and changing engines from Great Northern to North Eastern 'Atlantics' at Clifton Road Junction, abreast of York running sheds. With the load reduced usually to something under 300 tons, the Great Northern drivers were soon showing that they had not forgotten how to run fast and there was much sparkling performance, especially north of Grantham, where the train was then worked by Doncaster engines and men, in the course of a round evening trip from their home station. This book has already included many examples of actual running, but I cannot resist setting out two further performances, which are interesting not only for their own merit, but as showing the work of the pioneer engine of them all, No 251, which by that time was superheated, though retaining the original balanced slide valves. For a train of no more than eight coaches the schedule timing was not unduly fast, but on both occasions, worked by different crews, No 251 was driven away from Grantham as though a new 'Race to the North' was on (see table on page 92).

If strict point-to-point booked times were to be kept, much harder running was needed on the Great Northern part of the journey, passing Doncaster in 56 minutes, compared to the 43 minutes allowed for the remaining 32½ miles, even though the latter provided for the usual slow running through Selby and through York station. The drivers of engine No 251 certainly did not mince matters on these two occasions. The first one was 3 minutes early as soon as Retford and the second would have done even better after his lightning start from Grantham had he not eased the engine considerably after Crow Park. The second man ran much harder from Doncaster to Selby, and passed the latter station 5½ minutes early.

The process of improving the '251' class had been carried a stage further in 1919, when engine No 1403 was fitted with a 32-element Robinson superheater and 8-inch diameter piston valves. This involved a considerable rearrangement of the tubes and a reduction in diameter of the small ones from 2¼ to 2 in diameter. For ready reference, the details of the boilers with 24- and 32-element superheaters are tabulated hereunder.

GNR 'Atlantic' large superheated boilers

	24	32
Number of elements	24	32
Small tubes, number	137	133
outside diameter, ins	2¼	2
Flues, number	24	32
outside diameter, ins	5¼	5¼
Heating surfaces sq ft		
Tubes	1,290	1,121
Flues	526.5	703
Elements	427	568
Firebox	141	141
Total	2,384.5	2,533
Grate area, sq ft	31	31
Boiler pressure psi	170	170

This notable development put the finishing touch on the design of these engines and, coupled with the excellent structural and mechanical design which, of course, dated back to the year 1902, it paved the way for the

road performances in the years to 1937 which thrilled all their admirers and many 'doubting Thomases', beyond belief.

The exhilarating revival of speed on the Great Northern was cut short in 1921 by the occurrence of a lengthy coal strike which began before Easter and lasted until the summer. But it once again showed the capacity of the large-boilered 'Atlantics' for heavy train haulage to an extent perhaps that had never been displayed before. Because, although certain trains were cancelled and others combined, the schedules remained unaltered at the levels to which they had climbed back in the post-war revival. At the same time there was still a disposition, on the part of some commentators to regard the 'Atlantics' as a class of 'has-beens' and the introduction of the Gresley 3-cylinder 2-6-0s of the '1000' class with a nominal tractive effort of no less than 30,031 lb, and their use on heavy express passenger trains during the strike era was seen as a marked portent of the future. That an engine of such tractive power could be satisfactorily steamed from a boiler with a total heating surface smaller than that of the 'Atlantics' was considered to indicate a marked improvement in front-end design, and particularly in respect of the three-cylinder layout and its patented arrangement of the conjugated valve gear.

I have often wondered if any thought was ever given at Doncaster to the rebuilding of one of the 'Atlantics' experimentally, with three cylinders and the conjugated valve gear. The four-cylinder rebuild of No 279 was not entirely a success from the viewpoint of power output although, according to the records compiled by R.A.H. Weight, that engine amassed a notably high annual mileage.

So far as maximum loads during the coal strike are concerned, Cecil J. Allen has described vividly the travelling conditions when he was on the 8:00 am from Newcastle, after it was combined with the 9.35 am from Leeds at Doncaster and the total load became one of 14 eight-wheelers, 2 twelve-wheeled dining cars and a modern Gresley articulated twin vehicle, 526 tons *tare*. He goes on to say that 'as the number of passengers was in the neighbourhood of 800, and in addition to their luggage in the compartments every brake van and locker was piled with heavy luggage literally to the roof (passage from the back of the train to the dining cars was an absolute impossibility), the gross load behind the tender of superheated 'Atlantic' No 295 was, as

GNR 10:59 am
Doncaster–Peterborough

Load: 18 coaches, 526 tons tare, 600 tons full
Engine (large superheater 4-4-2) No: 295

Distance miles		Schedule min	Actual m s	Speeds mph
0.0	DONCASTER	0	0 00	—
4.7	Rossington		8 40	47½
6.6	*Pipers Wood Box*		11 25	39
8.3	Bawtry		13 35	—
12.1	Ranskill		17 30	60
17.4	RETFORD	22	23 40	—
4.9	*Markham Box*		11 55	26
6.7	Tuxford		14 25	—
12.2	Carlton		19 45	69
18.5	NEWARK		25 45	60
23.2	Claypole		30 40	48
28.9	Barkston		37 40	37½
33.1	GRANTHAM	44	44 20	—
5.4	*Stoke Box*		13 30	30½
8.4	Corby		17 15	—
13.3	Little Bytham		21 35	72½
16.9	Essendine		24 30	75
20.7	Tallington		27 40	70½
26.0	*Werrington Junction*		32 25	65
29.1	PETERBOROUGH	36	36 05	—

GNR Peterborough – Kings Cross

Load: 18 coaches 526 tons tare, 600 tons full
Engine (large superheater 4-4-2) No: 290

Distance miles		m s	Speed mph
0.0	PETERBOROUGH	0 00	—
3.8	Yaxley	8 05	—
7.0	Holme	11 40	58½
12.9	Abbots Ripton	18 30	39
17.5	HUNTINGDON	24 05	68
24.7	St Neots	31 00	55
32.3	Sandy	39 00	62½
39.4	Arlesey	47 00	—
44.5	HITCHIN	53 35	—
47.8	Stevenage	59 30	33
58.7	HATFIELD	72 25	69
63.7	Potters Bar	78 00	51
67.2	New Barnet	81 35	67
—		pwr	—
71.4	Wood Green	85 50	—
73.8	Finsbury Park	88 25	—
76.4	KINGS CROSS	92 35*	—

*Schedule time 93 minutes.

nearly as I could calculate, exactly 600 tons'. It would have been a daunting proposition for a locomotive having no greater tractive effort than 17,340 lb and an adhesion weight of only 40 tons, but for two things — the superb mechanical condition of this engine and of the one that relieved it at Peterborough, and the enthusiasm and skill with which the drivers and firemen went for the job. Allen had no conversation with either crew beforehand; it would be more than his life was worth to forsake a seat in the train!

The running that ensued is set out in two tables and collectively can be set down as one of the phenomena of Great Northern 'Atlantic' history. From the details tabulated, one can be fairly sure that both engines were going pretty well all-out the whole way. So far as No 295 is concerned, one or two features may be specially pinpointed. At the very start there are only 4 miles of level track before the 1 in 198 rise to Pipers Wood box begins and to accelerate this colossal load up to 47½ mph with the engine starting 'cold' from Doncaster was an impressive beginning. Then from Retford up to Askham there is 1¼ miles of 1 in 178, followed by 2 miles at 1 in 200 to be mounted and, by the top, the engine had been pounded up to 26 mph. Fortunately the rail conditions were good and it was possible to

make an even finer start from Grantham up the 5 miles continuously at 1 in 200 up to Stoke summit. The attained speed of 30½ mph here represented output of about 950 equivalent drawbar horsepower and the related drawbar pull of 12,000 lb (5.35 tons) was nearly 70 per cent of the nominal tractive effort of the locomotive — as near 'flat-out' as one was ever likely to see with steam. The joyous subsequent gallop down to Peterborough, with a top speed of 75 mph did not mean so much effort for, on a descending gradient of 1 in 200, it would require an equivalent drawbar horsepower of no more than about 400.

At Peterborough, No 295 and her crew were relieved by No 290 and another Herculean performance began. At Holme, they had this enormous train running at 58½ mph on level track and from there to Arlesey, where the moderately undulating road for 32.4 miles is equivalent to an average rise of 1 in 1700, the average speed was 55.1 mph. The average drawbar horsepower was 832 and the drawbar pull 32.7 per cent of the nominal tractive effort. This again was an altogether outstanding sustained effort. In the days of the nationalised British Railways, when all-out tests with the dynamometer car were being conducted with certain famous engine classes under strictly controlled conditions, the drawbar pull at 55 mph was generally under 30 per cent of the nominal tractive effort, while in ordinary service these locomotives rarely came anywhere near such heights of power output.

'Atlantics' transferred to the GCR section: engine No 4428 working through from Swindon to Sheffield on a through express from Swansea, here seen on the Great Western line near Steventon (M.W. Earley).

After this long sustained maximum effort, this incomparable 'Atlantic' topped Stevenage summit at 33 mph after the long bank up from Arlesey, and then averaged 51.5 mph over the undulations thence to Potters Bar. A brisk finish, despite the slight slowing through Wood Green tunnel, brought the train into Kings Cross half a minute inside schedule time — a magnificent effort by engine and crew. Enthusiastic as one can justifiably be over the locomotive work, one must nevertheless spare a thought for many of the passengers, particularly those at the rear of the train, in coaches that would be beyond the end of the platform, if not actually in the tunnel (!) and for the job of the station staff in unloading those mountains of luggage. One can well wonder how long it was after No 290 came to rest before some of those passengers managed to get away from Kings Cross.

On all the British railways, conditions had hardly settled down again after the long coal strike of 1921, before new excitement was generated with the prospects of Grouping, which it was decreed would take effect at the end of 1922. With the form of amalgamation decided upon and the 'Eastern Group', as it was at first referred to, consisting of the Great Northern, Great Eastern, Great Central and North Eastern, of the major English companies, there was naturally keen speculation as to who would get the job of Chief Mechanical Engineer. The situation was not clear-cut by any means. Sir Vincent Raven, of the North Eastern Railway, CME since 1910, had attained a position of great eminence in the railway world, particularly towards the development

of main-line electrification; and it was on his recommendation that the Board of the North Eastern Railway had actually decided to electrify the main line between York and Newcastle. But in 1922 he was already 63 years of age and he was appointed Technical Adviser to the new London and North Eastern Railway, rather than to any direct executive position. Largely at Lord Faringdon's suggestion the Board approached J.G. Robinson, who had been Chief Mechanical Engineer of the Great Central since 1902, the longest tenure in the most senior office of all the railway mechanical engineers; but he felt that the job should go to a younger man and recommended Gresley, who was then no more than 45 years old.

With Gresley in the chair, it seemed then that a continuance of Great Northern locomotive policy was assured, though there was an important change in the structure of the chief mechanical engineer's department. On all the consituent companies of the LNER, as on nearly all other British railway companies until Grouping, the chief mechanical engineer, or whatever title he held, had been the 'supremo' so far as everything to do with locomotives was concerned, responsible for design, manufacture, maintenance and running. An important change in this respect had, however, been made on the Midland Railway in 1907 with the transfer of responsibility for running to the traffic department, when the great Cecil W. Paget was appointed General Superintendent. This precedent was followed in the organisation of the LMS, in 1923, but on the LNER the newly appointed

The 4-cylindered engine, re-numbered 3279, in LNER livery, on the 5:30 pm Kings Cross-Newcastle express, in 1925, near Finsbury Park (Rail Archive Stephenson).

Locomotive Running Superintendents for the Southern, North Eastern and Scottish Areas were independent officers responsible to the respective Divisional General Managers. It is important to appreciate the impact of the appointments because they were to have some effect upon the future history of the Great Northern 'Atlantics'.

For the Southern Area, W.G.P. Maclure was appointed Running Superintendent. He had held the same post on the Great Central Railway for many years and, somewhat naturally, had a very high opinion of J.G. Robinson's locomotives. Gresley himself had a special regard for Robinson, feeling much indebted to him for his recommendation; so that when Maclure suggested trials of certain Great Central engines on the Great Northern there was no opposition from Gresley. To the North Eastern Area also he was much beholden, because from it he drew a most important tool of management in the Darlington dynamometer car and with it the skill and experience of its team of test engineers. On the running side J.H. Smeddle was the natural man for the job, having held the same appointment on the North Eastern Railway. He was the father of R.A. Smeddle, who 30 years later became Chief Mechanical Engineer of the Western Region of the nationalised British Railways.

With a dynamometer car at his disposal, Gresley was anxious to examine the relative potentialities and economy of the variety of locomotives for which he was now responsible and, after running trials between a Raven 'Pacific' and one of his own, in the summer of 1923 he turned his attention to the 'Atlantics', and an important series of tests was conducted between Newcastle and Edinburgh, involving engines of Great Northern, North Eastern, and North British design. Each engine made five return trips with service trains, taking whatever loads were offered, and also one return trip with a special train of maximum load. The engines were worked by crews from their own sheds, to whom full discretion was allowed in the way they worked the engines. The Great Northern sent engine No 1447, with the same Kings Cross driver, Albert Pibworth, who did so well with the Gresley 'Pacific' in the famous Interchange Trials with the Great Western in 1925. While both the North Eastern and the North British competitors in 1923 were in standard condition, the Great Northern 'Atlantic' required to have its boiler mountings cut down a little to clear the Scottish loading gauge and, in view of the rather disappointing results, I have often wondered if the shortening of the chimney affected the draughting and made the steaming less free than usual.

The choice of trains was unusual, being the 3:26 pm relief to the down 'Flying Scotsman', non-stop over the 124.4 miles to Edinburgh, Waverley, in 154 minutes, and the 10:35 pm up 'Night Scotsman', nominally non-stop to Newcastle in 151 minutes, but including in the schedule a conditional stop at Dunbar to take up passengers for south of Newcastle.

Competition between East Coast Atlantics: a later picture of No 1447, re-numbered 4447, with boiler mountings as cut-down for running between Newcastle and Edinburgh in 1923 (Rail Archive Stephenson).

Both the Great Northern and the North British drivers had to learn the road, because although the NBR man was running over his own line southwards to Berwick, the men in the 'Atlantic' link at Haymarket shed did not normally work over this route. All the top East Coast expresses were worked by North Eastern engines and men. It cannot have been particularly easy for Tom Henderson, who drove the NB 'Atlantic' *Hazeldean*, or Pibworth from Kings Cross to work an important test train over a strange route at night, even though they each had a pilotman at their elbow. In the official report, which I had the privilege of studying, the leading particulars of the three competing engines were set alongside and one notes with interest that the cylinder diameter of GNR 1447 is quoted as 20⅛ in, no doubt signifying that in her case the cylinders had been bored out to a little more than their nominal dimension of 20 in. The data below is quoted exactly as it was presented in the official report.

I am indebted to the records collected by the

'Atlantic' engine trials in 1923
Leading particulars of engines

Railway	GNR	NER	NBR
Engine No:	1447	733	878
Weight in working order, tons			
Engine	69.6	77.1	76.7
Tender	43.1	45.6	45.4
Total	112.7	122.7	122.1
Heating surfaces, sq ft			
Firebox	141	185	184.8
Tubes	1,824	1,298	1,619.0
Total evaporative area	1,965	1,483	1,803.8
Superheater	568	392	263.0
Boiler pressure, psi	170	175	180
Grate area, sq ft	31	27	28.5
Cylinders			
Number	2	3	2
Diameter, ins	20⅛	16½	21
Stroke, ins	24	26	28
Driving wheel diameter, ins	80	82	81
Adhesion weight, tons	40.0	39.5	40
Tractive Effort, at 85% working pressure, lb	17,580	19,300	23,324

late E.L. Bell for the logs of four runs made during the experimental period, two with the GNR engine No 1447 and two with the NBR *Hazeldean*, on the night runs from Edinburgh down to Newcastle (see page 92). In October, when the Great Northern runs were made, the train was lightly loaded, and no difficulty was experienced in keeping time, in spite of various checks. On the first of the North British nights the conditional stop at Dunbar was called. On such occasions an extra 6 minutes was allowed in the overall time from Edinburgh to Newcastle; but the Haymarket driver on No 878 tended to disregard this extra allowance and to run harder than usual to make up for the time lost thereby. While on both runs tabulated, the Great Northern driver kept his overall time, because of the heavier loading and the exuberance of the North British driver, as locomotive performances they were overshadowed.

What is surprising is the extent to which engine No 1447 was overshadowed when it came to basic coal consumption, for it will be seen from the table of results that related to the work done she used 5.08 lb per drawbar horsepower hour, against the 4.45 of the North Eastern 'Z' engine and the 4.12 lb of *Hazeldean*. Relating these to pounds per mile run, the respective figures work out at 40, 35.5 and 44.7 lb per mile. The North British engine would be expected to use more because of her heavier average load. When it came to the special trains, each of which was made up to 406 tons tare, the North Eastern figure

quoted of 3.63 lb is so suspect as to be unacceptable, because it would mean that the 406-ton train would have had to be worked at a speed very little less than that of the service trains, and yet the coal per train mile would be only 30 lb, against 35.5 for the 311-ton average load. One would think that 4.63 lb per DHP hour would be nearer the mark. This would be in line with the results from another series of tests with a 3-cylinder 'Z' class 'Atlantic' over this same route a year later. This does not disguise the fact that the performance of the Great Northern engine was disappointing.

It is evident that much store was set by those who scrutinised the results on the climbing of the Cockburnspath bank. Apart from the immediate start out of Kings Cross, which was in any case much shorter, this was a far more severe incline than any on the Great Northern main line. The bank itself is just 6 miles long and begins at Innerwick station with 1¾ miles at 1 in 210. Then there are 4¼ miles unbrokenly at 1 in 96, with the short Penmanshiel Tunnel just before the summit. The official report gives details of the climbing of the bank. Climbing banks of this severity was not the strongest feature of the Great Northern 'Atlantic' performance, in circumstances where the lack of tractive effort would be felt; but here it would seem that No 1447 was not being worked nearly so hard as No 295 was in that Herculean start out of Grantham with a 600-ton train when she put forth a drawbar pull of 5.35 tons at 30 mph.

One of the North Eastern competitors: a 3-cylinder 'Z' class (LNER class C7) (O.S. Nock).

The 5.92 tons recorded with No 1447 on the Cockburnspath bank at 20 mph would have involved an equivalent drawbar horsepower of about 700, compared to the 950 of No 295. Judging from the table of results in the official report there was some very level pegging between the three engines, 1447, 733 and 878, on the Cockburnspath bank. So far as the last engine was concerned, on her southbound journey with the special train, a severe check was experienced, which made comparison with the other two not possible and the performance shown in the table was that made on the nearest equivalent run with a service train.

For the Great Northern 'Atlantics', the foregoing were the only dynamometer car tests ever made with the superheater engines and it is a great pity that the results were relatively unrepresentative of the best the engines could

do. But they had one result that was important so far as the future of the pre-Grouping express locomotives were concerned. In such a closely fought contest it was evident that one design had no advantage over either of the others and each was left to carry on in its own area. There were no transfers and apart from the introduction of new standard 'Pacifics' little in the way of supersession took place for many years to come.

Gresley, as an old Great Northern man, would have been conscious enough of the lack of tractive effort in the superheater 'Atlantics'. His attempt to remedy this by rebuilding engine No 279 with four cylinders had not been entirely successful and the remarkable work of the standard engines fitted with 32-element superheaters had shown clearly that their only weakness, if it could be so

LNER 'Atlantic' Tests in 1923
Performance on the Cockburnspath Bank

Railway:	GNR	NER	NBR
Engine No:	1447	733	878
Load, tons	406.5	406.5	366
Average boiler pressure, psi	162	175	175
Steam chest pressure, psi	140	147	138
Average cut-off, per cent	40	56	52
Speed on bank, mph			
at foot	47.5	50.5	44.0
minimum	20	22.5	21.5
Drawbar pull tons at foot	2.45	2.20	2.35
maximum actual	4.75	4.80	4.70
maximum corrected for gradient	5.92	6.08	5.97

'Atlantic' engine trials
Test results

Railway:	GNR	NER	NBR
Engine No:	1447	733	878
Average load, tons tare			
Service trains	307	311	345
Special trains	406	406	406
Average speed mph			
Service trains	49.3	49.0	48.0
Special trains	46.0	47.2	47.5
Average drawbar horsepower			
Service trains	393	391	529
Special trains	527	529	525
Average steam-chest pressure psi			
Special trains	97	132	138
Average cut-off			
Special trains	40	42	38
Coal per DHP hour, lb			
Service trains	5.08	4.45	4.12
Special trains	4.42	3.63*	4.15
Average superheat temperature in deg(F)	624	577	520
Evaporation, lb of water per lb coal	7.2	8.6	8.2

*Highly suspect figure

described, was in sheer pulling power at low speeds. Once they were really going, at 50 mph or more, the freedom with which large quantities of highly superheated steam could be used by those relatively small cylinders and exhausted with remarkably low back pressure made them the equals, in heavy load haulage, of many other British designs of much higher nominal tractive effort. The use of a 'booster' engine therefore seemed a highly promising way of augmenting tractive power at low speeds and, as an experiment, in 1923, engine No 1419 was so equipped. This application was the first in British practice and, in so doing, Gresley undoubtedly had in mind the difficult start out of Kings Cross. As applied to engine No 1419 the booster was a separate 2-cylinder engine placed below the footplate which converted the trailing wheels into a pair of driving wheels, when required, and which supplied independent and augmenting power.

The booster engine had two inside cylinders of 10 in diameter by 12 in stroke, to which the steam distribution was by piston valves with direct valve motion. On the driving shaft of the booster was a pinion wheel from which, through an intermediate or idler pinion wheel, power is supplied to the trailing wheels of the locomotive, through a third pinion which was fixed on the trailing axle. The idler pinion was secured to the base of the booster by a rocking arm. When it was desired to put the booster gear into operation, the driver actuated a mechanism that moved the idler gear into mesh with the pinions on the driving shaft and the trailing axle of the locomotive. Then by means of an air-operated regulator valve, steam could be applied to the booster engine.

When steam was shut off from this engine, the idler gear was automatically taken out of engagement. The tractive effort of the booster engine was 8,500 lb, so working in conjunction with the tractive effort of 17,340 lb from the main engine the total power was increased by nearly 50 per cent. To accommodate the booster beneath the footplate, the main frames had to be extended and advantage was taken of this to fit a more commodious cab, after the style of that used on the 'Pacific' engines.

In July 1923, some trials with this modified engine were made in the London area on heavily graded sections, including a special demonstration trip with a load of no less than 18 bogie coaches. It was reported at the time that the advantages of the booster were practically demonstrated by the ease with which this very heavy train was started from rest and hauled up steep inclines. A photograph taken on one such run was reproduced in *The Railway Magazine*, but after that a great silence descended upon the entire project, until it was reported, some years later, that the engine was undergoing tests on the heavily graded Waverley Route, in Scotland, for which purpose the boiler mountings and cab roof had to be modified to clear the Scottish loading gauge, as had been necessary when engine No 1447 did her experimental running in 1923. The tests with No 4419, as she had then become, were conducted in 1927, when the possibility of using more powerful engines than the North British 'Atlantics' was being investigated to lessen the amount of double heading then common with the heaviest trains. The booster engine was run in competition with Gresley 'Pacifics'.

A North British 'Atlantic' in pre-grouping livery, No 906, Teribus, *in the Princes' Gardens, Edinburgh* (O.S. Nock Collection).

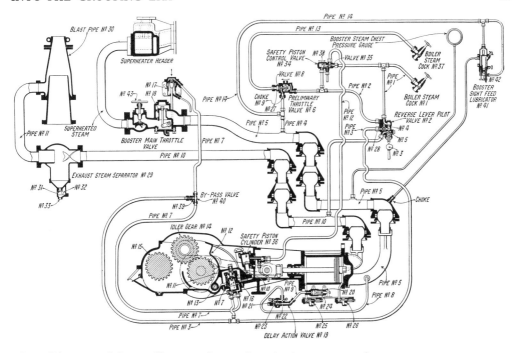

Above *Diagrammatic layout of booster and connections, showing steam control.*

Below *Elevation and plan drawings, showing general arrangement of Atlantic type locomotive with booster engine and fittings.*

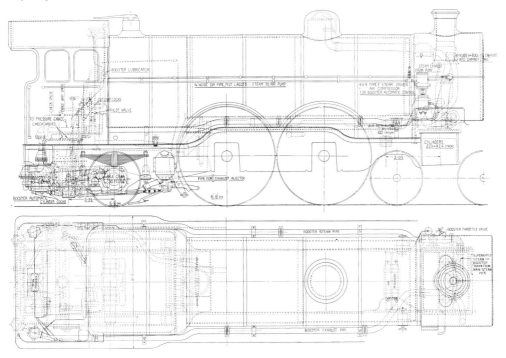

GNR Grantham–York (in 1920) (5:30 pm ex-Kings Cross)

Load: 8 coaches, 245 tons full
Engine (superheater 4-4-2) No: 251

Distance miles		Schedule min	Actual m s	Speed mph	Actual m s	Speed mph
0.0	GRANTHAM	0	0 00	—	0 00	—
6.0	Hougham		8 20	—	8 05	—
14.6	NEWARK	17	15 45	71½	15 30	74
21.9	Crow Park		22 30	—	22 10	—
28.2	*Markham Box*		29 10	52½	29 30	47½
33.1	RETFORD	37	34 00	68	34 40	54
38.4	Ranskill		eased		40 00	66
42.2	Bawtry		—		43 35	52
—			—		eased	—
50.5	DONCASTER	56	53 05		52 20	—
54.7	*Shaftholme Junction*		—		57 05	—
64.3	Templehirst		—		67 00	—
68.9	SELBY	79	75 25		73 35	—
—			signals		—	
82.7	YORK		signals		93 20	—
83.0	Clifton Junction	99	97 25		94 50	—

LNER Trial running 1923 Edinburgh–Newcastle

Engine (4-4-2) type:	GN	GN	NB	NB
Engine No:	1447	1447	878 *Hazeldean*	878 *Hazeldean*
Load, tons tare:	270	305	345	375

Distance miles		m s	Average speed, mph	m s	Average speed, mph	m s	Average speed, mph	m s	Average speed, mph
0.0	EDINBURGH (WAVERLEY)	0 00	—	0 00	—	0 00	—	0 00	—
3.0	Portobello	4 40	—	4 55	—	4 55	—	5 15	—
9.5	Prestonpans	—	—	12 40	50.3	11 35	58.5	—	—
13.2	Longniddry	—	—	16 45	54.2	15 20	59.2	16 45	53.7
17.8	DREM JUNCTION	21 55	51.5	21 30	58.1	19 35	65.0	21 15	61.3
23.4	East Linton	—	—	26 55	62.0	24 50	64.0	27 10	56.7
29.1	DUNBAR	33 20	59.6	32 50	57.8	31 30	51.3	32 40	62.1
33.8	Innerwick	—				8 25		38 05	52.0
36.5	Cockburnspath	42 25	49.0	41 25	51.7	11 35	51.2	41 40	45.2
41.2	Grantshouse	51 15	31.9	50 05	32.6	21 20	29.1	52 00	27.2
46.2	Reston Junction	—	—	55 25	58.2	26 45	52.1	57 30	54.5
51.9	Burnmouth	—	—	60 50	63.2	32 15	62.1	63 00	62.1
57.5	BERWICK	69 25	53.5	67 40	49.1	39 10	48.2	70 15	47.1
60.9	Scremerston	—		73 05	37.7	44 10	48.0	75 55	36.0
65.8	Beal	79 55	47.2	77 50	61.8	48 55	61.9	80 55	58.8
72.8	Belford	88 25	49.5	85 20	56.0	56 20	56.7	88 50	53.0
81.4	Christon Bank	98 35	50.7	signal stop		62 20	56.0	—	—
85.0	Little Mill	—		103 25	—	69 40	54.1	102 40	53.0
89.6	ALNMOUTH JUNCTION	107 25	48.8	107 45	63.8	74 20	59.2	107 25	58.1
95.9	Acklington	—		114 45	54.0	81 25	53.6	—	—
101.2	Widdrington	119 15	58.9	120 15	57.7	87 15	54.5	117 55	66.2
—		signals		pws		pws		signals	
107.8	MORPETH	129 35		129 25		96 20		130 20	
114.5	Cramlington	138 40		137 55		105 15		138 40	
—		signals		—		—		—	
124.4	NEWCASTLE	151 20		150 00		121 20		150 50	

Chapter 8

Challenge to the 'Atlantics'

With the introduction of the Gresley 'Pacifics' in 1922, it was clear that the Ivatt 'Atlantics' would be stepping down from their long-held place as premier express-passenger locomotives on the Great Northern main line. The onset of Grouping in 1923 began to cast further doubts as to their continuing in high favour, particularly when it was announced that a series of forty more Gresley 'Pacifics' were to be built. Although these were intended for general service on the East Coast main line, one could be sure that a generous allocation would be made to the Great Northern section. Apart from that, however, it seemed that the 'Atlantic' position was going to be challenged in other respects. It is true that the engine that had been tested between Newcastle and Edinburgh had not shown up too well but, even before the results of those tests were known, an infiltration from the North Eastern had begun. In the previous summer, the alteration in working of the principal London-Newcastle business expresses, the 8:00 am up and the 5:30 pm down, had led to the York stop being omitted in each direction and engines changed at Clifton Road Junction, abreast of York running sheds. In 1923, there was a new development, whereby the stop was omitted and the North Eastern engines worked through to Grantham.

It was not a very economical arrangement from the viewpoint of locomotive utilisation, because the North Eastern engine stood idle at Grantham all day and, to avoid its Gateshead crew having to do the same, those who took the morning train had to return to York 'on the cushions' and a second North Eastern set had to travel to Grantham similarly for the return working in the late evening. There is no doubt that the crews of the 3-cylinder 'Z' class 'Atlantics' did not a little 'showing off' on the evening train, largely for the benefit of the Great Northern pilotman who usually accompanied them from Grantham to York; and night after night they passed Selby well ahead of time. The schedule allowed 77 minutes for the 68.9 miles to this station, while the concluding allowance of 48 minutes for the 44.1 miles from York to their first stop at Darlington permitted some very easy running. The overall time of 142 minutes for the 126.8 miles from Grantham involved no higher average speed than 53.5 mph with a gross load of about 280 tons.

Occasionally there was a variation in the working of this train if for some reason a North Eastern engine was not available. One might have looked for something very interesting north of York, to see how a Great Northern 'Atlantic' would do on the magnificent racing stretch to Darlington; but on two recorded occasions the circumstances were not favourable. On the first, the North Eastern engine that had worked the up train had failed fairly early in the day, early enough for the evening working of the North Eastern crew to be cancelled, and the train sent north with GNR engine No 1446 and Grantham men, to pick up a North Eastern pilotman in a brief stop in York station. On the second, the Gateshead crew were already at Grantham and the driver rode on No 1438 from the start, to take over duties as pilotman as they passed through York. On neither occasion was the running north of York in any way representative. Neither Great Northern man had ever been north of York before and even with a pilotman one could hardly expect them to run hard after dark. Both engines had been run splendidly on their own line, passing Selby between 4 and 5 minutes early but, even with ample allowance north of York, both trains were several minutes late on arrival at Darlington. One could not really expect otherwise. It might have been much better if they were running in daylight.

Further south, no doubt at the instigation of the newly appointed Locomotive Running Superintendent of the Southern Area, there had begun a long-term trial and usage of Great Central locomotives on the Great Northern main line. Because of the continued lightness of the principal expresses on the Great Central line, Mr J.G. Robinson's *magnum opus*, the 4-cylinder 4-6-0s of the 'Lord Faringdon' class, had been somewhat under-utilised on their own line, at any rate so far as tractive power was concerned. These massively handsome engines had a nominal tractive effort of 25,145 lb and Maclure evidently felt there was better use for them on some of the heavier East Coast trains, for which 'Pacifics' were not yet available and on which the superheated large-boilered 'Atlantics' appeared to be extended almost to their limit. In 1923, the Great Central 4-6-0 engine, No 1166, *Earl Haig*, worked for a time on one of the hardest Doncaster turns, the 10:51 am up to Kings Cross, returning with the very heavy 4:00 pm express. This latter was not then one of the fastest trains out of Kings Cross, but as far as Peterborough it took a load little short of 500 tons. The Great Central engine is reported to have made some impressive starts out of Kings Cross, passing Finsbury Park in about 6 minutes.

Instead of the heavy, hard-slogging East Coast trains, however, Maclure found a more spectacular use for these Great Central engines, on the newly instituted Pullman trains between London, Leeds, Harrogate and Newcastle. These were booked to run the 186 miles between Kings Cross and Leeds Central in 205 minutes, and to work these trains two of the Great Central 4-6-0s Nos 1165, *Valour*, and 1166, *Earl Haig*, were transferred to the former Great Northern shed in Leeds, Copley Hill. North of Leeds, the new train was at first worked by North Eastern 'Atlantics'. This move put these big Great Central 4-6-0s into direct competition with the Great Northern 'Atlantics' because, on alternate days, the train was worked by Kings Cross shed on a 'double-home' basis. At first, although the Pullman train was booked to make an average speed of 54.3 mph in each direction on its non-stop runs between Kings Cross and Leeds, one sensed in the railway press an inclination to decry its achievement because of the relative lightness of the load, compared to some of the heavier East Coast trains. At the

Below *Engine No 4426 (superheated) on a class 'A' up express goods train passing Langley Junction water troughs, south of Stevenage* (Rail Archive Stephenson).

Bottom *A fine action shot of No 3288, pounding up the bank towards Hadley Wood, with the very heavy 5:35 pm out of Kings Cross* (Rail Archive Stephenson).

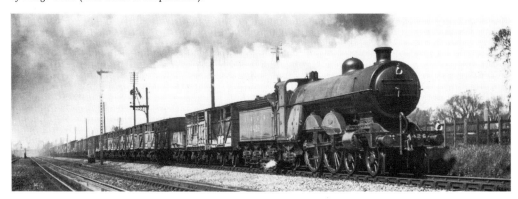

start, its usual load was one of six Pullman cars, with two ECJS full-brake vans for the heavy luggage many of the earlier patrons took with them, and this totalled about 290 tons in all, behind the tender.

In view of the use of two types of locomotive from the start of the new service, one based at each end, it is interesting to compare the basic proportions of the engines that were thus thrown into competition with the large boilered Great Northern 'Atlantics'.

Railway	GNR	GCR
Type	4-4-2	4-6-0
Cylinders number	2	4
Diameter ins	20	16
Stroke, ins	24	26
Coupled wheel diameter, ft-in	6-8	6-9
Heating surfaces, sq ft		
Tubes	1,824	1,881
Firebox	141	163
Superheater	568	343
Grate area, sq ft	31	26
Boiler pressure, psi	170	180
Adhesion weight, tons	40	57.2
Nominal tractive effort, lb	17,340	25,145

The 'Lord Faringdon' class was sometimes criticised for its use of the same proportions of firebox and grate area as on the 4-4-0 'Director' class, also designed and built at the Gorton Works of the Great Central Railway. But well enough aware of the express train running conditions on his own line, Robinson in all probability did not enlarge the grate area on his big 4-6-0s in order to avoid using too much coal just to keep the firebars covered. Great Central engines used hard coal, from the South Yorkshire and Nottinghamshire pits, and were usually run with a thin fire. There was plenty of tractive effort for a big effort in starting or in climbing a gradient and, that done, one could run on a light thin fire at high speed on the fast stretches. It is a great pity that no comparative figure of coal consumption on the Pullman trains of Great Northern and Great Central engines were ever made public. Records show that four out of the six 4-cylinder 4-6-0s were at various times engaged on these trains. The two of which I have not seen any report were 1164, *Earl Beatty*, and No 1169, *Lord Faringdon*. When it was first allocated to the Great Northern section, No 1167 bore the name *Lloyd George*, no doubt in honour of the wartime celebrity; but after a time the political implications of such a name in the stormy peacetime atmosphere led to its removal. When the

Pullman train was extended to Edinburgh in 1925, this engine, as plain 6167, in LNER colours, worked the inaugural down train.

A year earlier, the LNER had experimentally tried an extension of the Pullman train idea, with one from Kings Cross to Nottingham and Sheffield, recalling the working of the pre-war competitive 'flyers' by running via Grantham. The inaugural train at 11:05 am, which ran on June 2 1924, was hauled by a Great Northern 'Atlantic' but, like the Edinburgh train, it was frequently worked by Great Central engines. The inside cylinder 4-6-0, No 5425, *City of Manchester*, was frequently on the job and it was a strange experience, one Saturday morning when I was out on the line photographing at Hadley Wood, to catch in a ten-minute period two essentially Great Northern trains, coming past hauled by ex-Great Central engines, with the Edinburgh Pullman being hauled that day by the GCR 4-cylinder 4-6-0, *Valour*. The 'Director' class 4-4-0, No 5435, *Sir Clement Royds*, was also frequently on the the Sheffield Pullman. This train however was not a financial success and was soon withdrawn. So, until 1927, the only Great Central engines regularly working into Kings Cross were the 4-cylinder 4-6-0s.

In the meantime the 'Atlantics' themselves, displaced from some of the most important East Coast turns, were moving farther afield. A group of them were transferred to Sheffield, Darnall shed, and they were soon to be seen very far from their native haunts. Under the LNER renumbering scheme, they all had 3000 added to their original numbers, and by the end of 1925, engines 3272, 3280, 3285 and 4402 had been reported working on the Cheshire Lines Committee system on local trains, while 3254 ('Klondike'), 3277, 3295 and 4449 had been seen at Banbury working on through expresses to the Great Western line. The Sheffield 'Atlantics' also worked right through to Swindon on through trains to and from South Wales, and another interesting turn was the train carrying the Penzance–Aberdeen through carriages, non-stop between Sheffield and York. Although they were so different from their own engines the Great Northern 'Atlantics' became well-liked on the Great Central section. The one remaining 4-cylinder compound, No 3292, was stationed at Peterborough and worked on the East Lincolnshire line to Grimsby. She was scrapped in 1927.

The large-boilered 'Atlantics' that remained

on the Great Northern main line seemed to be in finer form than ever in the mid-1920s. This however was no more than an exciting prelude to the astonishing climax that broke upon the East Coast mainline railway scene from 1932 onwards, when those who knew the Great Northern 'Atlantics' in the years 1905–14 might well have rubbed their eyes in sheer disbelief at the feats of high speed and tremendous load haulage to which those of us who were travelling regularly from Kings Cross became accustomed. I am going to pass over some of the fine examples of running on the ordinary trains in the 1920s and draw attention more to the work of the London drivers on the Pullman trains, because the healthy rivalry that grew up between the Copley Hill men, with Great Central engines, and Top Shed, Kings Cross, with the 'Atlantics', established traditions of running and determination to surmount the effects of all signal and permanent-way checks en route that gave those beautiful trains a wonderful record of punctuality. Not only that, but it gave the traffic department sufficient confidence in the motive power to cut 10 minutes off the already sharp London–Leeds non-stop timing in the notable accelerations of 1932.

Before coming to details of actual running on the Pullman trains and comparisons of 'Atlantic' performance with that of their friendly Great Central rivals on the same trains, some reference must be made to the work of the Atlantics on the Great Central line itself. The Darnall engines used to take over haulage of the 6:20 pm express from Marylebone to Bradford at Leicester, but at that time in the evening there was an unbalanced working for a Leicester 'Atlantic' and it was customary to attach it as pilot to the Bradford train, so that on the sharply timed run from Leicester to Nottingham one usually had two 'Atlantics', one Great Central and one Great Northern, for a load of under 300 tons. On the difficult stretch north of Nottingham the Darnall engine was on its own. One evening when I was a passenger I was interested to see that our train engine from Leicester was to be the one-time Royal 'Atlantic', No 4442. In partnership with a Robinson 'Atlantic', No 6092, they hurtled a 290-ton train over the 23.4 undulating miles to Nottingham in 24 minutes. This was exciting enough to clock, but it did not demand much in the way of power output from two engines; things changed completely however at Nottingham when No 4442 was left to haul the 290-ton

train unaided over the hilly road to Sheffield.

It is really hard going for the first 10¾ miles out of Nottingham. Except for a respite of 1¼ miles at Bulwell Common, where the line is level for half a mile and then down at 1 in 330 for three-quarters, the gradient is 1 in 130–132 for the entire distance from the very start, through almost continuous tunnel to New Basford, right up to Kirkby South Junction. Once we came out into the open it sounded from the noise of the exhaust that the engine was going absolutely all out. We had then accelerated to 35 mph and, when we tore away to 53 mph on the Bulwell common breather, the noise was terrific; on the long, continuing ascent to Kirkby South Junction we settled down to a steady 45½ mph, which is equivalent to over 1,000 drawbar horsepower and a pull of about 50 per cent of the nominal tractive effort — a tremendous feat, taking us over that summit point in just 17 minutes from Nottingham (10.8 miles). But one could not continue thus on that part of the old Great Central main line. It ran through an intensely mined colliery area, which, incidentally, produced some of the finest locomotive coal, and there were places where speed had to be reduced, due to mining subsidence. Although we practically kept our booked running time to passing Staveley, 26.2 miles in 33 minutes, checks came thick and fast thereafter and we were 5 minutes late into Sheffield (38.2 miles) in 53 instead of 48 minutes.

On another occasion, I had a run behind another of these engines, No 3287, on the 10:09 pm from Sheffield to York, conveying the Penzance–Aberdeen through carriages and hauling, therefore, a total load of 335 tons behind the tender. The route followed was no speedway and in its first 12 miles it included more permanent speed restrictions, due to curves, than any other line in England over which important express trains ran. This section concluded with the extraordinary layout at Mexborough West Junction, where the speed limit was 5 mph! After that one got a mild 'spin' over the sharply undulating Swinton and Knottingley Joint line, with speeds varying between 50 and 70 mph. After joining the one-time York and North Midland line at Burton Salmon, the gradients are virtually level for the rest of the journey and, with time well in hand, we pottered along at between 53 and 61 mph to pass Copmanthorpe 43.1 miles from Sheffield in 55¾ minutes. After that there were signal checks running in to York.

Above *Cromer portion of the train due to arrive at Kings Cross at 4:30 pm, photographed near Stevenage in 1924, hauled by 'Klondike' No 256 (the tender is lettered in first post-Grouping style 'L & NER 256')* (Rail Archive Stephenson).

Below *The celebrated large 'Atlantic' No 4404 on the short-lived Sheffield Pullman arriving at Kings Cross in 1925* (Rail Archive Stephenson).

One of the most interesting runs I had with a Great Northern 'Atlantic' on the Great Central line came several years later, when I had the privilege of a footplate pass to ride the 9:35 am express from Sheffield to Leicester. I will not dwell upon the technicalities of driving and firing these remarkable engines at this stage, as it is more convenient to describe these, together with other footplate experiences, at some length in a later chapter; but the particular point about this run was that our engine was No 3276, which as GNR No 276 was involved in the unexplained smash at Grantham, in 1906. Because of the mystery surrounding it, she came to be regarded as an unlucky engine, at any rate on the GNR itself. When the question came of transferring some of these engines to the Great Central, it seemed that Doncaster took good care to include 276 among those to go! More about my ride on her, however, in a later chapter.

The year 1927 saw some important changes in the Pullman workings between Kings Cross, Leeds and Harrogate. During the summer service the Edinburgh train was re-routed, avoiding Leeds altogether and running non-stop between Kings Cross and Harrogate; and at about the same time the Great Central 4-cylinder 4-6-0s were taken off the job and replaced by 4-4-0s of the 'Improved Director' class. Whether this latter was a 'confession of failure' or of some engineering restriction on the line between Shaftholme Junction and Harrogate that precluded the use of such large and heavy engines I do not know; but so far as the lofty Crimple Viaduct was concerned there cannot have been any weight restriction there, because the North Eastern Area was frequently working the train north of Leeds with 'Pacifics'. I cannot however allow the Great Central 4-cylinder 4-6-0s to pass from the scene without a farewell gesture to engines that were friendly rivals and colleagues of the 'Atlantics' in inaugurating and running this prestige service in its first four years. So I have set out details of a typical run with the War Memorial engine, No 6165, *Valour*, when the load was one of six Pullman cars and two GNR-type bogie brake vans.

From the start, the big 4-6-0 got smartly away from Leeds and climbed the 1 in 100 to Ardsley at 30 mph; then, after slowing through Wakefield, they ran fast down the West Riding line and were getting ahead of time when a bad signal check came at Ranskill and this put the train a minute late by Retford.

LNER The 'Harrogate Pullman'

Load: 291 tons tare, 300 tons full
Engine (ex-GCR 4-6-0) No: 6165 *Valour*

Distance miles		Schedule min	Actual m s	Speed mph
0.0	LEEDS (CENTRAL)	0	0 00	
2.5	Beeston		5 55	45½
5.6	Ardsley		11 25	30
9.9	WAKEFIELD	19	16 55	slack
11.6	Sandal		19 30	49
15.4	Nostell		24 55	40
23.2	Hampole		32 40	74
29.8	DONCASTER	41	39 25	slack
34.5	Rossington		45 05	55½
36.3	*Pipers Wood*		47 15	50
—			signals	67 (max)
41.9	Ranskill		53 15	—
47.2	RETFORD	59	59 55	—
52.1	*Markham Box*		65 50	—
59.4	Carlton		72 30	77½
65.7	NEWARK	77	77 55	68
70.4	Claypole		82 30	60
76.1	Barkston		88 10	49
80.3	GRANTHAM	94	93 15	57½
85.7	*Stoke Box*		99 30	53½
97.2	Essendine		108 50	85
106.3	*Werrington Junction*		116.10	—
109.4	PETERBOROUGH	124	120 15	slack
116.4	Holme		128 20	68
122.3	Abbots Ripton		134 15	48
126.9	HUNTINGDON	143	139 10	66
—			signals	—
134.1	St Neots		147 15	—
141.7	Sandy		154 50	—
153.9	HITCHIN	170	168 20	—
157.2	Stevenage		172 45	47
168.1	HATFIELD	185	184 10	74
173.1	Potters Bar		189 15	—
180.8	Wood Green		196 15	—
183.2	Finsbury Park		198 50	—
185.8	KINGS CROSS	205	202 55	—
Net time, min			**199½**	

The recovery was not especially vigorous until after Grantham, when the 5½ mile climb to Stoke was taken at a minimum speed of 53½ mph and a high-speed run was made on the descent towards Peterborough, sustaining 85 mph around Essendine. In consequence, the train was nearly 4 minutes early on passing Peterborough and the effort had already begun to be eased down before the severe signal check at St Neots, which cost about 2½ minutes in running. The timing southwards from Huntingdon allowed some margin for recovery and no very substantial effort was needed to keep comfortably ahead of time for the rest of the journey. The performance showed an easy competence in doing the job. How the coal consumption of these engines compared with that of the 'Atlantics' was never made public and the only figures ever published for the latter engines, from the Newcastle-Edinburgh trials of 1923, did not exactly flatter the Doncaster design.

Four of the 'Director' class 4-4-0s were at times stationed at Copley Hill shed, from 1927 onwards, for working the Pullman trains. These were 5506, *Butler Henderson* 5507, *Gerard Powys Dewhurst*, 5510, *Princess Mary* and 5511, *Marne*. The last-mentioned engine, together with No 5507, 'opened the ball', so to speak, with the Harrogate–Kings Cross non-stop run in the summer service of 1927, while the Great Northern 'Atlantic' No 4404 worked on the alternate days from Kings Cross. Details are tabulated of a run with this latter engine, not long after the service was inaugurated. From the timekeeping point of view, it was unfortunate that the signal stop came when the easiest part of the journey was over. With a load of no more that 265 tons, it had been a simple matter to pass Doncaster nearly 3 minutes early, but the check cost at least 5 minutes and the driver had the job of trying to make up the lost time on a stretch of line beset by a rapid succession of permanent speed restrictions, due to curves and difficult

LNER 11:20 am Kings Cross–Harrogate Pullman non-stop express

Load: 7 cars, 256 tons tare, 265 tons full
Engine (GN 4-4-2) No: 4404

Distance miles		Schedule min	Actual m s	Speed mph
0.0	KINGS CROSS		0 00	—
2.6	Finsbury Park		6 30	—
12.7	Potters Bar		20 05	42½
17.7	HATFIELD		25 10	72½
31.9	HITCHIN		38 00	—
44.1	Sandy		49 20	76½/66
58.9	HUNTINGDON		62 20	75
—			—	57/80½
76.4	PETERBOROUGH		78 35	slack
—			—	64/45
105.5	GRANTHAM		111 05	easy
120.1	NEWARK		124 35	—
138.6	RETFORD		143 55	—
156.0	DONCASTER	165	162 10	—
160.2	*Shaftholme Junction*		167 10	30*
—			signal stop 2½ min	
170.7	Knottingley		187 25	25*
173.8	Burton Salmon		192 10	35*
179.7	Church Fenton		199 55	65/25*
184.4	Tadcaster		206 25	60/66
193.8	Spofforth		216 10	33/26
198.8	HARROGATE	223	224 05	—
Net time, min			219	

*Speed restrictions

The ex-Great Central 4-cylinder 4-6-0, No 6167, on the up Harrogate Pullman near Potters Bar (C. Laundy).

junction layouts. The slacks permitted no more than a brief spurt up to 65 mph between Burton Salmon and Church Fenton, where the rising gradients begin. Although the train was doing 66 mph before Spofforth, the final 5 miles at 1 in 86–91 are a 'killer' and speed had fallen to 33 mph by Crimple Tunnel and finally to 26 mph before steam was shut off for Harrogate.

The ex-Great Central 'Director' class 4-4-0s stayed on the Pullman jobs for about four years. Again one would dearly have liked to know how their running costs compared with those of the Great Northern 'Atlantics'; but the fact that they were eventually taken off and 'Atlantics' stationed at Copley Hill in their place suggests that the latter engines had withstood the challenge. In the latter years of the Great Central sojourn on these trains, I made a number of journeys, but on the days I was able to travel I always found a Great Northern engine on the job. Those who, like R.A.H. Weight, kept a close watch on nearly all happenings on the East Coast main line did not note any occasion of sensational recovery of lost time such as were sometimes reported with Great Northern 'Atlantics'; though, as I saw myself in later years, the Copley Hill men in the Pullman link were not averse to really hard running, when occasion demanded it. So far as Kings Cross was concerned, due to Weight and his coterie of fellow recorders, the Pullman men got perhaps more than their fair share of the locomotive running limelight and the names of Drivers Barnes, Rumble and Topliss became familiar to readers of railway literature. The best known of them all at that time was W. Sparshatt, who was something of an exhibitionist and often ran unnecessarily hard. Like others of his kind elsewhere, he was not popular with his fellow workers.

So far as the Great Central engines were concerned, Cecil J. Allen logged a good run with No 5511, Marne, on the Harrogate–London non-stop in the summer of 1927, when it was carrying the minimum load of six Pullmans. The times and speeds are set out in the accompanying table. The sharply falling gradients from Harrogate made possible a rapid start, though even before Tadcaster the curves in the line precluded any really high speed and afterwards there came a succession of severe speed restrictions. It was clear that the booked point-to-point times provided for their careful observation, but even with this it will be seen that the train was already 4¾ minutes early when it passed on to the East

Coast main line at Shaftholme Junction. Time gaining continued, though without any running of special distinction, and it was, perhaps, to be expected that the train was stopped dead by signal at Newark, which would otherwise have been passed more than seven minutes early. The recovery was not particularly fast for a train of this moderate weight, taking all but 20 minutes for the 14.6 miles from Newark to Grantham. Then came a good spin down the bank from Stoke, with a maximum speed of 83½ mph, which was cut short by the permanent-way slowing at Helpston.

Having regard to there being another

LNER Harrogate & Edinburgh Pullman

Load: 6 cars, 248 tons tare, 255 tons full
Engine (ex-GCR 4-4-0) No: 5511 Marne

Distance miles		Schedule min	Actual m s	Speed mph
0.0	HARROGATE	0	0 00	—
5.0	Spofforth		6 50	70½
8.0	*Wetherby South Junction*	11	9 40	55/69
14.4	Tadcaster		15 25	40*
19.1	Church Fenton	25	21 20	35*
25.0	Burton Salmon	32	28 40	30*
28.1	Knottingley	36	34 00	30*
32.2	Womersley		39 10	64
38.6	*Shaftholme Junction*	50	45 20	45*
42.8	DONCASTER	55	50 10	61½
51.1	Bawtry		58 45	52/68
60.2	RETFORD	74	67 25	—
65.1	*Markham Box*		72 50	49½
71.4	Crow Park		78 35	76½
78.7	NEWARK	93	86 10	signal
—			86 40	stop
93.3	GRANTHAM	109	106 35	52½
98.7	*Stoke Box*		113 35	41½
110.2	Essendine		123 30	83½
—			pws	—
122.4	PETERBOROUGH	139	136 10	—
129.4	Holme		145 00	61½
135.3	Abbots Ripton		151 30	46½
139.9	HUNTINGDON	158	156 20	71½
147.1	St Neots		163 10	54
154.7	Sandy		170 45	65
—			pws	—
166.9	HITCHIN	185	183 45	30
170.2	Stevenage		188 45	40
181.1	HATFIELD	200	200 20	71½
186.1	Potters Bar		205 25	57½
—			signals	—
196.2	Finsbury Park		217 00	—
—			signals	
198.8	KINGS CROSS	220	221 20	
	Net time, min		210½	

*Speed restrictions

permanent-way slowing to come, in an awkward location on the long bank leading to Stevenage, the running from Peterborough southwards was not very vigorous and, in fact, a minute was lost between there and Huntingdon; with the effect of the slack itself, the train was barely on time on passing Hatfield. With a clear road, there would have been no difficulty in reaching Kings Cross on time, or a little too early but, due to signal checks, the arrival was 1¼ minutes late. It would be unfair to hold this up as a poor comparison between the capabilities of the 'Directors' and the GN 'Atlantics', because I know from experience on their own line that the Great Central engines can do very much better; but south of Peterborough this was not one of their best performances.

An interesting addition to the Pullman link at Kings Cross in 1927 was the booster-fitted 4419, after her experimental working in the North. I remember talking to one of the drivers I knew well and he told me she was a good engine, albeit something of a rough rider. Judging by the standards of many other locomotive designs *all* the Great Northern 'Atlantics' might well be judged as rough riding and from men having a lifelong experience of this, for one of them to be specifically described as 'rough' must have signified something especially wild! This same driver told me that Mr Gresley had said she must be in the Pullman link; but knowing a little of the

workings of that small headquarters staff in the building at Kings Cross station, from one a little further down the ladder, I would guess that it was not Gresley but Bulleid, then his personal assistant, who made the stipulation. After a time No 4419 was running with the booster gear disconnected, though at least one early photograph of her climbing Holloway bank with one of the Pullman trains shows the booster in action.

Another event of 1927 was the conversion of the last of the large-boilered 'Atlantics' as yet non-superheated; this was No 4443, which until her conversion had been stationed at Darnall shed, Sheffield. Like very many of the class she retained her original cylinder and balanced slide valves after she was superheated. So far as the modernisation of the whole stud was concerned, while many of them retained their slide valves to the end, eventually all of them had 32-element superheaters. In this connection there might be a point of confusion arising from the series of line diagrams with leading dimensions published serially in *The Railway Gazette* during the early part of 1937 and republished subsequently in booklet form. In this series the boiler dimensions related to the 24-element Robinson superheaters first applied to these engines in 1914, and with which many were afterwards fitted. By the time those articles were published most, if not all, of them had 32-element Robinson superheaters.

Large 'Atlantics' on the GCR section: No 3295 leaving Nottingham Victoria with a Southampton–Glasgow train (Great Western coaches) (Rail Archive Stephenson).

Chapter 9

Indian summer—'Atlantics' to the rescue

The early months of the year 1930 did not give promise of any very enterprising developments in the British locomotive world. The great depression that had struck so viciously at the economy and general livelihood of the USA was then settling upon Europe, and when the time came, in October of the year, for *The Railway Magazine* to issue its 400th number, the veteran Editor, J.F. Gairns, in the measured phraseology of the day had to confess that 'The railway outlook, as a whole, is by no means favourable, and No 400 appears at a time when the situation is most seriously depressing'. One could well imagine that a modern feature writer would have expressed it in far terser language. This may seem a strange opening to a chapter that I have entitled 'Indian Summer', yet that year saw the raising of the curtain on a series of events in express-train running that put the Great Northern 'Atlantics' in a class by themselves. In setting on record the stories of outstanding achievement that are contained in this and the succeeding chapter, I have not followed strict chronological order, but rather grouped them according to like circumstances.

That otherwise dismal year, 1930, gave me my first experiences of the Pullman trains. Although at that time my parents were still living in Barrow-in-Furness, four-day breaks at each Bank Holiday weekend gave a chance to go north, with variations of route from London each time. The 'Queen of Scots' Pullman, as it had then been named, was not the most convenient of trains to fit in on my return journey. It then left Leeds at 4:10 pm and to catch it meant leaving home on the first train in the morning — a train which incidentally would have got me to Euston by 4:15 pm — and making a somewhat halting journey across country from Carnforth. That rather dull prelude however brought a rich reward later, for not only did we have a load of eight of the latest all-steel Pullmans, with a tare weight of 318 tons and, with every third class seat taken, at least 335 tons full, but with a late start of 5 minutes, 5 minutes further lost by checks on the way, we sailed into Kings Cross 5 minutes early, with a net time of 190

minutes for the run of 185.8 miles. The engine was No 4444 and the driver the fiery Sparshatt.

Later that year, after a holiday in Scotland, I arranged my return south so as to travel by the Harrogate Sunday Pullman, which then ran to the same schedule as the 'Queen of Scots'; at the end of the summer tourist season it was also carrying a maximum load. I was hoping that we might have a Great Central engine, but another of the Kings Cross stalwarts was on the job, No 4450, with the famous driver, J. Rumble. Three years earlier he had made quite a name for himself in working the train for *nineteen weeks* continuously, north from Kings Cross one day and back the next, entirely on 'Atlantics'. In the earlier part of my own journey behind him, although leaving Leeds on time his running was at first even faster than Sparshatt's. But after experiencing a slight permanent-way check to 35 mph through Grantham and passing that station 4½ minutes early, he began to ease down, albeit touching 85 mph on the descent from Stoke. After Peterborough the pace became so leisurely that we were no more than exactly on time, to the very second, on passing Hitchin, though the driver put on a good concluding spurt from there and finished nicely ahead of time. This included one flash of real brilliance, with a top speed of 79 mph before Hatfield and a minimum of 63½ mph over Potters Bar summit. More details of these two fine runs are included in a summary of all my seven runs on the Pullman trains with 'Atlantics' later in this book.

In the spring of 1932, despite the continuing depression, came a welcome acceleration of Anglo-Scottish services by both East and West Coast routes; the previous work of the Great Northern 'Atlantics' gave the operating authorities confidence enough to cut 10 minutes from the already fast timing of the 'Queen of Scots' Pullman between Kings Cross and Leeds. But my first journey by one of the ordinary accelerated trains, the 1:20 pm Scotsman from Kings Cross brought an unexpected experience. We had taken a heavy train of 497 tons tare out of London and, after making a normal start out to Hatfield, passing

Top *Deputising for a Pacific: No 4436 on the 'crack' 5:30 pm Newcastle express, just out of Hadley North tunnel in the early 1930s* (Rail Archive Stephenson).

Above *On the GCR section: No 3286 passing Bagthorpe Junction, Nottingham, with the empty stock for a return 'race special' from Nottingham to Kings Cross* (Rail Archive Stephenson).

that station in 24¾ minutes, our 'A3' 'Pacific' put on a tremendous spurt, averaging 73.5 mph throughout the 57.3 miles from Hatfield to Fletton Junction and passing Peterborough 7 minutes early. Things were justifiably taken easily on the climb to Stoke, and Grantham was reached in 111½ minutes, 2½ minutes early. Then we started away again and made good speed on the descent to the Trent valley, until nearing Newark, where we slowed down and came to a dead stop ¼ mile south of the station — with all signals off. Looking ahead I was surprised to see our 'Pacific' being un-

coupled and then backed into a nearby siding. An 'Atlantic' was standing alongside and to this, after certain representations, our driver and fireman transferred, and so, with No 4422 instead of a Pacific, we set off for York, still with a modest 530 tons full behind the tender.

Between that time and 1938 there were three further instances on which 'Pacific' drivers had to give up their own engines, on this self-same train, all with hot middle big-ends; but this first instance was the most difficult of all for the driver and fireman. On the other three occasions the impending failure of the 'Pacific' was discerned before Grantham. At that time the East Coast main line had a fairly lavish provision of standing pilots. That on the up side at Hitchin has been mentioned earlier in this book; Peterborough and Grantham had one for each direction and the North Eastern had similar provision for both directions at Darlington and Tweedmouth Junction. The pilots in both Southern and North Eastern Areas were 'Atlantics' in good condition and, if not necessarily ready for an immediate maximum effort, it was not long before they could be appropriately worked up. But with No 4422, which was commandeered at a moment's notice, it was far otherwise. She was taken off a slow, lightly loaded train, in no way prepared for such a task. Until the accelerations of 1932, one was inclined to take the schedule of the pre-war 2:20 pm from Kings Cross as a basis for comparison where running of the day Anglo-Scottish expresses were concerned, with its 97-minute timing from Grantham to York, and it certainly makes a good basis in this case.

The 2:20 pm Scotsman was allowed 80 minutes for the 68.1 miles from Newark to York; but this was from a 'flying' start, passing Newark at between 65 and 70 mph, and covering the next 6.3 level miles to Carlton in about 6 minutes. Our driver and fireman did extremely well to work this 'scratch' engine up to 57½ mph in this distance, with such a load as 530 tons, and the great merit of what they did afterwards can be assessed by a comparison with the pre-war schedule, from a zero at Carlton, assuming that as usual the 2:20 would pass there in about 23 minutes from Grantham.

Above *The up Newcastle express on Langley Junction troughs, hauled by No 3300* (Rail Archive Stephenson).

Below *Two large 'Atlantics', No 4445 and 4418, on the summer 11:40 am Scottish express approaching Hadley South tunnel* (Rail Archive Stephenson).

Distance miles		2:20 pm Schedule min	Actual m s
0.0	Carlton (pass)	0	0 00
12.2	Retford	16	15 23
29.6	Doncaster	35	33 28
33.8	Shaftholme	40	38 13
—			signals
48.0	Selby	56	55 48
61.8	York (arr)	74	76 28

Thus, until the signal check at Selby, which cost about 1½ minutes in running they were not only keeping but improving upon the pre-war schedule, with a load that would have been unheard of at that time. Not only this but, from the dead start in Newark yard, they covered just over 50 miles in the first hour, having passed Templehirst, the last station before Selby, in 59¾ minutes. The average speed over the 43.4 miles from Carlton to Templehirst was 53.3 mph with sustained speeds of 57 mph on level track. At York, the North Eastern Area had a 'Pacific' waiting to take over; but she did very poorly losing 7¼ minutes to Darlington, without any checks, and a further 3¾ minutes to Newcastle. This was a sad anticlimax to what had gone before.

It is disturbing to think that the second instance of this kind, which took place two years later, might have remained unknown, although it was far more spectacular — brilliantly so in fact. The circumstances were these. The run was recorded in meticulous detail by my friend and fellow graduate at Imperial College, Mr A.F. Webber, then well established as a consulting engineer in Birmingham and having close connections with the steel industry. He was travelling from Kings Cross to Darlington, en route for Tees-side, when the 'Pacific' on the 1:20 Scotsman failed and was replaced by the down-side pilot at Grantham. Thrilled beyond measure at the run that followed, he sent full details to Cecil J. Allen, but was rather surprised that not the slightest reference was made to it in *The Railway Magazine*. Allen apparently just did not believe it! I can quite imagine his reluctance to publish something of so exceptional a nature and I remember only too well an occasion, in more recent times, after I myself had become author of the 'Locomotive Practice and Performance' feature in *The Railway Magazine*, when I was sent details of a run of an apparently exceptional nature which on further investigation proved to be entirely fictitious! But, coming from a man of Webber's status as an engineer, one might have thought that it would have been worth Allen's while to ask his colleagues on the LNER to refer to the guard's journal, when the authenticity would have been shown beyond any doubt.

As it was, the news of one of the most epoch-making of Great Northern 'Atlantic' achievements lay in 'cold storage' for another two years, until Allen himself had a closely similar experience, in identical circumstances. Even then it was only coincidence that brought the earlier epic to light. Allen, like Webber two years earlier, had been bound for Tees-side, and that very night, in the course of steel-industry business, Webber himself was at the Zetland Hotel in Saltburn. There he noticed someone, whom he recognised as Allen, dining with the General Manager of the Skinningrove Iron Works. After dinner he made himself known as a fellow locomotive enthusiast and, somewhat naturally, Allen could talk of nothing else but the run he had experienced from Grantham to York that very afternoon. Waiting for a pause in his flow of enthusiasm, Webber reminded Allen of the run he himself had enjoyed two years earlier and of which complete details had been sent. Apparently it took a little time for Allen to acknowledge that he had ever received the log and the relevant details; but then he passed it to one side remarking, 'Quite honestly, I didn't believe it'. Even then, to Webber's great disappointment it was only Allen's own run that was published in *The Railway Magazine*. I saw Webber a short time afterwards and he gave me the full details; but it was not until many years later that, in my book *The Great Northern Railway*, I was able to set the two runs alongside in tabular form.

As if this were not enough, there was a fourth instance in 1938 when closely similar times were made. The only difference in the three 'Atlantic' runs through from Grantham to York was in the manning. At the time of the 1932 accelerations, a link of eight senior drivers was set up at Kings Cross to work double-home turns to Newcastle. There were three of these daily, on the 10:00 am, 1:20 pm and 5:30 pm expresses, and they were balanced by reciprocal workings from Tyne-side sheds, one from Heaton and two from Gateshead. The particular circumstance of Allen's run in 1936 was that the driver, Walker by name, was a Gateshead man and had never previously been on a Great Northern 'Atlantic'. The other three runs, mine from Newark in 1932, Webber's, in 1934, and the third, which was not logged in detail, were all made by Kings Cross top link-men, all of whom had grown up with 'Atlantics'. The three runs from Grantham to York were:

Year	Engine No	Driver	Load tons full	Time to York Actual min	Time to York Net min
1934	4415	Samwells	545	87	87
1936	4404	Walker	585	87¾	86½
1938	3285	Peachey	540	89	86

Engine No 4404, maker of the historic run with the 585-ton 1:20 pm 'Scotsman' from Grantham to York (Rail Archive Stephenson).

The schedule time was then 90 minutes. Moreover, all three Great Northern engines and their crews continued to Newcastle, though in each case the North Eastern Area, warned in advance, had pilot engines waiting to couple on ahead, at York.

The superlative performance put up by the 'Atlantic' engines, 4415 and 4404, is set out in the table on page 111. Details of the run with No 3285 are not available, but from the overall result it is clearly evident that its quality was equal in every way. According to earlier records, the engines 3285, 4415 and the one involved on my own run from Newark, 4422, had their original cylinders and slide valves, though whether the front ends had been renewed at the time of these memorable exploits I cannot say. Certain it is, however, that all of them by that time had 32-element superheaters, which seemed the principal factor in making such outstanding work possible. If one turns back in this book to details of earlier runs from Grantham to York, it can well be understood how a traveller with the vast experience of Cecil J. Allen found a run like that of No 4415 utterly unbelievable, especially with such a huge load as 545 tons. It naturally took time to get under way but, once on to the falling gradients from Peascliffe Tunnel to the Trent Valley, speed was soon into the 70s and, assured that the engine was sound in limb as well as wind.

Driver Samwells and his fireman really began to pile it on! The minimum speed of 53 mph at Markham summit suggests little less than absolutely 'all-out' driving and to reach 'even time' from the start as early as Bawtry and to pass Doncaster in 49 min 34 sec, could well have seemed incredible feats to anyone used to normal East Coast running in the heyday of the 'Atlantics'.

In the meantime, reference to the tabulated details will show that the North Eastern driver on engine No 4404 was doing very nearly as well with a tremendous load of 585 tons. He fell behind a little from Newark and on the climb to Markham, but even so a minimum speed of 48 mph was phenomenal by earlier standards. It may well be asked how a strange driver could have coaxed such work out of the engine? I think the answer is that those engines were among the easiest of any to drive. In the following chapter I shall have a good deal to say about footplate working and I shall give examples of how differing methods gave equally brilliant results; I came to the conclusion that it did not really matter how you set the reversing lever. Although the closely toothed notches on the quadrant and the catch block would allow of a fine adjustment, nothing of the kind seemed necessary, and I have seen one of them driven for 150 miles of high-speed work with the cut-off unchanged at 50 per cent. As to the fireman's side they were marvellous steamers and no doubt the Grantham pilots would be well supplied with first-class Nottinghamshire coal.

There is no doubt that Walker was going all out from Markham, passing Retford at 77½ mph and then, on little easier than level track, going on through Ranskill and Scrooby at 74–75 mph. He had caught up a little on the London driver by this time, but from Doncaster onwards both trains did some very level pegging, at magnificent speed, over the dead-level stretches towards Selby. The average speeds over the 17 miles from Doncaster to Brayton Junction, near which steam is shut off in readiness for the Selby speed restrictions, were 62 mph in each case. The North Eastern driver went the faster through Selby and recovered more rapidly afterwards, so that he had taken the lead by Naburn. The concluding check on this occasion was not severe and did not prevent an overall time 2¼ minutes inside schedule. The North Eastern Area had a 3-cylinder 4-4-0 of the 'Hunt' class waiting to pilot the train on the first occasion and, on the second, a veteran NER 2-cylinder 'Atlantic' of Class V. Although time regaining continued, the Great Northern engines were of course by then hauling no more than half the load.

Before coming to a detailed analysis of the very important technical features of these two runs, which would undoubtedly apply equally to that of engine No 3285 in 1938, there are two other instances that came to my notice of 'Atlantics' coming to the rescue. The first came on September 4 1936, when the streamlined 'A4' 'Pacific', No 2510, *Quicksilver*, hauling the up 'Silver Jubilee' express ran hot and had to come off the train at York. The driver was Samwells, of Kings Cross shed, he who had made the remarkable run from Grantham to York with the 'Atlantic' engine

No 4415 two years earlier. The up-side station pilot at York on that day was a 3-cylinder 'Z' class 'Atlantic' that had been fitted with rotary-cam poppet-valve gear and to this Samwells and his fireman transferred. Unlike the GN 'Atlantics', this engine was not an easy one for a stranger to drive and Samwells, after experimenting with various positions of the reverser, gave up and stopped at Doncaster in the hopes of getting a 'Pacific'. No such engine was available, and they got instead a GN 'Atlantic', actually No 4452, the first of the Ivatt superheater engines of 1910, though by now fitted with a new boiler and 32-element superheater. This engine also had 20-inch cylinders and piston valves.

They had the standard 'Silver Jubilee' 7-car train of 220 tons, about 235 tons full, and the following details are compiled from examination of the guard's journal. Judging from the relatively slow start, probably due to the engine having no more than a light head of steam when suddenly called upon for such an important duty, the fire had to be built up, and it took 19 minutes to cover the first 17.4 miles to Retford; but after that there was some grand running, as will be appreciated from the tabular summary below.

To drop only 5½ minutes on the schedule of the 'Silver Jubilee' between Retford and Hatfield was a fine piece of work.

The next 'rescue operation' was on the down 'Flying Scotsman', of all trains. I was travelling on a Saturday on heavy traffic when we took a load of 545 tons out of Kings Cross with one of the three Gresley 'Pacifics' stationed at Heaton shed. From the very start we seemed to be limping and very soon there developed every sign that the engine was not steaming well. After a laborious climb to Potters Bar, we made no appreciable speed on the faster stretches and eventually we staggered to a stop in Peterborough station in

Distance	Schedule	Actual	Average speed	
miles	min	min	Schedule	Actual
0.0 Doncaster	0	0	—	—
17.4 Retford	14	19	74.6	44.1
35.9 Newark	29	34½	74.0	71.6
50.5 Grantham	41	47	73.0	70.2
79.6 Peterborough	64½	71	74.1	72.7
97.1 Huntingdon	79½	88	69.9	61.7
124.1 Hitchin	100½	110	77.1	73.6
138.3 Hatfield	111½	122	77.3	71.1
156.0 Kings Cross	127½	139	66.4	62.5

Booked average speed Retford–Hatfield 74.4 mph
Actual average speed Retford–Hatfield 70.2 mph

93 min 35 sec, from Kings Cross. In quick time the standing down-side pilot, 'Atlantic', No 4407, coupled on ahead and we set off again, now 20 minutes late. Not being on the footplate of either engine, I cannot say how much of that big load was being taken by the pilot, though from its efforts down from Kings Cross it did not seem as though the 'Pacific' was good for much at all — *Dick Turpin* of all engines; not one of its best rides to York! With No 4407 to assist, however, we were soon making splendid time. From 61 mph as early as Werrington Junction, we averaged over 60 right up to Stoke summit, reaching a maximum of 68½ mph at Tallington, and not anywhere falling below 54½ mph. If one credits No 4407 with no more than half the load, say 275 tons, she was putting in the shade all pre-war standards of running, to say nothing of doing so from what could be called an impromptu start. The 'Flying Scotsman' was then allowed 34 minutes from passing Peterborough to the stop at Grantham; we took 31¾ minutes start to stop.

From Grantham however real record-breaking began. So rapid was our progress that I have set out the details in tabular form (see page 110). Compared to the 97-minute schedule of the pre-war 2:20 pm, the 'Scotsman' of 1937 was a tremendous flyer, allowed no more than 83 minutes and these two engines drew in to a signal stop at the York ticket platform, 81.9 miles, in no more than 74 min 55 sec. The effort was sustained without a break from start to finish, with an average speed of exactly 70 mph over the 63.3 miles from Barkston to Brayton Junction. Then again there was a most vigorous recovery from the Selby slack to the unusual maximum of 72½ mph at Naburn. All this was nevertheless to no avail, for York was in the usual state of traffic confusion that prevailed at busy weekends before the installation of colour-light signalling and we stood for a solid 9 minutes at the ticket platform before there was a line clear for us to enter the station. The 'Atlantic' No 4407 had not

enough coal to go further and had to couple off, and no fresh help was available for poor old *Dick Turpin* and his crew. They had to struggle on as best they could and we were about 40 minutes late into Newcastle.

Lest this saga of rescue operations gives the impression it was only the Gresley Pacifics that failed in those days of more than 50 years ago, I must tell the story of 'Atlantic' No 4420 on the 6:21 pm from Sheffield to Leicester one evening when I was a passenger. It was the 5:00 pm from Bradford Exchange to Marylebone, at that time always brought into Sheffield by a rebuilt 4-cylinder 4-6-0 of the Lancashire and Yorkshire type. The ex-GNR engine took over a load of 285 tons and started briskly enough, but before we got to Staveley she was dragging her feet, and it then took us 25 minutes to struggle up the 10 miles to Tibshelf. Eventually, having taken 67½ minutes to cover the 38¼ miles from Sheffield to Nottingham, No 4420 gave up the ghost and was replaced by an early Robinson 4-4-0, which proceeded to lose more time on to Leicester. When next I travelled by that train, however, engine No 4456 fully redeemed the reputation of the 'Atlantics' and gave me an excellent run.

In concluding this chapter, I must turn now to an analysis of those two remarkable runs from Grantham to York, continuing with the 1:20 pm Scotsman. I am taking the stretch of line between Newark and Brayton Junction (Selby) for examination, because this is, in the aggregate, dead level. The rise from Crow Park to Markham Box is balanced by the succeeding descent to Retford, and it is the same with the 'hump' that begins just north of Scrooby troughs and flattens out to dead level again before Black Carr Junction. The descents can be taken at full speed and the slight easings sometimes made through Retford, Doncaster, and over the facing junction at Shaftholme are of no consequence. On these occasions, it seemed, the drivers took them with hardly any slackening at all. I have divided the section of line under examination into three and, for the first, a small allowance

Engine No:		4415			4404	
Load, tons full:	Average speed mph	540	DHP	Average speed mph	585	DHP
Newark-Black Carr Junction						
(33.1 miles)	66.8		953	63.6		922
Shaftholme Junction-Brayton						
(12.8 miles)	62.8		825	63.6		922
Crow Park-Brayton (45.6 miles)	64.0		876	63.2		910

Above *A celebrated Kings Cross Pullman engine, No 4444, here seen on the 5:35 pm Hull express near Potters Bar* (Rail Archive Stephenson).

Below *The 1:15 pm 'Scotsman', 'Atlantic'-hauled from Kings Cross, here seen passing Wood Green hauled by No 4409* (Rail Archive Stephenson).

must be made for the trains still having a little impetus from the downhill run from Peascliff Tunnel.

It is when these results are compared to the nominal tractive efforts of the engines and then to the work of other British Locomotives that the outstanding nature of these performances are revealed. Taking three of the above results, further analysis works out as follows:

Speed mph	Drawbar hp	Drawbar pull lb	Percent of nom TE
62.8	825	4,930	28.4
63.6	922	5,340	31.4
66.8	953	5,340	30.8

After nationalisation, tests were made, on one or other of the stationary plants and with dynamometer cars in strictly controlled conditions, to determine the maximum output of certain pre-nationalisation designs. The aim was not to register high transitory efforts, but what could be sustained for half an hour or more. Now these Great Northern 'Atlantic' runs were nothing if not sustained efforts and with them must also be bracketed the run of engine No 3285, when the performance must

have been fully comparable to enable such an overall time to be made. To complete the comparison I am anticipating the results from yet another remarkable run to be described in the next chapter, which included some high power outputs at lower speed. Thus, ordinary service performance of engines 4404, 4415 and, from the next chapter, 4456, stand against the all-out test results of a Gresley 'V2' 2-6-2 and a Great Western 'King'.

Ratio of drawbar pull to nominal tractive effort

Speed mph	40	55	60	65
LNER 'V2' 2-6-2	43.0	29.7	26.7	23.8
GWR 'King' 4-6-0	42.2	27.8	24.3	21.2
GNR 'Atlantic'	60.0	38.0	34.0	31.0

The reader may well question how it was that an engine design that originated in 1902 and was developed to finality in 1919, by the incorporation of a 32-element superheater, could show such results. In the next chapter, with the aid of some most enlightening footplate experience I hope, in all modesty, to offer an explanation.

LNER Grantham–York, 'The Flying Scotsman'

Load: 16 coaches 509 tons tare, 545 tons full
Engines: (GN 4-4-2) No 4407 and (4-6-2) No 2579, partly disabled

Distance miles		Schedule min	Actual m s	Speed mph
0.0	GRANTHAM	0	0 00	—
4.2	Barkston		6 00	70½
6.0	Hougham		7 30	77
9.9	Claypole		10 29	81/75
14.6	NEWARK	15	14 12	78
21.9	Crow Park		20 15	72
26.4	Tuxford		24 28	58½/60
28.2	Markham Box		26 18	57½
33.1	RETFORD	33	30 33	77½/70
36.2	Sutton		33 10	74
38.4	Ranskill		34 57	75
40.3	Scrooby		36 28	75
44.0	Milepost 149½		39 43	62
47.7	Black Carr Junction		42 52	80½
50.5	DONCASTER	49	45 23	64
54.7	Shaftholme Junction		49 07	69
57.5	Moss		51 32	70½
60.5	Balne		54 05	67½
64.3	Templehirst		57 24	72½
67.5	Brayton Junction		60 05	75
68.9	SELBY	67	61 40	30*
73.0	Riccall		66 29	63½
78.5	Naburn		71 19	72½
80.7	Chaloners Whin Junction		73 14	—
81.9	Ticket platform (signal stop)		74 55	—
			83 55	
82.7	YORK	83	85 47	

*Speed restriction

In 1938, No 4446 having taken over the up 'Silver Jubilee' streamliner, in the snow near Potters Bar (E.R. Wethersett).

LNER Grantham–York

	Engine:			4415		4404	
	Driver:			Samwells		Walker	
	Coaches:			16		17	
	Load, tons tare/full			506/545		546/585	

Distance miles		Schedule min	Actual m s	Speed mph	Actual m s	Speed mph
0.0	GRANTHAM	0	0 00		0 00	
4.2	Barkston		8 22	61	8 17	—
6.0	Hougham		10 05	71	10 03	—
9.9	Claypole		13 22	74	13 23	74
14.6	NEWARK	15	17 13	68/73	17 23	—
21.9	Crow Park		23 18	—	24 19	64
25.8	Dukeries Junction		27 01	57½	28 30	48
28.2	*Markham Box*		29 41	53	31 31	48½
33.1	RETFORD	35	34 16	72½	36 15	77½
36.2	Sutton		36 56	69	38 49	72½
38.4	Ranskill		38 52	71½	40 37	74
40.3	Scrooby		40 26	72	42 08	75
42.2	Bawtry		42 04	—	43 43	—
44.0	*Milepost 149½*		43 44	67	45 22	61
47.7	*Black Carr Junction*		46 56	70½	48 38	72½
50.5	DONCASTER	53	49 34	59½	51 19	55
54.7	*Shaftholme Junction*		—		55 36	62½
57.5	Moss		56 34	64	58 15	64
60.5	Balne		59 23	—	61 02	60
64.3	Templehirst		63 03	65	64 42	66
67.5	*Brayton Junction*		66 04	—	67 41	—
68.9	SELBY	73	67 35	24*	69 17	30*
73.0	Riccall		75 08	50	75 18	55
78.5	Naburn		81 11	58	80 56	60
80.7	*Chaloners Whin Junction*		83 33	—	83 09	—
—			—	—	signals	
82.7	YORK	90	86 56		87 40	

*Speed restrictions

Chapter 10

The Pullman links—footplate work

While occasional opportunities to burst briefly into fame, like the remarkable occasions highlighted in the previous chapter, showed the continuing potentialities of the large-boilered 'Atlantics', even to as late as 1938, it was the accumulated record of the five years, from the May accelerations of 1932 to 1937, in working the Pullman trains that will for ever remain a lasting memorial to these engines in the history of steam-locomotive operation in this country. But, although a most brilliant climax, it was also a culmination of their long innings as main-line motive power units. Although for ten years, from 1922, they had been supplanted as the top line express-passenger locomotives of the East Coast route, one could not describe the schedules of the Pullman trains as requiring anything less than the highest quality of locomotive work, relating the speed to the tonnage hauled and the tractive power available. It is true that after the withdrawal of the ex-Great Central engines from those turns worked by Copley Hill shed, the Pullman trains required the services of only four 'Atlantics' daily, out of a total stud of 91 of the large-boilered variety, but so much of the running was of so spectacular a character as to symbolise the work of the class as a whole.

It was not age, nor deterioration in their mechanical quality that led to their removal from the Pullman trains in 1937. For some time, since the large-scale introduction of the new Stanier locomotives all over the LMS system, there had been a relentless drive on all British railways generally to get increased monthly mileage out of all the main-line passenger and mixed-traffic engines, and complicated rosters had been worked out, involving multiple manning that sometimes extended to locomotives being worked by six or seven crews in the course of a single journey. On paper the results were spectacular, but unfortunately the servicing arrangements did not everywhere match the ingenuity of the diagramming and engine failures occurred. The principle was nevertheless accepted to some extent on the LNER, particularly with respect to the 'Pacifics' on the East Coast route, and some elaborate new diagrams were

worked out. With considerably increased mileages being worked by individual engines, sheds like Doncaster and Grantham found they had more 'Pacifics' than they needed, and two of the Doncaster engines were transferred to Copley Hill for the Pullman trains. I had my first trip behind one of them in April 1937 and, to the honoured memory of the 'Atlantics', it was only for a few minutes south of Retford that a close observer of the running would have discerned that a locomotive of far greater tractive power was at the head of the train.

So, now, to a survey and statistical analysis of my own personal experience of 'Atlantic' running on the Pullman trains. These consisted of eight non-stop runs from Leeds to Kings Cross; three on the Harrogate Sunday Pullman; one on the 'Queen of Scots' before its acceleration; and four on the 'Queen of Scots', scheduled 195 minutes for the run. Of my two down journeys, one was on the 'West Riding Pullman', stopping intermediately at Wakefield and one on the 'Queen of Scots'. So far as the up journeys were concerned, except for my first on the Sunday train, on which we had a punctual start from Leeds and very few incidental delays, the running on the 205-minute schedule was usually indistinguishable in its vigour and efficiency from that required by the 195-minute schedule of the 'Queen of Scots' from May 1932. Frequently in his long authorship of the 'Locomotive Practice and Performance' feature in *The Railway Magazine*, Cecil J. Allen would present a summary of minimum times from an extensive group of runs over a particular route, ostensibly to show that even the fastest of overall times made on any journey did not represent the ultimate capacity of the locomotive type concerned; and as this chapter is in some ways a culminating eulogy of Great Northern 'Atlantic' performance, I have done the same with these Pullman runs.

In this case it refers only to the journeys I have experienced personally. There are, first of all, two points to be made; first, that on no occasion was there any time to be booked against the locomotive, even though three of these runs were made in very stormy wintry

Above *The 6:05 pm down Sheffield Pullman approaching Hadley South tunnel, hauled by 4-4-2 engine No 3284* (Rail Archive Stephenson).

Below *The 11:20 am Edinburgh Pullman, later named the 'Queen of Scots', climbing Holloway bank hauled by engine No 4419 with booster in action* (Rail Archive Stephenson).

Above *The down 'Queen of Scots' approaching Grantham hauled by Leeds-based 4-4-2 No 4423* (Rail Archive Stephenson).

Below left *Engine No 4423 at Copley Hill sheds after the author had ridden her down from Kings Cross* (O.S. Nock).

Below right *The driver's corner: the cab of the large-boilered 'Atlantic', No 4423* (O.S. Nock).

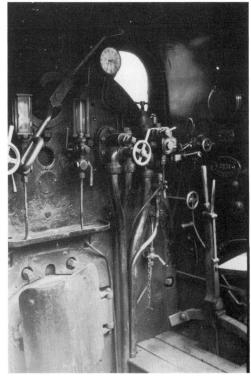

weather and, second, that overall booked time was kept, except on two runs with the Sunday train, when a succession of permanent-way checks caused more delays than could be recovered. The total net gains on schedule time on eight runs amounted to no less than 90 minutes and while 49½ minutes of this total was registered on the four runs made on the 205-minute schedule, that still left 40½ minutes for the four made on the accelerated timings of the 'Queen of Scots' express from 1932 onwards. The load was never less than 7 Pullmans, with a gross load of 285 tons, while the maximum, with 8 cars, was 335 tons. The average on the eight occasions was 311 tons. Seven different engines were involved. Of these, six were regulars at Kings Cross and one likewise at Copley Hill; the eighth was a scratch engine obtained by Copley Hill at relatively short notice and which, as it turned out, provided by some margin the fastest run of all.

To set out full details of each of these eight runs with the times at around 70 passing places on each, with accompanying speed readings of the maximum and minimum rates throughout, would be an altogether too massive and probably indigestible a document. So I have picked out the two most noteworthy for detailed tabulation (page 124) and have prepared a smaller table covering all the eight runs, but with passing times only at those stations where a time was given in the working timetable. In this smaller table (page 120), I have not distinguished between those made on the 205-minute schedule and those on the faster. The two runs on which overall time was not kept require some mention. Number 8 was a very fine piece of work in the face of a most disheartening series of signal checks. This driver contributed quite a lot to the summary of fastest times, by his extremely vigorous running south of Huntingdon and, on the form he was showing, I judged that with a clear road inwards from Hitchin he would have been on time in Kings Cross. But the final checks were crippling. Run no 6 was also very interesting as featuring the pioneer engine, No 3251. It was the only time I ever travelled behind her until after she had been restored and was put again into working order.

This run was made on a stormy January night, when a succession of permanent-way slowings and associated signal checks made us 9¾ minutes late through Grantham, and then at so low a speed as to make the subsequent time up to Stoke summit little faster than from a dead stop. But from Grantham we had a completely clear road, and covered the 105.5 miles to Kings Cross in 104 minutes 16 seconds, regaining 7 minutes on the Sunday schedule and slightly improving upon the 1932 schedule of the 'Queen of Scots' express. In view of the historic interest of this engine I have tabulated the details of this fine run between Grantham and Kings Cross. It was all the more enjoyable in the pleasant surprise it provided at the end of a busy and tiring weekend of work out on the line. At first, when speed restrictions had caused a loss of nearly 10 minutes on schedule by the time we passed Grantham, I was not very hopeful, but then all changed and, although I had clocked faster descents from Stoke to Peterborough, the running was uniformly hard all the rest of the way to London, culminating in a minimum speed of 59 mph over Potters Bar and a rousing 79 mph through Wood Green. On arrival at Kings Cross my pleasure was consummated on discovery that our engine had been the very historic '251' itself.

The two most outstanding runs that I was able to record on these trains, Nos 3 and 7 in the table on page 119, were made in rather different circumstances. No 3 took place on Whit Tuesday, after I had enjoyed a railway photographic weekend based upon Berwick-on-Tweed. I began my return journey on the up 'Flying Scotsman', being hauled by one of the Raven 'Pacifics' as far as Newcastle. There I changed trains, waiting for the 'Queen of Scots' which was hauled to Leeds by a Gresley 'Pacific'. At the Central station the 'Atlantic' No 3284 came on, driven by W. Payne, though I did not alight during the engine change and had no conversation with him. This was the first of many runs I had behind him. He was typical of the finest type of steam locomotive engineman. After he had moved up into the link working the Newcastle double-home turns, he was one of the four specially selected to work the 'Silver Jubilee' streamliner, when that epoch-making train was put on in the autumn of 1935. His run with the Pullman was a classic of its kind, in the vigour with which he set out to recover a 4-minute late start from Leeds and then his skill in avoiding delays from a late-running train ahead.

The companion run, No 7 in the summary table, was made three years later when I had the privilege of an engine pass and rode with Driver Worboys and Fireman Fisher on a journey that still remains one of the most memorable experiences I have ever had on railways, anywhere in the world. But before referring in any detail to this run or to that made with engine No 3284 by Driver Payne, some notes as to the footplate conditions and techniques of driving those wonderful engines are necessary. My place of business was close to Kings Cross station in those days and, in that lunch-hour pastime so happily described by another author as 'station sauntering', I had often looked in some trepidation into the cabs of the Great Northern 'Atlantics', particularly when engine passes began to come my way and the suggestion was made that I might care to ride one of the Pullman trains. Unlike in some of the more modern engines that I had already ridden, there seemed absolutely nothing in the way of creature comforts in those starkly furnished cabs. There was a small tip-up shelf on the fireman's side; one could not call it a seat and it was mounted so high up, to give vision through the front glass, that balancing on it would leave my short legs dangling.

Quite apart from comfort, however, there was in those Spartan cabs little by which an observer could form any assessment of the extent to which an engine was being opened out. The catchblock on the reversing lever had a number of finely spaced serrations, enabling quite fine adjustments of the lever position to be made, but there were no markings on the quadrant to indicate the corresponding point of cut off in the cylinders. The regulator was a traditional type, working in a quadrant across the face of the firebox back-plate. There was no steam-chest pressure gauge as was usually found on British locomotives in that era and I had already found that the position of the handle in relation to the quadrant plate on other British locomotives was no real guide as to how far the actual valve was open. The Gresley 'Pacifics' were then exceptional in having steam-chest pressure gauges. But as I peered into those 'Atlantic' cabs on Kings Cross station I wondered how on earth I was going to get a steady enough stance to *write* when those engines got going and, even from my lineside observations, I could see that they were not particularly steady at speed.

The first one of the class that I rode was No 4423, on the north-bound 'Queen of Scots', non-stop to Leeds. When I climbed aboard at Kings Cross and scrambled experimentally onto that high ledge I found there was a convenient bolt on the firebox front against which I could brace my right foot, at the same time

wedging my back against the cab side; and so supported, front and rear as it were, my hands were free, the one to hold my notebook and the other to write in it. As I settled down to three hours rolling, pitching and tossing I just wondered if I should get cramp in this strange position; but all was well, except that between the ambient temperature and the heat in that confined cab I was just about roasted. It was a gloriously fine day of almost unbroken sunshine and by the time we got to Leeds the thermometer was creeping into the eighties. As to recording the cut-offs, that proved simplicity itself. No driver with whom I rode indulged in any 'fine adjustment' of the reversing lever. As for the quiet old Yorkshire-man who took No 4423 down to Leeds, as we passed Belle Isle box, midway between the first and second tunnels out of Kings Cross, he brought the lever back to about a quarter of the way between full and mid-gear and left it there without the slightest change for 175 miles, until, indeed, we were coasting down the final descent into Leeds. So far as the actual cut-off was concerned, I counted the number of serrations on the quadrant ahead of the catch block and my friends in the loco-motive department gave me the actual per-centage of cut-off afterwards. I did the same on all my footplate runs on these engines.

At that time in British locomotive history there were pundits writing in the railway press and instructors in enginemen's improve-ment classes, who were flogging the principle that the only correct and most economical way to drive a locomotive was with the regulator full open and using as early a point of cut-off in the piston stroke as possible. From the viewpoint of theoretical thermodynamics this was undoubtedly correct and the Gresley 3-cylinder designs, from the largest types to the smallest, responded readily to that treat-ment; but elsewhere, even on the Great West-ern, there were wide divergencies in driving practice, however much certain publicists tried to make us believe it was not so. No engines, however, flouted theory to such an extent and still turned in such a superb per-formance as did the Great Northern 'Atlan-tics', and none of them more so than No 4423. For that setting of the reverser represented a cut-off at 50 per cent in the piston stroke — 50! And it was only when climbing the Holloway bank and on the hard gradients of the West Riding line, between Doncaster and Ardsley, that the regulator was as much as half over on the quadrant plate. On one of the flying stretches, when Driver Rogers took me over the 27 miles from Hitchin to Huntingdon in only 12 seconds over the even 20 minutes, giving me my first-ever personally recorded maximum of 90 mph, the regulator was little more than a quarter open.

Returning in the late afternoon of the same day, the London driver used a shorter cut-off of 35 per cent, again unchanged throughout from Wakefield, but a rather wider regulator opening, though never more than half way over on the quadrant. The theorists would have told us that, in using such long cut-offs, the engines would have choked themselves and never been able to develop any appreciable speed, but on these engines practice gave the lie to theory so completely that I have often wished that an opportunity could have been made for a full thermodynamic analysis of their performance, as was later conducted with many more modern types. But it would have been important for such tests to be made with the engines working just as the Pullman link drove them, or as they were driven when going to the rescue of disabled 'Pacifics'. I am sure there would have been much to be learned. The fact that these engines could run with the utmost freedom and economy up to maximum speed, working on a cut-off of 50 per cent, goes some way to explain those monumental occasions when they took over the haulage of the 540-ton 1:20 pm Scotsman at Grantham. To my mind, it all depended upon a free steam flow through the valves and cylinders. The valve events themselves do not entirely give the answer. As running in the final state, with 32-element superheaters, the relevant dimensions were as follows:

GNR 'Atlantics' motion details

Type	Slide valve engines	Piston valve engines
Valves	Balanced slide valves	8 in diameter piston valves
Maximum valve travel, ins	$4\frac{3}{8}$	$4\frac{3}{8}$
Steam lap, ins	$1\frac{3}{16}$	$1\frac{1}{4}$
Exhaust clearance, ins	$\frac{1}{8}$	$\frac{5}{16}$
Lead (in full forward gear), ins		
Front	$\frac{3}{32}$	$\frac{3}{32}$
Back	$\frac{3}{32}$	$\frac{3}{64}$
Cut-off in full gear (%)	70	70

At the very time of writing this chapter an interesting correspondence has been running in the technical journal CME, the monthly magazine of the Institution of Mechanical Engineers, on the possible development of the steam locomotive, and some highly controversial views have been expressed, mainly by men regarding the subject from a theoretical viewpoint, few of whom had any actual dealings with the steam locomotive in their own professional work. I was very interested when argument centred upon the degree of superheat provided, because theoretically there are several sides to this question. But when it came to practical politics I am sure that the use of high-degree superheat was one of the biggest factors of all in the success of the large-boilered 'Atlantics' in their final form, because it was the extreme fluidity of the steam in this state that enabled such volumes to be passed through the cylinders with no constraint in the exhaust. If there was one retrograde feature introduced on to those engines in their later days I think it was the Ross 'pop' safety valves which, when they lifted, allowed such a rush of steam to escape as to lower the boiler pressure. The old Ramsbottom type of valve could be kept at 'sizzling' point without full blowing off. I noticed that the fireman of No 4423 kept the pressure at about 160 lb per sq in, to avoid full lifting of the 'pop' valves and thus sacrificed about 10 lb per sq in of potential boiler capacity.

Before coming to a detailed commentary on the down Pullman runs, I must get back to my two outstanding up journeys, logs of which are set out in the accompanying tables. There was one initial difference between the two, which might have been significant but which, in the event, did not prove so. On the run of Whit Tuesday 1932, Driver Payne had one of the regular Kings Cross Pullman engines, a superb unit with a notable record of high mileage express running to its credit. On my footplate run with Driver Worboys, the regular engine had developed a slight defect and had been stopped. Copley Hill had appealed to Doncaster for help and they had sent No 4456. Where she had been obtained from I do not know, but the last time previously I was aware of her activities she was working on the Great Central line and based at Darnall shed, Sheffield. The engines at that shed worked to almost every point of the compass, to Liverpool over the Cheshire lines, to York, to Cleethorpes and even to Swindon; and it may well be that being in Doncaster on her normal peregrinations she had been commandeered and sent to Copley Hill for the Pullman. She was certainly not in the state of pristine cleanliness that we always associated with the Pullman engines and Driver Worboys and his fireman, Fisher, knew no more about her attributes then anyone else at Copley Hill.

Coming now to Payne's run with No 3284; as was normal practice, the engine that had brought the train in from the north gave a rear-end push out of the platform, after which the train engine proceeded by itself to surmount the quarter-mile at 1 in 50 after Holbeck station. Then — always a thrilling experience at this point — one heard the thunderous exhaust beat change to a rapidly quickening tattoo as the train accelerated in the dip across the valley towards Beeston. Then came the 3¼ miles at 1 in 100 up to Ardsley; a formidable start indeed to an engine starting 'cold' on a long, fast run. It was splendidly managed with this 8-car train though, after mounting the 4-mile bank at 1 in 150 from Sandal, the usual fast run down the West Riding line was interrupted by a perma-nent-way check and adverse signals in the approach to Doncaster reminded us that the line was still thick with the tail end of the Bank Holiday week-end traffic. Then we got going in grand style, topping Markham summit at the notable minimum speed of 60 mph and sustaining 85 down to the Trent Valley. The slight signal check before Newark was at the level-crossing with the LMS cross-country line to Lincoln. In pioneer days, the Midland Railway was first on the ground here, and when the Great Northern main line was built and crossed it on the level, it was the Midland who built the signal-box, with the result that in the Grouping era an LMS signalman controlled the traffic at this point over the East Coast main line. On this occasion I think he must have been a little slow in 'pulling off', because, although the distant signal was 'on' when first sighted and caused the shutting off of steam and a touch of brake, it cleared almost at once.

The recovery up the rising gradients from Newark was splendid and, by Grantham, the late start of 4 minutes from Leeds had been wiped out and we were nearly 2 minutes early. The descent from Stoke summit to Peter-borough was always exciting on the Pullman trains and this time Payne gave me the fastest I had clocked up to that time, with an average speed of 84 mph from Corby right through to Werrington Junction and a maximum of 88 mph. The days were long past when a slowing to 40 mph over water troughs was required on the Great Northern main line. We were in good form to pass Peterborough about 6 minutes early, but then we encountered the bane of the up 'Queen of Scots' Pullman, the 3:10 pm up from Leeds, which was due into Kings Cross 10 minutes ahead of us. Heavy traffic and protracted station working had delayed her and she had only just cleared the platform when we were passing New England sheds. Then, as Payne explained it to me afterwards, it was 'no good chasing her out to Holme. It would only mean more checks'. So he hung back at first, hoping that with a 'Pacific' and an incentive to make up time the Leeds train would get well away. So it turned out, and with only one signal check, and that not a bad one, he was able to make the fine average speed of 62.9 mph over the 65.9 miles from Holme to Haringey. As usual at such times, the approach to Kings Cross was congested and we were stopped for several minutes at Belle Isle; but we managed to clock in almost exactly on time.

The second run tabulated, made three years later, had uncertainties and hindrances of a different kind. There was first of all the big query as to how that hastily acquired engine would turn out; and then the water troughs on the up line at Werrington Junction were empty, because of repair work. On such a demanding duty there was no question of trying to get through from Muskham, north of Newark, to Langley Junction, 96 miles away, without intermediate replenishment. We would have to stop at Peterborough to take water. From the moment we were away from Leeds however it was evident that No 4456 was a very strong engine and in excellent mechanical condition. Going up to Ardsley, Worboys had her in 50 per cent cut-off with the regulator full open and the minimum speed of 39 mph was by far the highest I have ever clocked there with one of the Pullman trains. We were through Wakefield in record time and then the fun really began. At any appreciable speed she became one of the wildest things I have ever ridden. I have certainly been faster down the West Riding line, which perhaps was just as well, because she pitched, corkscrewed and the tail-wag at the cab end was transmitted to the tender. No coal pusher was needed on this engine and by the time we began to slow down for Doncaster the footplate was ankle-deep in coal. When passing through Wakefield the cut-off had been shortened to 35 per cent and there it remained all the way to Peterborough.

We had left Leeds on time, but in anticipa-tion of the time that would be spent stopping for water, Worboys was trying to get as much

LNER Leeds-Kings Cross, The 'Queen of Scots' Pullman

Load, cars:		8		7	
tons E/F:		314/325		277/290	
Engine (4-4-2) No:		3284		4456	
Driver:		Payne		Worboys	
Distance	**Schedule**	**Actual**	**Speed**	**Actual**	**Speed**
miles	min	m s	mph	m s	mph
0.0 LEEDS (CENTRAL)	0	0 00		0 00	
2.5 Beeston		6 47	41½	6 12	43
5.6 Ardsley		12 07	31¼	10 52	39
7.5 Lofthouse		14 17	60	13 12	59
9.9 WAKEFIELD	18	16 55	40*	15 52	35*
11.6 Sandal		19 15	56	17 53	59
15.4 Nostell		23 40	48½	22 10	50
—		pws	35	—	—
25.8 Carcroft		33 25	78	31 26	76½
—		signals		signals	—
29.8 DONCASTER	39†	38 10	30*	36 05	—
34.5 Rossington		43 15	62	41 48	59
36.3 *Milepost 149½*		45 10	55	43 48	52½
41.9 Ranskill		50 00	75	49 15	69
47.2 RETFORD	57†	54 25	70½	54 00	73
52.1 *Markham Box*		58 55	60	58 33	60
59.4 Carlton		64 42	85	64 20	82
—		signals	66	—	—
65.7 NEWARK	75†	69 50	60	69 30	64
70.4 Claypole		74 22	64½	73 52	68
76.1 Barkston		79 45	55½	79 10	58
80.3 GRANTHAM	90	84 10	62	83 24	64
85.7 *Stoke Box*		90 00	48½	88 55	55
88.7 Corby		92 55	72	91 38	77½
93.6 Little Bytham		96 35	87½	95 10	90
97.2 Essendine		99 02	88	97 32	93
101.0 Tallington		101 40	86½	100 03	92
103.9 *Helpston Box*		—	—	102 01	88
—				pws	35
106.3 *Werrington Junction*		105 30	81	104 91	
109.4 PETERBOROUGH	119	109 20	20*	109 40	water
—		signals		114 25	stop
113.2 Yaxley		115 40	52½	121 00	54
116.4 Holme		119 00	66	124 07	68½
122.3 Abbots Ripton		124 42	53	129 44	57
126.9 HUNTINGDON	137	129 13	77½	133 58	79
134.1 St Neots		134 57	69	139 40	71
138.4 Tempsford		138 30	76½	143 11	76½
—		signals	40	—	70
141.7 Sandy		141 35	—	145 58	72
147.2 *Langford Bridge*		147 50	55	150 47	65
150.1 Three Counties		150 47	64½	153 24	69
153.9 HITCHIN	162	154 35	56	156 66	62½
157.2 Stevenage		158 25	49½	160 29	53½
160.8 Knebworth		162 20	56	164 08	64/60
168.1 HATFIELD	176	169 00	75	170 23	82
173.1 Potters Bar		173 55	54	174 40	69
176.6 New Barnet		177 22	69	177 40	74
180.8 Wood Green		180.45	79	181 09	70
—		signals	—	—	—
183.2 Finsbury Park		183 45	—	183 25	—
—		signal stop		signals	
185.8 KINGS CROSS	195	191 15		189 35	
Net times, min		181¼		176	

*Speed restrictions. †On second run 38 min to Doncaster, 73 min to Newark, 88 min to Grantham and 2 less than shown thereafter.

in hand beforehand. The running had been excellent from the start, but it was after Newark that it became really exceptional, with no lower speed than 58 mph at Peascliffe Tunnel and a sustained 55 mph up the last mile to Stoke. With the lever still in 35 per cent, the regulator was one half open from Newark and then, having topped the summit, no change whatever was made in the controls and we continued so for the whole of the ensuing descent. The result was an *average* speed, over the 10.3 miles from Little Bytham to Helpston signal box, of exactly *ninety miles per hour.* Strangely enough, at this tremendous speed, which reached a maximum of 93 mph near Essendine, the engine itself was riding quite smoothly. So we drew up in Peterborough 7 minutes before we were due to pass through. Very fine running continued all the way to London, culminating in the remarkable minimum speed of 69 mph over Potters Bar; and it was only when we had passed Finsbury Park that there were any signal checks. I calculated the net time on this magnificent run as 176 minutes and only 2¾

minutes more than the summary of minimum times from Leeds to Kings Cross.

Going down the same day, with the engine No 4423, we had a net time of 183¼ minutes, again with some superb running, as will be appreciated from a study of the table on page 123. Beside it is another very fine run with Driver Payne, on the 'West Riding Pullman', which in 1933 had a slightly easier timing of 187 minutes to the stop at Wakefield, against 177 minutes passing through by the 'Queen of Scots', but he started very vigorously and was beating the faster schedule until the signal stop at Langford Bridge box. The recovery was swift and included the unusually high minimum speed of 57 mph in climbing the bank from Huntingdon to Milepost 62. The checks before Peterborough were not severe and, with time now in hand on the slower schedule, things were taken easily on the ascent to Stoke. Even so, the net time to Grantham of 106½ minutes was inside the faster 'Queen of Scots' schedule. Then there came a whole series of signal checks which began at Claypole, continued through Newark

LNER Pullman Trains Leeds–Kings Cross

Summary of fastest times

Distance miles		Times m s	Average speed* mph
0.0	LEEDS (CENTRAL)	0 00	—
5.6	Ardsley	10 52	30.9
9.9	WAKEFIELD	15 23	57.1
15.4	Nostell	21 41	52.4
25.8	Carcroft	30 26	72.8
29.8	DONCASTER	34 21	61.3
34.5	Rossington	39 26	55.5
47.2	RETFORD	50 28	69.2
52.1	*Markham Box*	55 01	64.5
65.7	NEWARK	65 55	74.9
80.3	GRANTHAM	79 42	68.5
85.7	Stoke Box	85 13	58.8
88.7	Corby	87 56	66.3
106.3	*Werrington Junction*	100 11	86.2
109.4	PETERBOROUGH	103 13	61.0
116.4	Holme	111 19	52.0
126.9	HUNTINGDON	121 05	64.7
153.9	HITCHIN	143 38	71.9
157.2	Stevenage	147 11	55.8
168.1	HATFIELD	157 06	65.9
173.1	Potters Bar	161 23	70.0
180 8	Wood Green	167 41	73.3
183.2	Finsbury Park	169 45	69.7
185.8	KINGS CROSS	173 22	—

*Overall average speed 64.3 mph.

LNER Harrogate Sunday Pullman
(As from Grantham to Kings Cross)

Load: 8 cars, 309 tons tare, 325 tons full
Engine (4-4-2) No: 3251

Distance miles		Schedule* min	Actual m s	Speed mph
0.0	GRANTHAM	0	0.00†	—
5.4	*Stoke Box*		8 06	46
8.4	Corby		11 08	73
13.3	Little Bytham		15 00	80½
16.9	Essendine		17 45	82
26.0	*Werrington Junction*		25 25	—
29.1	PETERBOROUGH	30	29 06	15‡
36.1	Holme		37 42	68½
42.0	Abbots Ripton		43 27	53
46.6	HUNTINGDON	49	47 57	76½
53.8	St Neots		53 58	66½
58.1	Tempsford		57 37	74
61.4	Sandy		60 31	67
64.4	Biggleswade		63 08	69
66.9	*Langford Bridge*		65 31	62
69.8	Three Counties		68 11	67
73.6	HITCHIN	76	71 55	57½
76.9	Stevenage		75 48	51½
80.5	Knebworth		79 37	57
87.8	HATFIELD	91	86 11	77
92.8	Potters Bar		90 58	59
96.3	New Barnet		94 13	73
100.5	Wood Green		97 31	79
102.9	Finsbury Park		99 41	—
105.5	KINGS CROSS	111	104 16	—

*From passing Grantham at full speed.
†Times from passing at 20 mph.
‡Speed restriction.

and we were still sighting adverse distant signals at Muskham, half way across the Trent Valley. The offending train was side-tracked after Carlton and, after climbing to Markham, Payne put on a terrific burst of speed, doing 79 mph before Retford and again at Scrooby troughs, and clearing Pipers Wood summit (Milepost 149½) at 64½ mph. Having gained nearly 3 minutes on the 'Queen of Scots' schedule between Retford and Doncaster, things were taken more easily and we should have been on time at Wakefield but for the signal stop outside.

Roger's work on the 'Queen of Scots' was splendid throughout. Quite apart from the burst of speed from Hitchin to Huntingdon, with its maximum of 90 mph, the uphill work was also excellent and there was further fast running north of Grantham. I should be giving a one-sided view of these two runs if I gave all the credit to the drivers, because both of them were backed up by absolutely first class firemen, Walsh, as mate to Payne, and Hunt, to Rogers. It is certainly true that these 'Atlantics' are not difficult engines to fire and the 'tail-wag' that went on practically without a break on No 4423 certainly spread the coal into the back corners of the wide firebox and eliminated any need for careful placing of the coal. In a report I wrote of the 'Queen of Scots' journey, not long after it was made, I estimated that the coal consumption did not greatly exceed 30 lb per mile; and as we were averaging 70 mph the firing rate would have been approaching 2300 or 2400 lb per hour. This was hard work for a fireman and those chaps deserve a special word of praise for the success of their efforts.

While the Kings Cross-Leeds Pullman trains naturally claim most of the limelight, I must not forget those experiences on the Great Central and I have tabulated the details of two runs between Sheffield and Leicester. The first is interesting as being with the same engine that gave me such a truly record run up on the 'Queen of Scots' and it was made not long after that engine had first been transferred from Doncaster to Darnall shed. It was remarkable in that not a single restriction due to colliery workings was in force. From the initial pull up to Darnall we went easily down the steep bank to Woodhouse and then speed lay between 53 and 60 mph on the undulating, but rising, length to Staveley. Then came the big bank, nearly at 1 in 100 up to Heath and easing to 1 in 300 for the last 1½ miles to Tibshelf. With no speed restrictions to come, the engine was not pressed here and speed fell to 30 mph; but we ran merrily enough afterwards, touching 71½ mph in the dip before Kirkby and sustaining 68 mph down the long 1 in 132 from Annesley.

On my footplate run with No 3276, we had four slowings for permanent-way work. The first three were no more than moderate, but the one before Basford was for relaying and was severe. The main feature of this run, apart from the general excellence of the engine was the very fine climb from Staveley to Heath. This driver worked for the most part in 40 per cent cut-off, with the regulator about two fifths open; but for the Staveley bank he advanced to 50 per cent and the regulator about three-quarters open. As a result we were still doing 40½ mph as far up the climb as Duckmanton South Junction and did not fall

The down 'Queen of Scots' Pullman passing Wood Green, hauled by 4-4-2 engine No 4450 (Rail Archive Stephenson).

LNER (GC line) Sheffield–Leicester

			6:21 pm		9:35 am	
Train, ex-Sheffield:						
Load, tons E/F:			261/285		264/280	
Engine (GN 4-4-2) No:			4456		3276	

Distance miles		Schedule min	Actual m s	Speed mph	Actual m s	Speed mph
0.0	SHEFFIELD– VICTORIA		0 00	—	0 00	—
—			signals	—	—	—
2.0	Darnall		5 55	—	5 20	—
5.0	Woodhouse		9 45	53	8 52	60
8.2	Killamarsh		13 30	57/53	12 43	53
10.1	Eckington		15 35	60	14 45	56
—			—	—	pws	43
12.0	Staveley		17 40	55½	17 17	50
14.9	*Duckmanton South Junction*		21 55	34	21 15	40½/37
17.9	Heath		27 35	30	25 47	41
20.3	Pilsley		31 35	—	29 15	39
21.7	Tibshelf		33 10	57½	30 55	64½
—			—	—	pws	43
26.5	Kirkby		37 25	71½	36 12	53
27.4	*Kirkby South Junction*		38 15	62½	37 12	53
28.6	*Annesley North Junction*		—	—	38 27	68
—			—	—	pws	50
32.4	Hucknall		42 55	68	42 12	—
34.9	Bulwell		45 10	68	44 47	67
—			—	—	pws	—
36.6	Basford		46 50	—	47 52	—
—			signals	—		
38.2	NOTTINGHAM	51	49 55		51 07	
0.9	Arkwright St.		2 30		2 20	
4.4	Ruddington		6 50	57/63½	6 20	62/65
9.0	East Leake		11 30	54	10 48	56
10.6	*Barnston Box*		13 15	52½	12 25	55
13.6	LOUGHBOROUGH		16 00	72½	15 10	71
15.6	Quorn		17 55	62½	17 02	60
18.4	Rothley		20 45	58/61	20 00	56/60
21.1	Belgrave		23 30	56/60	22 49	55/62
23.4	LEICESTER	26*	26 20		25 55	—

*Schedule 27 min on 6:21 pm.

---

below 37 mph. Despite the four slacks, we practically kept time from Sheffield to Nottingham. Because of its susceptibility to colliery subsidences this part of the old Great Central main line has not such a good road-bed as elsewhere and this did not help the naturally lively riding of the engine, though after my experiences on the Pullman trains the antics of No 3276 seemed mild. Whatever reputation she may have had since the mystery of the Grantham accident of 1906, no strictures could be applied 30 years later. I found her a lovely engine. She was one of those that had retained her original balanced slide valves, though at the time of my trip she had a 32-element superheater.

The section from Nottingham to Leicester was completely free of restrictions and both engines ran smartly. Number 3276 was quicker off the mark, working again in 40 per cent cut-off with the regulator two-fifths open. The rise to Barnston is nearly 4 miles long, mostly at 1 in 176, and after the descent to Loughborough the gradients are adverse again, though not quite so steep, practically to Belgrave. Yet it will be seen that the two engines made average speeds of 60.2 and 60.7 mph over the 16.7 miles from Ruddington to Belgrave, which is adverse on the whole. I found that the Great Northern 'Atlantics', though different in so many ways from their own engines, were generally popular on the Great Central section, particularly from their constant ability to steam very freely.

LNER Kings Cross–Leeds Pullman trains

Train:			'West Riding'		'Queen of Scots'	
Load, ton E/F:			287/300		277/290	
Engine (4-4-2) No:			3288		4423	
Driver:			Payne		Rogers	

Distance miles		Schedule* min	Actual m s	Speed mph	Actual m s	Speed mph
0.0	KINGS CROSS		0 00	—	0 00	—
2.6	Finsbury Park		6 28	—	6 32	—
5.0	Wood Green		9 30	55½	9 47	59
9.2	New Barnet		14 17	51½	14 13	53
—			—		signals	—
12.7	Potters Bar		18 32	48½	18 34	35
17.7	HATFIELD	24	23 20	76½	23 57	75
23.5	*Woolmer Green*		28 30	58	29 15	59
28.6	Stevenage		33 14	69½/66	33 55	70½/67½
31.9	HITCHIN	37	35 57	82	36 33	84
35.7	Three Counties		38 42	84	39 10	90
—			signal stop	—	—	82
44.1	Sandy		49 27	72½	45 08	86½
51.7	St Neots		55 55	66½	50 58	69½
58.9	HUNTINGDON	59	61 52	74½	56 45	77½
62.0	*Milepost 62*		64 50	57	59 43	55½
—			—	82	signals	30
69.4	Holme		71.03	78	67 18	74
—			signals		pws	32
76.4	PETERBOROUGH	77	78 00	22[†]	76 37	20[†]
79.5	*Werrington Junction*		83 13	55½	81 27	60
84.8	Tallington		88 32	66	86 33	65
92.2	Little Bytham		95 40	58	93 39	58½
97.1	Corby		101 26	46½/50	99 08	50½/54
100.1	*Stoke Box*		105 22	41	102 43	48½
105.5	GRANTHAM	108	110 55	69	107 39	77/73
111.5	Hougham		117 00	78	112 27	83½
—			signals	2	—	79½
120.1	NEWARK	120	128 57	20	118 49	80½
126.4	Carlton		137 40	62	123 48	74
133.7	*Markham Box*		145 28	52½	130 45	56
138.6	RETFORD	138	149 52	79/75	135 10	76½
145.6	Scrooby		155 29	79	141 15	69/73
149.5	*Milepost 149½*		158 34	64½	144 33	61
153.2	Black Carr Junction		161 40	75	147 46	75
—			—		signals	—
156.0	DONCASTER	155	164 07	30[†]	153 42	
162.6	Hampole		172 05	58½	161 47	66
170.4	Nostell		180 00	48	170 01	53½
174.2	Sandal		184 27	75½	173 19	75
—			signal stop		—	—
175.9	WAKEFIELD	177	189 15		175 15	—
180.2	Ardsley	185			182.45	32
183.3	Beeston				186 34	60
185.8	LEEDS	194			191 27	—
	Net times, min		177		183¼	

*Schedule of 'Queen of Scots' only; 'West Riding' booked 187 min to Wakefield.
[†]Speed restrictions.

LNER Leeds–Kings Cross Pullman Trains

Run no:	1	2	3	4	5	6	7	8
Year:	1930	1930	1932	1932	1933	1935	1935	1936
Train:	Queen of Scots	Harrogate Sunday	Queen of Scots	Queen of Scots	Queen of Scots	Harrogate Sunday	Queen of Scots	Harrogate Sunday
No of cars:	8	8	8	7	7	8	7	7
Load, tons full:	335	335	325	300	285	325	290	295
Engine No:	4444	4450	3284	4444	4436	3251	4456	3280
Driver:*	Sparshatt	Rumble	Payne	Taylor	Hollands	—	Worboys	Bird
Distance miles	m s	m s	m s	m s	m s	m s	m s	m s
0.0 Leeds (Central)	0 00	0 00	0 00	0 00	0 00	0 00 pws	0 00	0 00
9.9 Wakefield	18 25	18 02	16 55	17 25	17 42	19 20 checks	15 52 signals	17 05 signals
29.8 Doncaster	38 00	38 15	38 10 pws	38 05	38 32	47 07 signals	36 05	38 53
47.2 Retford	55 35 signals	55 05	54 25 signals	55 17	55 18	67 53	54 00	56 35 signal stop
65.7 Newark	75 35	72 20 pws	69 50	72 37	71 22	86 50 pws	69 30	81 04 signals
80.3 Grantham	92 20	89 25	84 10 signals	87 55	86 33 signals	103 14	83 24	97 50
							109 40†	
109.4 Peterborough	118 55	119 50	109 20	115 45 signals	117 20	132 20	114 25	132 13
126.9 Huntingdon	137 05	140 55	129 13 signals	135 42 signals	135 55	151 11	133 58	150 28
153.9 Hitchin	162 60	170 00	154 35	161 35	160 42	175 09	156 56	173 32 signals
168.1 Hatfield	177 10	184 30	169 00 signals	175 55 signals	174 23 signals	189 25	170 23 signals	188 15 signals
185.8 Kings Cross	194 45	203 45	191 15	195 25	193 00	207 30	189 35	209 55
Schedule time, min	205	205	195	195	193	205	193	205
Net time, min	190	201½	181¼	190	188	198	176	186½

*Drivers all Kings Cross except run 8
†Stop to take water.

Chapter 11

Into the sunset—withdrawal—preservation

The year of the Silver Jubilee of His Majesty King George V, that brought such glory to the latest express passenger locomotives built at the Doncaster Plant, saw the beginning of the end for the 'Klondikes' for, in November 1935, the first of them was withdrawn. This was No 3982, which as GNR No 982 had been one of the first to be superheated, as early as February 1914. Three of them, namely Nos 255, 950 and 989, at one time had the 17-element version of the Gresley twin-tube apparatus, but all the class eventually had 18-element Robinson superheaters, with a heating surface of 254 sq ft. Once withdrawal began, with a second engine in December 1935, the process continued steadily, with six more in 1936, including the inside-cylinder No 271, another six in 1937, this lot including the celebrated pioneer No 990, *Henry Oakley*, and three in 1938. There were no withdrawals in 1939 and, at the outbreak of the second world war, five of them remained in traffic. These were Nos 3250, 3252, 3254, 3256 and 3259. The first two of these survived long enough to have new numbers allocated to them, under the Thompson renumbering scheme of 1943 as Nos 2893 and 2892 respectively, though they never bore those numbers. No 3252 was the last to go, in July 1945, at the ripe old age of 42 years.

The preservation of No 990 and its enthronement in the York Railway Museum was an event that proved of far greater significance than was realised at the time. Prior to its withdrawal in October 1937, the engine had for some time been stationed at Mexborough and, like the majority of her class, engaged on quite humdrum secondary duties; but when the sharply timed buffet-car services were put on between Kings Cross and Cambridge in 1932, there were opportunities for them to sparkle, as of old. The schedules were originally planned for three-car trains and working by the large boilered 'Atlantics'; but the popularity of what became universally known as the 'Beer Trains' was such that five coaches soon became the minimum load and six and seven were frequently taken. Several 'Klondikes' were then stationed at Cambridge and they occasionally took a turn on these fast trains. The total distance was 57.9 miles and the schedule time for those trains which made four stops was no more than 71 minutes, coming up. Details are tabulated of two runs with 5-coach trains, together with one of my own, on which I joined a 7-coach train hauled by one of the large 'Atlantics' at Hitchin.

The Cambridge branch is by no means an easy one, even with such relatively light trains as these, especially in the up direction. There is first of all a severe speed restriction at Shepreth Branch Junction and then, after undulations to Meldreth, there is a steep climb at 1 in 120 up to Royston. The gradients continue adverse to Ashwell, including such inclinations as 1 in 163 and 1 in 183, after which there is a welcome dip through Baldock. On the first run, engine No 3257 lost a minute to Royston, but had won it back by Hitchin, though the minimum speed of 55½ mph before Royston was excellent. On the second run, No 3252, the longest lived of them all, ran quite brilliantly. She tied with No 3257 to Harston, but then got away in great style to attain 73½ mph after Shepreth and speed had not fallen below 61 mph when steam was shut off for Royston. This engine also ran very smartly on to Letchworth, beating the smart sectional time here by more than 1½ minutes.

Once on to the East Coast main line and with the large-boilered No 4402 providing further comparison, both the 'Klondikes' did splendidly, attaining speeds of 53 and 56½ mph up the continuous 1 in 200 to Stevenage and following up with lightning accelerations to nearly 70 mph on the level and slightly rising length to Knebworth. Engine No 4402, with two additional coaches, was naturally not so rapidly away from Hitchin but she kept the sharp allowance to Welwyn Garden City, planned originally for a 3-coach load! The falling gradient from the re-start makes a considerable help in getting away smartly on the final run and all three engines were inside 'even time' by Finsbury Park. Their use on the 'Beer Trains' was however the swansong of the 'Klondikes' on fast express work, though more than 20 years later we were to see what the preserved '990' could still do in the way of express running.

LNER Cambridge–Kings Cross

Run No:			1		2		3	
Engine No:			3257		3252		4402	
No of cars:			5		5		7	
Load, tons E/F:			153/160		153/160		217/230	
Distance		**Schedule**	**Actual**	**Speed**	**Actual**	**Speed**	**Actual**	**Speed**
miles		**min**	**m s**	**mph**	**m s**	**mph**	**m s**	**mph**
0.0	CAMBRIDGE	0	0 00	—	0 00	—		
2.6	Shepreth Branch Junction		4 28	—	4 30	—		
5.3	Harston		7 58	62	8 01	—		
8.1	Shepreth		10 52	67	10 40	73½		
10.0	Meldreth		12 46	55½*	12 18	61*		
13.0	ROYSTON	15½	16 31	—	15 39	—		
3.9	Ashwell		6 30	—	6 21	51		
8.3	Baldock		11 40	70	10 42	71		
10.4	LETCHWORTH	14½	13 42	—	12 58	—		
2.6	HITCHIN	5	4 45	—	4 53	—	0 00	
3.3	Stevenage		5 42	53	5 21	56½	5 52	50
6.9	Knebworth		9 00	68	8 36	69	9 27	65½
9.9	Welwyn North		11 36	73	11 10	75	12 03	75
11.6	WELWYN GARDEN CITY	14	13 37	—	13 09	—	14 10	—
2.6	Hatfield		3 53	—	3 46	60	3 52	57½
7.6	Potters Bar		9 00	59	8 34	65	8 46	63
11.1	New Barnet		12 14	—	11 44	—	11 50	73
15.3	Wood Green		15 38	74	15 11	75½	15 13	76½
17.8	Finsbury Park		17 42	—	17 24	—	17 18	67½
—			—		signals		signals	—
20.3	KINGS CROSS	22	22 03	—	22 47	—	23 30	

*Minimum speed before shutting off steam for Royston.

By 1924 all of them had been superheated, although eleven of them retained their balanced slide valves to the end. The majority had extended smoke-boxes in their latter days, engines 3984 and 3985 being the exceptions. This did not have any connection with the superheating equipment, because on these engines, both with the Gresley 'twin' and with the Robinson, the apparatus was accommodated in the recessed portion of the boiler barrel, ahead of the front tube-plate. An extended smoke-box was first fitted to engine No 252 in 1913, as a form of spark arrester and this, proving efficacious, was applied to most of the class, whether superheated or not, even before Grouping in 1923. Unlike the larger-boilered 'Atlantics', the 'Klondikes' had screw reversing gear. When originally built in in 1898, engine No 990 had lever reverse, but this was subsequently altered to correspond with subsequent engines of the class. It is sometimes thought the use of a very wide firebox precluded the use of a screw reverser on the large-boilered engines; but a study of the drawings shows that there would be no structural difficulty in arranging for screw actuation of the lever and a link mechanism for adjusting the valves.

So far as the large-boilered engines were concerned, there is one last development to be referred to, although it did not actually prove to be a 'development' in the truest sense of the term. In the autumn of 1936 the 4-cylinder simple 'Atlantic', No 3279, arrived at the Doncaster Plant for general repairs. Although it had never come into the limelight as the nominally most powerful of all the 'Atlantics', even after receiving, in 1932, a new boiler with 32-element superheater, the engine had by that time amassed a mileage of 629,300 since its conversion to four cylinders in 1915. In the intervening 21 years it had thus averaged 575 miles per week. Despite his continuing pre-occupation with his ever-increasing family of 3-cylinder types, Gresley retained a great affection for the 'Atlantics' and, rather than apply a routine overhaul to No 3279, he decided to rebuild it once again, as a virtually new type of engine but carrying the standard 32-element superheater boiler. It was a remarkable project for Doncaster, at that period, for the engine had a modernised version of the 'K2' cylinders, of 20 in diameter and 26 in stroke, with 10-in diameter piston valves, actuated by outside Walschaerts valve gear, with the lengthy maximum travel of 6 in, at 70 per cent cut-off. With entirely new frames, the so-called 'rebuilt' locomotive was actually an entirely new one, on which was mounted a standard boiler.

The new engine left the plant in April 1938, and Gresley was sufficiently interested in it to criticise use of the old short cab and to require its lengthening. This involved welding of an 8¼ in extension on to the rear end of the frames to carry it. Thus modified, the engine went into traffic in June 1938. It was stationed at New England shed, Peterborough, and although working to Kings Cross on occasions, I have not been able to trace any records of its performance in the remaining months before the outbreak of the Second World War. As far as I can ascertain, it worked mainly on the Lincolnshire lines. But, by 1938, the day of the 'Atlantics' generally was passing, and it is difficult to imagine just what was in mind in undertaking such an extensive and probably expensive renewal of this old engine. Before the introduction of the 'Pacifics', the entire stud of large-boilered 'Atlantics', including the three compounds, was stationed only at four sheds, namely Kings Cross, New England, Grantham and Doncaster; by 1938 the allocation had changed and those four sheds then had respectively 17, 23, 11 and 12 engines of the class. The remaining 29 were allocated as follows: Hitchin 8; Cambridge 3; Colwick 3; Sheffield 7; Copley Hill 6 and York 2.

Although war conditions came to introduce a wider, if promiscuous, sphere of activity for these engines, it is perhaps not generally known that even before the autumn of 1939, special train workings took them far to the north of York. In view of the constraints that were imposed upon them at the time of the 'Atlantic' trials between Newcastle and Edinburgh in 1923 and the cutting down of the boiler mountings of engine No 1447, it is surprising to recall that authenticated reports exist of No 4443 (New England shed) in Edinburgh in 1933, of No 4405 also there in 1935 and, in July 1939, of No 4452 working an NB section express from Waverley to Perth — all apparently without suffering damage through striking overhead structures! When wartime loads began to mount up, 'Atlantics' of the GN type were sometimes used for piloting 'Pacifics' and Class 'V2' 2-6-2s between York and Newcastle. At the time of Gresley's death in April 1941 the whole stud of 92 was still intact, excepting of course the two compounds 292 and 1300. By that time however shortages of materials and labour, and war conditions generally, were taking their toll, and causing rapid deterioration, not only in aging units like the 'Atlantics' but also in the heavy first-line power. Consequently it was no surprise to learn that in 1943 the first of them had to be withdrawn. This was No 4459, one of the batch built new in 1910 with Schmidt superheaters and its departure fanned the ever-smouldering fires of partisanship into a brief burst of flame.

As was partly to be expected, the scrapping of 4459 stirred that evergreen enthusiast for

The one-time 4-cylinder engine, No 3279, rebuilt with two 20 in by 26 in cylinders and outside Walschaerts valve gear at Skegness in 1939 (Rail Archive Stephenson).

Engine No 3293 fitted with Westinghouse continuous cab-signalling equipment; here seen at Nottingham in 1946 (Rail Archive Stephenson).

anything Great Northern, R.A.H. Weight, into a characteristic 'funeral oration' in the *Journal of the Stephenson Locomotive Society* and this touched one or two others, whose sympathies lay westward, distinctly on the raw. One of them wrote indignantly to the *Journal*, 'Is not far too much fuss being made at the scrapping of the first GN large 'Atlantic'? The enthusiasts of other lines have seen their old favourites go, and we have not seen much evidence of grief in the Journal, or elsewhere. Far better-looking types and equally efficient machines have disappeared — usually in the interests of standardisation [!] — and we have seen no tearful references to their departure'. He went on to list some of those on the LMS and the Southern that were on the danger list, though curiously enough none of those on the Great Western.

On the score of efficiency, during the summer of 1944, Edward Thompson arranged for a series of coal consumption trials to be run between the first of his new 'B1' 4-6-0s, No 8301, *Springbok*, and the various pre-grouping classes, which included the large-boilered GN 'Atlantics'. Compared to what the latter engines had been called upon to do in pre-war years these runs were a mere 'doddle' so far as speed was concerned; but it was interesting to find that on stopping trains between Kings Cross and Cambridge there was absolutely nothing in it, between the 4-6-0, No 8301, and the 4-4-2, No 3285. Details of the working on two typical round trips were as shown below.

The figures below are what one might expect, with a train making a considerable number of intermediate stops.

On the Lincolnshire line, No 8301 was tested against the much rebuilt 3279. From Peterborough they went out in the early morning with the 3:00 am express to Grimsby. This was the wartime equivalent of the old 3:10 am mail that connected with the 1:10 am from Kings Cross. It took just over two hours for the 78½ mile run, with seven intermediate stops. The return working was on the 9:05 am up, successor to the pre-war 9:25 am, which had been a through buffet-car train to Kings Cross. In 1944, when

| Engine No | Load tons | | Average load | Coal lb/train | Coal lb/train |
	Down	Up	out & home	ton mile	mile
3285	175.9	223.8	199.9	0.220	43.9
8301	194.8	221.8	208.3	0.220	45.9

| Engine No | Load tons | | Average load | Coal lb/train | Coal lb/train |
	Down	Up	out & home	ton mile	mile
3279	283.5	484.2	383.8	0.164	63.0
8301	293.5	419.2	355.6	0.158	56.3

Thompson's tests were made, it was loading very heavily, (see table above).

No particular significance can be attached to these coal consumption figures which, in terms of pounds per train ton mile, were roughly double those returned by engine No 1447 in the Newcastle-Edinburgh tests of 1923 and merely reflect the high consumption inevitable in the working of a train making a number of intermediate stops, as distinct from a long non-stop run.

It was in 1946 that Thompson ordered the complete renumbering of the LNER locomotive stock and the ex-GNR 'Atlantics' lost their old identity. From 3251 onwards they were numbered from 2800 in order of construction, including those which had already been scrapped. A total of 49 of the standard engines received their new numbers, 8 of which still retained slide valves. There was in addition the rebuilt 3279, which became No 2808. But scrapping was then proceeding rapidly and another 3 were scrapped in 1946 very soon after receiving their new numbers; no fewer than 29 were withdrawn in 1947. For the record, the 16 that entered British Railways ownership in January 1948 were, using their old LNER numbers, 3279, 3281, 3288, 3293, 3300, 3301, 4409, 4419, 4424, 4440, 4441, 4445, 4446, 4447, 4451 and 4455, of which four still retained their slide valves. The pioneer engine, No 3251, later No 2800, had been withdrawn in July 1947, but fortunately set aside for preservation. The survivors had an additional '6' added to their numbers, but actually only two lasted long enough to carry them; these were 62822 (old 3294) and 62885 (old 4455). The former was the last to remain in traffic and it was not withdrawn until November 1950, after a life of more than 45 years.

One of the last survivors, No 3293, was the subject of a very interesting experiment in 1946. In the post-war recovery period intense interest was being shown in systems of automatic train control. The LMS, through papers and technical explanations at meetings of learned societies, was trying to stimulate interest in the system of inductive intermittent control that was being developed from the trial installation put down on the Southend line in pre-war years, in strong opposition to the well-established system in use over practically the entire main-line network of the Great Western. My then chief at Westinghouse, Major L.H. Peter, was a strong advocate of continuous, rather than intermittent cab signalling, and he persuaded the LNER to put in a trial installation on the down line between Greenwood signal-box and Potters Bar. This was before the widening of the line. The locomotive equipment was fitted to engine No 3293. When one of my electrical colleagues in the company told me which engine had been selected for the trial, I could not help feeling that the choice had been made by someone on the LNER with an impish sense of humour for there could not have been a more cramped and inconvenient cab for an observer or observers to ride in than an Ivatt 'Atlantic'. Fortunately for my colleague's peace of mind no appreciable speeds were attempted during the trials but, as it was, I gathered he found his footplate experience highly disconcerting.

The last run of a GNR 'Atlantic' was made the occasion of a special celebration. Old '294' has been stationed at Grantham and after careful preparation she made one or two trips to and from Kings Cross in mid-November. Then on Thursday, November 23 she left Grantham for the last time and went to Kings Cross, where she remained at Top Shed till the following Sunday morning. Then, at 11:00 am she worked a special express train non-stop to Doncaster on which there travelled Mr C.K. Bird, then Chief Regional Officer of the Eastern Region of BR, and H.G. Ivatt, son of the designer and the last Chief Mechanical Engineer of the LMS. After a very foggy start and some 'wrong line' running, the train was 13 minutes late on passing Huntingdon; but in clear weather the lost time was regained by the time Doncaster was reached. After certain ceremonies on Doncaster station, the old engine was taken into the Plant to be scrapped. One felt that no locomotive class had a more moving and spectacular end. At that time, of course, old 294, then BR No 62822, was painted black but the memory of the class, as it originally was, remained secure in the remarkable process of restoration that had been applied to the pioneer engine, No 251.

After this famous engine was withdrawn in July 1947, the aim was to restore it, as far as possible, to its original condition, externally at any rate. This was a much more ambitious project than that undertaken for the first of the Klondikes, No 990, which had extended to no more than repainting the engine in Great Northern livery, leaving it with a super-heater boiler, extended smokebox and cylinders with piston valves. It had so happened, however, that at about the same time as No 251 was withdrawn, engine No 2868, old 4438, arrived in the plant for scrapping. She was one of those which had retained her original slide valves and, with a view to the more complete restoration of No 251, it is believed that not only were the slide valves and cylinders from 4438 taken, but also the frames, while the boiler eventually fitted was one that had been spare at Doncaster since the withdrawal of engine No 3278, in July 1945. To complete the 'restoration', or rather the fabrication of a memorial engine, Rams-bottom safety valves were fitted, the super-heater was removed, and the chimney moved back to the position occupied when the original engines were non-superheated. The engine was then beautifully painted in the old GNR colours and stored for the time being in the paint shop at Doncaster Plant. How much of the restored engine actually belonged to the

original 251 it is hard to say; my guess is very little!

Apart from a visit to Kings Cross in 1952 on the occasion of the Centenary of the opening of the station, engine No 251 remained in the paint shop at Doncaster until the autumn of 1953. Then, when the time came to celebrate the centenary of the opening of the Doncaster Plant, at the suggestion of Mr A.F. Pegler, then a member of the Eastern Region Area Board, arrangements were put in hand for the running of a special train, to be named the 'Plant Centenarian' on two successive Sundays, on the 20th and 27th September. On the first occasion, the train was to be run from Kings Cross to Doncaster and back, with time in between the outward and return journeys for a quick tour of the plant. On the second Sunday, the special was to start from Leeds and, between Doncaster and Grantham, to take the original line for part of its route, via Lincoln. As patronage was expected to be heavy, provision was made for an 11-coach train, of nearly 400 tons tare weight, to be hauled by the *two* preserved 'Atlantics' in partnership. With the 'Klondike' No 990, *Henry Oakley*, there was no trouble; the superheated boiler steamed freely and it was only a case of giving her paint work a thorough cleaning. But No 251 would not steam! The idea of a large-boilered GN 'Atlantic' being so temperamental was so horrifying that the most urgent investigation was necessary.

The last survivor in ordinary traffic: No 3294, now numbered 62822 in BR stock at Grantham, ready to leave with a train for Boston in May 1949 (Rail Archive Stephenson).

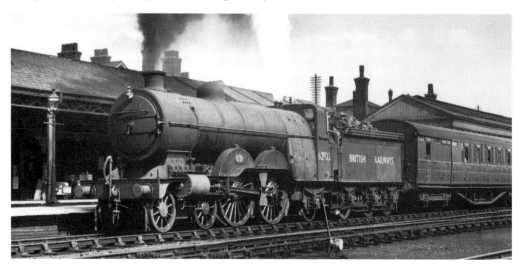

The boiler was one that had been super-heated but, at the time of the restoration, in order to set the chimney back to its original position and present a correctly restored appearance, the superheater had been removed; the boiler was left with 133 tubes of 2 in external diameter and 32 superheater flues of 5¼ in outside diameter. The tube heating surface had remained unchanged, but that derived from the large flues was of very little use. The furnace gases swept through the middle of these tubes imparting a much reduced amount of heat to the outside. It was only after some running trials from Doncaster that the reason for this deficiency was realised and it was then arranged for a set of dummy superheater elements to be inserted in each of the flues. This improvisation worked like a charm and though the steam as supplied to the cylinders was still in a saturated condition there was plenty of it, and it was considered that the engine could be used in partnership with No 990 on the 'Plant Centenarian' train. On a gloriously sunny morning, the two engines made a brave sight and between them put up an entirely adequate performance.

It was the following Sunday, however, that provided the real thrills, and on that day my wife and I were guests of Mr Pegler and his friends, and privileged to travel in the beaver-tail observation car attached to the rear of the train. This was one of the two cars that had been built by Sir Nigel Gresley for the rear end of the Coronation streamlined train and in which we had ridden when a maximum of 106 mph had been sustained on the descent when from Stoke tunnel towards Peterborough. On September 27 1953, we joined the train for the start from Leeds, whence a non-stop run to Doncaster was scheduled. With eleven coaches, as a week previously, plus the observation car, we had a load of 409 tons tare and, with a full load of passengers, a total of at least 435 tons behind the second tender. Engine No 990 was leading, manned by a renowned Copley Hill driver of the day, A. Cartwright, while on No 251 was W. Hoole, of Kings Cross, with whom I have ridden on the footplate of an 'A4' Pacific at more than 100 mph.

With the permanent-way restrictions so frequently experienced on a Sunday, signal checks and misty weather, nothing much could be done on the first section to Doncaster. There was a short interlude there, to give some time for such passengers as wished to make quick visit to the plant; during this period, some distinguished visitors joined our party in the observation car. First of these were the two Misses Ivatt, two elderly maiden ladies, daughters of the engine designer. Then there was Mr J.R. Bazin, who had joined the Great Northern Railway as a pupil of Mr Ivatt's, at Doncaster in 1897 and who was Assistant Works Manager at Doncaster at the time the first superheated 'Atlantics' were built. He subsequently became Chief Mechanical Engineer of the Great Southern Railway, in Ireland. It was good to meet him, still

In September 1953: the preserved 990 and 251 hauling the 'Plant Centenarian' special express from Kings Cross to Doncaster, approaching Stoke summit (W.A. Camwell).

so hale and hearty, and so intensely interested in all the proceedings of the day. We were also especially honoured by the genial presence of Sir Ronald Matthews, the last Chairman of the LNER. The re-start from Doncaster was scheduled for 11:15 am and, because of engineering work on the main line, we were to be diverted via Lincoln, with a leisurely non-stop run of 61.4 miles, to Grantham. It is not a fast running route in any case, but there was another reason for restraint; engine No 251 in her non-superheated condition was not so economical in her water consumption and a weather-eye had to be kept on the contents of the tender. Inspectors that I knew well rode on both the locomotives, Jenkins, the senior inspector at Regional headquarters, on No 990 and Dixon, of Kings Cross, on No 251.

Apart from the severe permanent speed restrictions, at Black Carr Junction, where we turned off the East Coast main line, on the sharp curves at Gainsborough and Lincoln, and on rejoining the main line at Barkston, there were no checks. We covered the first 3 miles to Black Carr Junction in 6½ minutes and then went quietly on over the level road to Gainsborough, not exceeding 54 mph. We had a spell at 57 mph on the level near Saxilby and took 55½ minutes to passing slowly through Lincoln, 37 miles from Doncaster. The last 24.4 miles to Grantham took 37 minutes, pass to stop. There opportunity was taken to top up the tender of No 251, because it had no water pick-up scoop, and then we were treated to a spell of real express running. Of course when the engines had been in their prime, no 'Atlantic' driver would think anything of taking a 435-ton load on his own, but with two museum pieces it was another matter and, with this wonderful precedent established, there were hopes of many more special trips. To ensure this, the two engines had to be treated gently!

We started well up the continuous 1 in 200 rise up to Stoke tunnel, attaining 42 mph, and then put on a grand piece of fast running. Speed rose quickly to 80 mph before Essendine and it was finely sustained after the gradients had flattened out to dead level after Tallington. The average speed over the 17.6 miles from Corby to Werrington Junction was 72.8 mph; but we were scheduled to stop again, to top up the tank on the tender of No 251. Nevertheless time was nicely in hand and after a halt of 4½ minutes we set out on the run to Kings Cross, for which the working time allowance was 92 minutes. Except that

the engines were eased a little on the descent from Milepost 62 to Huntingdon, the running as far as Hitchin was up to the best East Coast standards of that time. Looking through my last pre-war notebook I have details of seven runs, all with 'A4' class streamlined 'Pacifics', on which the time over the 37.5 miles from Holme to Hitchin was 34 m 28 s, 36 m 05 s, 36 m 13 s, 42 m 02 s, 39 m 57 s, 36 m 23 s and 37 m 41 s. On this run with the 'Plant 'Centenarian', the two veteran 'Atlantics' took 36 min 22 sec. They were, in fact, going magnificently, but were getting so far ahead of time that a marked easing down took place after Stevenage; and at Hatfield, where speed would normally be in the mid-seventies, we were drifting along at a mere 56 mph. Had the initial effort been continued we would have been in Kings Cross in 82 or 83 minutes, even

Eastern Region Grantham–Kings Cross
The 'Plant Centenarian'

Load: 11 coaches, 409 tons tare, 435 tons full
Engines: 4-4-2s, Nos 990 and 251

Distance miles		Actual m s	Speed mph
0.0	GRANTHAM	0 00	—
5.4	*Stoke Box*	9 41	42
8.4	Corby	12 50	68
13.3	Little Bytham	16 52	78
16.9	Essendine	19 35	80
20.7	Tallington	22 37	75
23.6	*Helpston Box*	25 10	68
26.0	*Werrington Junction*	27 19	—
29.1	PETERBOROUGH	31 32	—
1.4	*Fletton Junction*	3 37	—
3.8	Yaxley	6 56	—
7.0	Holme	10 10	64½
12.9	Abbots Ripton	16 07	51½
14.4	*Milepost 62*	17 50	—
17.5	HUNTINGDON	20 55	66
20.4	Offord	23 40	63
24.7	St Neots	27 50	57
28.9	Tempsford	31 52	67½
32.3	Sandy	34 52	65/69
35.3	Biggleswade	37 31	65
37.8	*Langford Bridge*	39 55	57½
40.7	Three Counties	42 47	64½
44.5	HITCHIN	46 32	55½
47.8	Stevenage	50 57	40½
51.4	Knebworth	55 17	—
—		eased	
58.7	HATFIELD	64 02	56
—		pws	10
63.7	Potters Bar	71 13	—
71.4	Wood Green	81 20	62 (max)
73.8	Finsbury Park	84 09	
—		signals	
76.4	KINGS CROSS	89 35	

Above *The second 'Plant Centenarian', on the following Sunday, leaving Grantham for Kings Cross with engines 990 and 251* (Rail Archive Stephenson).

Below *Engine No 251, heading the 'Farnborough Flyer' special train on September 9 1954 for the Air Show taking the curve at Reading West Junction* (M.W. Earley).

Bottom *Engine No 251 on shed at Basingstoke, coupled to a 'King Arthur' class 4-6-0 and the ex-GCR 4-4-0* Prince Albert, *which had been train engine of the special train* (Ivo Peters).

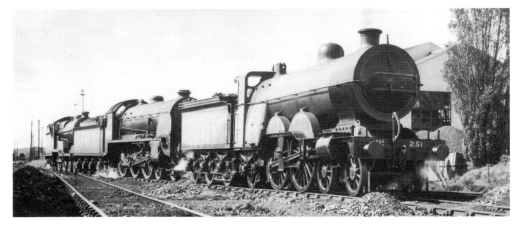

with the drastic slowing over the constructional works at Potters Bar.

As we hoped, haulage of the 'Plant Centenarian' in 1953 was not the last occasion that these two engines appeared in steam. A.F. Pegler's dual association with the Eastern Region and with the Northern Rubber Company, at Retford, led him to organise several summer outings by special train to various resorts, often by routes that were unusual and interesting from the railway point of view. In 1954, the trip was from Retford to Liverpool (Riverside) and it was worked as far as Edge Hill by the GNR 'Atlantic' No 251 in partnership with an ex-Great Central Railway 'Director' class 4-4-0, the *Prince Albert*. Eight days later, on Sunday, September 12, the same pair of engines worked a special from Leeds conveying spectators from North Country stations to the air display at Farnborough. The route was via Doncaster, Tuxford, Mansfield, Nottingham and the former GCR line, thence on to the Great Western at Banbury and so via Oxford and Reading West to Basingstoke. I drove thence to witness and photograph the arrival of the train, and to enjoy a leisurely walk around the two engines in the locomotive yard, after the train had been taken over by a Southern locomotive for the last stage of the journey to Farnborough. This, so far as I know, was the last time No 251 was in steam.

The 'Klondike' No 990, *Henry Oakley*, was one of the preserved steam locomotives chosen to take part in the 150th anniversary celebrations of the Stockton and Darlington Railway in August 1975. Until then it had, since 1953, occupied an honoured place in the old Railway Museum; but for the Shildon pageant it was steamed once again and, as the very first British tender engine of the 'Atlantic' type, was the object of much interest. Afterwards an appropriate place was found for it in the new National Railway Museum. Even then, however, the working life of this great old engine was not finished. In May 1977, it was once again brought out of the Museum, and put into running order. On June 1, piloting an ex-LMS 'Black Five' 4-6-0, it pounded up the steep bank out of Keighley at the head of a schoolchildren's special to Oxenhope on the Keighley and Worth Valley Railway. On a sunny day the handsome green engine made a brave sight among the hills. It was to remain there for some weeks working occasional trains and was maintained at Haworth. Great Northern enthusiasts hoped that a place might have been found either for this engine or No 251 in the Rainhill celebrations of 1980, but this event was primarily a party for LMS interests and the East Coast had to be content with *Flying Scotsman* and *Green Arrow*

So the saga of the Great Northern 'Atlantics', as working engines, has come to an end. But the preservation movement and the ever-increasing interest in special steam-hauled trains being what it is, who can tell? We can only rejoice that two such beautiful and historic examples of British steam locomotive practice remain, as museum pieces.

No 990, Henry Oakley, *in service again in 1977, piloting a 'BR5' 4-6-0 on an SRPS special on the Keighley and Worth Valley Railway* (Brian Stephenson).

Index

Leeds Central: 4-4-2 engine No 4456 has just backed on to the 'Queen of Scots', ready for the non-stop run to Kings Cross (O.S. Nock).